Ducati Desmo

THE MAKING OF A MASTERPIECE

Ducati Desmo

THE MAKING OF A MASTERPIECE

MICK WALKER

OSPREY

Dedicated to John Fairclough

Published in 1989 by Osprey Publishing Limited
59 Grosvenor Street, London W1X 9DA

British Library Cataloguing in Publication Data
Walker, Mick
Ducati Desmo
1. Ducati motorcycles, 1983
I. Title
629.2'275
ISBN 0—85045—879—X

Design Simon Bell

Filmset by Tameside Filmsetting Limited,
Ashton-under-Lyne, Lancashire
Printed by BAS Printers Limited,
Over Wallop, Hampshire

Contents

Introduction

An often overlooked fact is that without people motorcycles would simply remain lumps of metal, with an assortment of rubber, plastic and even glass thrown in for good measure.

With people, bikes come alive. It is people who create the history, because without them a motorcycle wouldn't turn a wheel, let alone win a race, set a new speed record, or even get its owner down to the 'local' for a Sunday lunchtime pint!

Because of this I have always made it a policy to include people as well as the machinery in my various books—in *Ducati Desmos* I've taken this a stage further and looked at the influence of men such as Ing. Fabio Taglioni, Mike Hailwood and Paul Smart and the effect they have had on Ducati's success.

This is not just a story of past achievements, it is also a continuing story, for unlike many other classic marques, Ducati Meccanica S.p.A. is very much alive and kicking today—thanks in no small part to brothers, Claudio and Gianfranco Castiglioni.

After my two previous books for Osprey on the Ducati marque, the question has to be asked, why another one on Ducati? The answer is simple— demand. I have received scores of letters from around the world asking for one specifically on the famous Desmos—in both road and racing form.

It is fitting, therefore, that the first chapter of the book is devoted to Ing. Taglioni, as this great designer, now retired, has been almost single-handedly responsible for having the vision to follow an idea through from the drawing-board to the race circuit, and finally to the public highway. In doing so his name has become synonymous with the word *Desmo*, which today is just as significant to enthusiasts around the world, as the name Ducati itself.

I am not only indebted to Ing. Taglioni, who has been kind enough to reveal personal facts about his career and life, but also to the many other people who have given me their time, and in doing so contributed greatly to this book's interest. These include Nadia Pavignani and Franco Valentini of Ducati and Luigi Giacometti of Cagiva—all of whom it has been a great pleasure to have known over the years; World Champion on both two and four wheels, John Surtees; Australian grand prix star of the 1950s Ken Kavanagh, now resident in Italy; my many friends in the British Ducati Owners Club, and in particular Paul Weston; four times World Formula 2 Champion Tony Rutter; Imola hero Paul Smart and his charming wife, Maggie.

A very special word of thanks must go to my Italian friend Gerolamo Bettoni, who has provided more than his share of help and encouragement with the project, together with Giorgio Grimandi—who was and still is one of Franco Farnè's right-hand men in the experimental department at the Bologna factory.

The majority of the photographs came from my own personal collection, but credit should also be given to the following: Doug Jackson, Don Upshaw, Philip Tooth, Alan Cathcart, Mike Clay and Alan Kirk. In addition, the few holes that remained were filled with the help of my good friends from the EMAP archives in Peterborough, headed by the custodian of the old *Motor Cycle* and *Motor Cycling* files, Brian Woolley.

I have taken the liberty of dedicating *Ducati Desmo* to John Fairclough, without whom it is unlikely that I would have ever put pen to paper . . . and none of my books would have been written—thanks John.

To my loyal and long-suffering wife Susan, and equally loyal secretary/typist Carol Green; also the many others who have by their interest and efforts made it possible—thank you all.

Last, but not least, to the super-efficient Osprey editorial team of Helen, Val and editor Ian Penberthy, not forgetting former editor Tony Thacker who gave the green light to my original idea.

Here it is then, the full story of what went on—both in public and behind the scenes—during the creation of a motorcycling legend, the Ducati Desmo story.

Mick Walker
Wisbech, Cambridgeshire
December 1988

1

Ingegnere T

In many ways the story of Ducati Desmo is the story of Ing. Fabio Taglioni—one of Italy's greatest motorcycle designers. As already recorded in my two previous works on the legendary Bologna marque *Ducati Singles* and *Ducati Twins* (Osprey Publishing), it is to Taglioni that the hordes of committed Ducati enthusiasts around the world look up to as the father of the company's motorcycles.

But amazingly, until now virtually nothing has appeared in print to reveal the man behind the name. Very few, outside the factory's gates, have any idea whatsoever who this almost god-like figure, known to many simply as Doctor T (a title which incidentally he dislikes), really is.

So it is only fitting and correct that in this book, which sets out to record the full development history of the Ducati Desmo line, its creator should come under the spotlight.

Fabio Taglioni was born on the 20 September 1920 in a little group of houses called *Ducato di Fabriago*—the actual address was Via della Viola 13, in the country town of Lugo in north-eastern Italy. Lugo is in the area known as Emilia Romagna, which also encompasses Ravenna, Ferrara, and Forlì, and has a population of some 50,000. The region has a long-standing enthusiasm for all forms of motor sport *and* mechanical engineering. And its predominantly agricultural economy is being caught up by an industrial one.

His father, Biagio, was an engineer who ran his own company specializing in the repair of agricultural machines, engines in particular. From an early age, the young Fabio showed that he was at his happiest when assisting his father and learning from him, and displayed a natural flair for anything mechanical.

He grew up in Lugo, where his early schooling took place. He was the eldest of three children. Besides Fabio, there was a brother Athos, born in 1922, and a sister Maria—the youngest—born in 1926. Athos was for many years employed by the Forestry Department in Forlì, where he made his home and is now retired. While Maria, as a housewife, still lives in Lugo to this very day.

After his primary education at the local school, Fabio progressed first to Imola and later to Bologna University. However, his education was interrupted by the Second World War which Italy entered into in June 1940. Aged 21, Fabio was called up for military service in February 1941. He first served with the army in the *Carristi Divisione Ariete* (Tankman Ariete Division). In May 1942 he was transferred to Mechanical Transport.

Soon he found himself in charge of a workshop in Sicily repairing military vehicles. Not only things like trucks and field equipment, but also aircraft which had been shot down or damaged on the ground during the fierce fighting which took place in both North Africa and later Sicily itself. And it was during this time that Taglioni first began his close association with the art of refined engineering principles. He noted that the piston aero-engine was a particular work of art. And as Massimo Clarke so rightly confirms in *La Moto Classica*: 'This was a very significant experience. Indeed, for a long time after piston aerodynamics were replaced by jet propulsion, the development of competition engines (and later of production engines), both for cars and bikes, drew heavily on the technological advances and the rich experience gained in this sector.'

It was also during his war service in Sicily that he was able to renew his pre-war interest in motorcycles. Amongst those he rode, he remembers best a Motosacoche with belt final drive, a Peugeot from the 1920s, a 1924 ohv AJS, a Rudge Ulster, a BSA Gold Star and a Guzzi Airone 250. But the only machines he came into contact with in Sicily were various Italian brands of military two-wheelers—such as Guzzi and Gilera singles, which he spent much of his spare time tuning.

During the allied landings in Sicily, he was wounded and ultimately transferred to a military hospital until 8 September 1943 with serious injuries to his left leg. Thanks to his mechanical knowledge he spent the next two years, following his release from hospital, instructing army recruits on engines and shaft-drive assemblies, amongst other subjects. He was discharged from military service in 1945.

After the conflict he resumed his studies at Bologna University where he gained a degree in industrial engineering (mechanical section) in 1948, and also at the *F. Alberghetti Istituto Magistrale* (Teaching Institute) in Imola. In fact, when I asked him what he would have liked to have done had he not been an engineer, Ing. Taglioni replied, 'a teacher of technical subjects'.

It was whilst completing his studies that he first began his involvement with the motorcycle industry—as a design consultant with the Ceccato concern. This company had just begun trading, the year was 1950 and

Year 1932—AJS 350 owned by Taglioni's father. The young Fabio (left) was able to ride it from 1930, aged ten. His younger brother Athos is seated on the pillion

although never a large marque Ceccato was none the less relatively important in the field of ultra-lightweight motorcycles at the time.

The company produced a wide range of bikes, both two-and four-stroke, ranging from 49 cc to 173 cc. At Ceccato, Taglioni assisted mostly in the development of their top-of-the-range overhead-cam models—first 75 cc and later 100 cc. Not only this, but he also conceived a double overhead-camshaft cylinder head, which although never ultimately used, clearly showed his skill at such an early stage in his career.

His first real appointment of note came when he joined the FB (Fratelli Boselli) Mondial factory based in Milan. At that time Mondial had won three successive 125 cc world road racing championships and were therefore world leaders in the field of lightweight four-stroke engine development. All three of Mondial's titles had been awarded in respect of designs for overhead-camshaft power units by Alfonso Drusiani.

Taglioni was doubly fortunate because he was put to work straightaway in the Mondial race shop of the Via Corso Vercelli firm. The Boselli brothers were racing enthusiasts who had manufactured three-wheel trucks before the war. Two-wheel production was re-started in 1948 and the following year their rider, Nello Pagani, won the first ever 125 cc World Championship. The following year they retained it through Bruno Ruffo and then in 1951 made it a hat trick with Carlo Ubbiali in the saddle. The same rider had finished third in the two previous years.

One of Taglioni's first tasks at Mondial was to further develop the 125 double knocker GP engine, and also a single overhead-cam version. Later, he also developed a 174 cc sohc unit for use in Italian Junior events. This featured a single overhead-cam driven by a train of gears derived from the 125 cc motor. After this he began the first tests of the 250 single-cylinder dohc GP engine, which was later to take the world title in 1957.

But in April 1954, he resigned from Mondial and on 1 May joined the Ducati factory as their head of the technical, planning and experimental department—in other words as their chief designer. His rapid rise to

Right **Twenty-three years on; this 1955 photograph shows the newly-appointed Ducati chief designer with an experimental prototype featuring hand-beaten alloy streamliner**

Moto da 125 cc A.C.T
186 Km/h

A babbo
Fulio
-IX-55

fame was a clear indication of his ability. Ducati boss Dott. Montano, recognizing his talent, had approached Taglioni. At Mondial he had reached something of a stalemate with little chance of early promotion and could not have achieved the level of design freedom and possibilities that the larger and more progressive Ducati factory could offer. Another factor was that following their three years of glory, Mondial were to be largely unsuccessful in racing until their double championship year in 1957—after which they quit the sport, never really to recover, before finally closing in 1979.

In contrast, Ducati under Montano's leadership was growing rapidly. Taglioni had also joined just after the company had been reorganized, separating the mechanical division to form Ducati Meccanica S.p.A.

His first brief was to design a 50 cc engine for a proposed record-breaker. This was to be blown with a volumetric supercharger, but shortly after its approval the whole project was cancelled, when the Ducati board decided it would be more beneficial to publicize the company through other sporting channels. Taglioni

was next asked to oversee the preparation of specially tuned versions of the 98 cc ohv sports model for both Reglarita (trials) and road racing.

And although, as recorded in Chapter 3, the factory riders not only gained bronze medals in that year's ISDT, and proved the pushrod engine relatively reliable in several long-distance classics of the day, such as the Giro d'Italia and Milano-Taranto, Taglioni quickly realized that the success the factory sought would not be gained without a totally new design.

The result of this was a completely new bevel-driven, overhead-cam single. The first engine, although of 98 cc, was always intended primarily as a 125 cc class machine. The smaller capacity was initially used because it allowed the factory to compete in the lower capacity 100 cc category in Italian road events.

This initial model, the 98 Gran Sport, was an instant success not only taking a class victory in its very first event but acting as the prototype for a long line of singles over the next two decades. Besides this, a development of this basic concept, with the larger 125 cc capacity, was to win its designer and factory worldwide acclaim as the first truly successful motorcycle engine to use positive-valve operation—in other words desmodromic, or desmo for short.

Later, Taglioni was to conceive the world's first

Ing. Taglioni (right) directs a couple of his race mechanics as they prepare desmo cylinder heads for the Bologna factory 1958 Grand Prix effort

production Desmo and ultimately the whole Ducati line would sport this innovation by the year 1980, something that is not only maintained to this very day, but has remained unique to Ducati in the production field (if one discounts factory prototypes and home-built specials!) of the two-wheel world. All this and more is covered in detail elsewhere in this book.

But why desmo? Taglioni's answer to this is that although desmodromic valve gear had been known since the early part of the twentieth century, it only became attractive 'because of the unreliability of competition engine valve springs—one of the biggest problems in the early 1950s; that's why the external hairpin springs were widely used, because they could be changed in a short space of time without removing the cylinder head. In fact, many set off on long-distance road races with a good supply of spare springs and the special tool for changing them!'

And don't forget his time at Mondial had fully conditioned Taglioni to the various problems in the development and running of small capacity high revving four-stroke engines.

As is revealed in Chapter 3, when Taglioni built the single-cylinder dohc GP racing Ducati—which came before the Desmo version—what really prevented its full potential from being realized most was the hairpin valve springs.

He had first considered reversing the central camshaft to provide a type of opposite valve operation—in other words closing the valves through double rocker arms instead of opening them and, at the same time, using the twin camshafts to open them. And that was precisely how the original *three* overhead-camshaft system of desmodromic valve operation came into existence.

Taglioni had earlier realized the potential of desmodromics whilst studying for his engineering degree at Bologna University. But like several other ideas which he also formed at the time he was not able to use these immediately—for obvious reasons.

Away from the world of engineering and motor-cycles, Fabio Taglioni got married and his wife Norina, who was very much a housewife rather than a career woman, gave him a daughter Piera, who later became a leading teacher of mathematics. The Taglionis became grandparents in 1977, when Piera gave birth to a boy, Luca.

Fabio Taglioni's other great love away from his family and motorcycling has been—and still is—exotic flowers. His orchids, in particular, have won him much acclaim. Now in retirement, he spends much of his time tending his beloved flowers in his greenhouse at home in Bologna.

In many ways it is fitting that his love of such tender static blooms should contrast so sharply with the breathtaking speed of his two-wheel creations. But even so they display more than anything the real man.

Proof that Taglioni's design flair was not restricted to machines with one or two cylinders. With development engineer/rider Franco Farnè, he shows off the jewel-like 125 dohc four-cylinder racer, circa early 1966

One who is patient, quiet, unassuming and loyal. Someone who likes peace and quiet, but at the same time has been able to display a rare gift which has seen his brainchildren leave the drawing-board and turn into cold metal. A man who has created some very special motorcycles—ones which clearly have the stamp of a single person, not a whole design team, ones which combine the techniques of an engineer with the beauty of an artist.

And what of cars, a Porsche or a Ferrari perhaps? No, he has owned relatively few—a couple of Alfa Romeos, a Giulietta 1300 and a GTV 1750. A Simca 1000, an Austin 1000 and an Innocenti 1000 with automatic shift—in consequence of his old war injury.

A question which has always intrigued me was why had he stayed at Ducati so long? His answer was simple and to the point—fidelity. In other words, Fablio Taglioni is not only a loyal man but a correct one too, one of the old school. He believes in old-fashioned values, someone who once he has given his word keeps it, someone who has conducted his life based on high moral principles. Not for him the 'dog-eat-dog' brand of commercial warfare, where yesterday's promises and

Imola 1973; Taglioni (second left) with the Ducati Formula 750 team bikes

goodwill are forgotten in the search for today's extra profit. For example, when I asked him what his opinion had been of the various managers at Ducati during his time there he would not answer the question. And in fairness to his request that I only write his *exact* answers I will not attempt to reply to this matter here, although the reader may well form his own judgement after reading the facts and events which are outlined within the following pages.

However, there were many other questions to which he was only too pleased to comment and I found this a rewarding experience. Previously, the writing on Ducati motorcycles has in the main concentrated on the machines themselves, rather than the personalities—which of course means that very little has been written about Ing. Taglioni. His opinion of the various riders who have ridden his creations in races around the world is particularly enlightening. He obviously has a high regard for the majority of the competitors who have ridden for him. But two in particular win special mention—Degli Antoni and Mike Hailwood. Degli Antoni 'because he was the first important co-operator for the setting up of the desmo operation', and 'Hailwood who was the unbeatable racer-man'.

Others who receive special mention are Franco Farnè—'a very good racer and also at the present time a wonderful co-operator and excellent tuner'. Paul Smart 'an example of courage and perseverance'. Others mentioned included Francesco Villa, Bruno Spaggiari and four times World F2 Champion, Tony Rutter.

But which designs are his favourites, the ones closest to his heart? 'The single-cylinder 100/125 Gran Sport, as ridden in events such as the Giro d'Italia; the Scrambler [street scrambler singles of the late 1960s and early 1970s which proved best-sellers in Italy]; the Imola '72 750 and derived models with bevel-driven engines and the Pantah series.'

And which, in his opinion, were the most important race victories achieved by his designs over the years? 'The Giro d'Italia, Milano-Taranto, Barcelona 24 hours and other such endurance events, because they show not only the power of the engines but also their technical validity and operation which are useful for standard production motorcycles.'

Why didn't Ducati build racers for sale to the public in the same way as Aermacchi or Yamaha? 'All Ducatis for racing were produced primarily to benefit the production models, or publicize them, not purely as racers in their own right.'

When asked which other motorcycle designers he holds in high regard his reply was typically simple and direct. 'All those which produced something different to others, but valid, reasonable and functional.'

Ing. Taglioni with 600TT2 frame, of type used by Tony Rutter to take four world titles (1981, 1982, 1983 and 1984)

And of all the designs which *didn't* make it? This was his V4 prototype of the early 1980s which he regrets most at not having been followed through, saying: 'This was developed with very good results, but not *one* of the managers of that time saw the opportunity to produce it in series production.'

What of current and future developments in the motorcycle industry? In his opinion, many modern machines have become 'sophisticated two-wheel cars and if we go on at this rate they will become a kind of plane without wheels'. Not so far-fetched as it seems! Electronic ignition is 'a great advantage—and gives results that cannot be achieved by any other method'. On the subject of water-cooling he sees it 'as a complication and one which adds weight. But is virtually indispensable for the latest breed of engines with four valves per cylinder and such high performance. Water can be made to go anywhere and cool exactly the right places.' Incidentally, he thinks *five* valves to be more of a marketing exercise, rather than anything else—Yamaha take note. . . .

He obviously regrets that it has not been possible to preserve a collection of his creations at the Ducati factory (like Moto Guzzi and Gilera, for example). A number of more recent prototypes have survived, in fact, although they are largely in a totally unrestored state hidden away out of sight, deep within the factory's bowels. But this motley collection is hardly worthy of the creative genius who gave over 30 years' service to the Bologna marque—a great pity in my opinion.

In his book *The Illustrated Encyclopedia Of Motorcycles*, the late Erwin Tratgatsch defines the most famous motorcycles as those that 'have been so good that they have been produced for many years with a minimum of modernization and development'. If one uses this as a yardstick, then Ing. Fabio Taglioni can truly be judged to have been not only one of Italy's top designers, but of the world too. His designs, such as the bevel-driven ohc singles and V-twins, belt-driven vees and the desmo systems for both racing and standard production machines, have stood the test of time over the years with the minimum of modifications.

To me, the name Taglioni sits proudly amongst the very top designers the motorcycle industry has produced, men such as Bradshaw, Norton, Marcellino, Guzzi, Turner, Page, Patchett, Küchen, Remor, Moore, Carroll, Craig, Riedel, Carcano and Kaaden—in no particular order of merit—but all worthy of the highest accolade as is the leading player behind the Ducati Desmo story, Ing. Fabio Taglioni.

A recent photograph of the man who was responsible for putting the Ducati and Desmo names on the world motorcycle map

2

Desmodromics explained

The word *desmodromic* will not be found in the Oxford English dictionary or any other. Instead, it was coined from two Greek words meaning 'controlled run'. And its mechanical usage is the idea of eliminating one of the chief bugbears of valve operation at high rpm—the phenomenon of valve float, or 'bounce'. This happens when the valve springs are unable to respond quickly enough to close the valve back on their seats. The desmodromic idea was to replace the troublesome springs with a mechanical closing system much like that used to open them, thus giving a positive action. Eliminate the springs and you eliminate the bounce and get a higher-revving engine, in theory. This had been known since the early days of the internal combustion engine but for many years no designer managed to *successfully* harness it.

The great British designer, James L. Norton, conceived his version of the positive-valve operation in the early 1920s

One of the first examples of completely positive mechanical valve operation was used by the French Delage concern in its grand prix car of 1914—and the French knew the method as *desmodromique*. The Delage engine employed four valves per cylinder in pent-roof combustion chambers. Twin overhead-camshafts were used and each valve pair was actuated through a stirrup-shaped tappet with an integral, duplex bridge-piece at its lower end. Two cams were used: one depressed the tappet to open the valve via the upper member of the bridge, the second cam raised the tappet to close the valve through the medium of the lower bridge member. Between this last item and a collar on the valve stem a small 'tolerance spring' was interposed to ensure that the valve was pulled positively on to its seat. It would not have been possible to manufacture sufficiently accurately then to provide positive seating without some degree of freedom.

The Delage system was not particularly successful and was not developed, but in the 1920s several other manufacturers tried out variants of it. One layout, the Vagova, utilized a cam track embodying inner and outer cam forms which guided a roller attached to one end of a 'rocker', the other end of the rocker was forked to embrace the valve stem. To provide the required freedom for seating, the pivot of the rocker was given a small amount of spring-loaded float parallel to the valve axis.

Alternative methods investigated were to use the cam track in conjunction with a tappet for direct operation of the valve, or to retain the rocker but incorporate two cams, one bearing on each end of the rocker. A more complicated version was that used by Bignan-Sport, also during the 1920s. It featured a bevel-gear driven face cam or swash plate provided with a vee-section periphery. Motion was conveyed from cam to valve by a crosshead running on a guide; the crosshead carried a pair of oppositely inclined rollers, one of which ran on each face of the swash-plate periphery.

In Britain, another form of desmodromic operation was patented in the early 1920s by none other than the legendary James L. Norton, founder of perhaps the greatest name in British motorcycling. This was similar to the Vagova design in that it employed a cam track and rocker. However, instead of Vagova's spring-loaded rocker trunnion the Norton rocker end entered

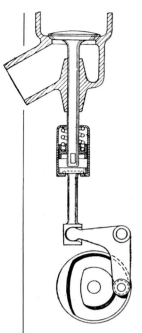

The grandfather of all desmodromic systems, F.H. Arnott's valve mechanism was patented in 1910. It incorporated a cam track, a bell-crank lever and a tappet

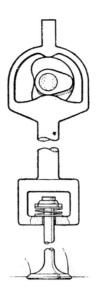

In 1914 the French Delage company employed a desmodromic layout of two cams and a stirrup member; each stirrup operated two valves

a slot in the valve stem and a small leaf spring was fitted on the rocker's upper surface. Complete closure was ensured by the provision of an adjustable abutment in the valve stem above the rocker. Ingenious, but one cannot visualize slotted valves standing up to today's thermal and mechanical stresses.

A complex variation of the Bignan-Sport face cam theme was patented by the car giants Fiat, also in the late 1920s. A spring-loaded crosshead was mounted on the valve stem, at each end of the crosshead was a roller and the rollers ran between a pair of face cams mounted coaxially with the valve and driven by spur gears. The direction of rotation of the rollers would, of course, be suddenly reversed as they transferred from the opening to the closing face cam, so that the rate of wear of the mechanism might well be high.

The double cam layout has had many adherents in the past. In 1916 J. M. Brewster invented an overhead valve arrangement operated by rods. The opening cam was followed by a roller-ended tappet connected to the valve-opening rocker by a jointed push-pull rod. On the tappet was a transverse peg engaged with the forked end of one arm of a bell-crank lever. The other arm of the bell crank carried a second roller which bore on the closing cam. But this layout included more pivots and arms than would appear desirable, though it would probably have worked well enough at the low engine speeds of the day.

A spring-loaded trunnion also appeared in the Vareille design in which, instead of the cam track as on the Vagova, there were two cams between which the rocker end was sandwiched. A shackle connected the rocker's other end to the valve stem. Technically, though, it would have been more practical to have had

a forked rocker end and abutments on the valve, otherwise the Vareille system was robust and simple—even by present day standards.

But one of the neatest and most sensible of the early designs, and which was similar to what both Mercedes and Ducati used years later, came from Ballot, a name once well known in French motoring circles during the veteran and early vintage period. This comprised a double cam and three arm rockers of Y form. One arm bore on the opening cam, the second on the closing cam and a third had a forked end which actuated the valve through abutments. Complete closure was ensured either through a spring above the fork or by allowing some spring controlled movement between the two cam follower arms of the rocker.

One of the last designs to appear prior to the onset of the barren years for desmodromics (1930–54) was the work of G. A. Mangoletsi, then a well-known sand racer

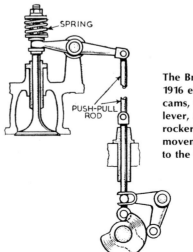

The Brewster system of 1916 employed a pair of cams, with a bell-crank lever, a push-pull rod and rocker to transmit the movement from the cams to the valve

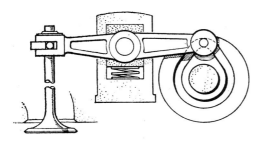

Vagova utilized a cam track and rocker; the rocker trunnion was spring-loaded to ensure total valve closure

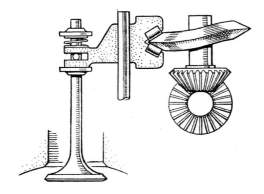

An interesting variation by Bignan-Sport was a face cam theme patented by the car giants, Fiat, circa late 1920s

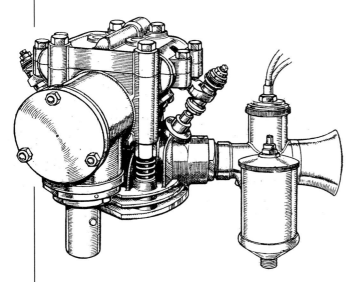

In the late 1920s the engineer G.A. Mangoletsi modified a Matchless single-cylinder motorcycle engine to positive-valve operation of his own design. Drawings show the complete cylinder head . . .

from Southport and later head of the G. M. Carburettor company in the 1950s. Not unlike the Ballot valve gear, Mangoletsi's scheme was even simpler in that the follower of the closing cam was embodied in the valve actuating arm. The opening cam follower ran on the same pivot as the arm, and a spring between the two components compensated for cam irregularities of manufacture or wear.

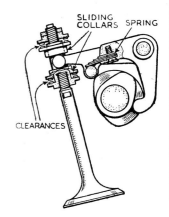

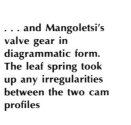

. . . and Mangoletsi's valve gear in diagrammatic form. The leaf spring took up any irregularities between the two cam profiles

Juan Fangio at the wheel of a 3-litre Mercedes-Benz
W196 during practice for the 1954 Buenos Aires GP.
Fangio went on to win the race from Stirling Moss in
another of the eight-cylinder desmodromic Mercedes

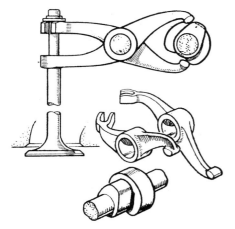

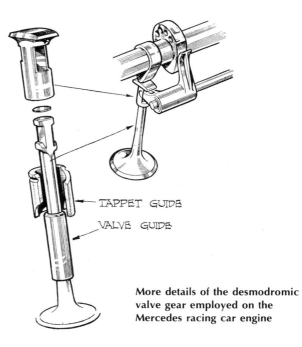

TAPPET GUIDE

VALVE GUIDE

Mercedes used a desmodromic system in their W196
grand prix racing car engine. The valves were operated
by a pair of cams and scissor-action rockers

More details of the desmodromic
valve gear employed on the
Mercedes racing car engine

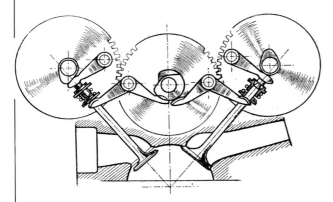

The original system used by Ing. Taglioni in the 1956 125 Ducati desmodromic single-cylinder GP racer. The lever type rockers absorbed cam loads and the axes of the valve stems and cams were offset to secure maximum mechanical advantage

Valve position was set relative to the rocker arm by means of adjustable collars on a threaded valve stem. Spring washers between the collars and rocker abutments provided a degree of freedom to ensure complete closure.

All the activities in the 1920s might suggest that, apart from Brewster and Delage, no one had done anything earlier on positive closure. However, that was not the case, because as far back as 1910, English engineer F. H. Arnott provisionally patented the grandfather of all desmodromic valve operations. The Arnott design employed a cam track and a bell-crank lever, also a small clearance between the cam follower and valve, and a closing spring—a formula subsequently utilized in varying degrees by other designers.

In comparison with Vagova and Norton, the Arnott valve lay on the other side of its rocker arm, so that the cam track had the same form as the *closing* cam of a twin-cam layout, instead of that of the opening cam.

It is interesting to recall that years later Arnott revived his interest in motorcycle engines with the advent of 500 cc car racing in the early 1950s. He remembered his old patent and decided to try his hand once more at desmodromics with the conversion of a 500 cc JAP ohv single in 1954. However, this later Arnott design differed considerably from the original and was reminiscent of the Ballot and Mangoletsi methods. There were two cams and a Y-shaped rocker having a forked leg bearing on collars on the valve stem. The rocker, unlike that of the two earlier inventions, had no spring-loaded tolerance and Arnott stated at the time that with the design and materials employed, no valve seating difficulties were experienced with his 1950s JAP engine. Arnott's statement in 1954 coincided with the rebirth of desmodromics—that the introduction of springs into a device intended to eliminate them had been an unnecessary complication, which in retrospect hampered the development of the principle—and was without doubt the reason it is not in wider use today.

Since those early days described above, interest in desmodromic valve operation waned until the immediate post-war days when it had almost been forgotten—until 1954 when the giant Mercedes-Benz concern decided that something better than spring return was required to ensure the utmost efficiency for

Here the theoretical valve diagram for the desmodromic valve layout is compared with that of an orthodox spring controlled system. A and B represent the respective amounts of overlap

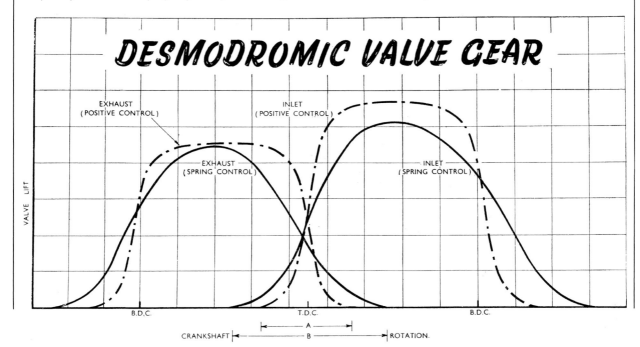

DESMODROMIC VALVE GEAR

its new W196 $2\frac{1}{2}$-litre grand prix engine. The German company therefore evolved a desmodromic layout, the success of which was evident if the car's 1954 racing record was anything to go by. The unsupercharged, straight-eight cylinder engine was reputed to develop over 260 bhp (or 104 bhp per litre). With an individual cylinder capacity of 312 cc it is easier to see that this design was still of interest to the motorcycle world.

Two cams per valve were used by Mercedes (as on the Delage engine), and each cam had its own rocker. The rockers were pivoted side-by-side on a common shaft and had a scissors' disposition. The opening rocker bore on a shoulder part way down the valve stem, and the closing rocker on a collar near the end of the stem. Originally the design embodied final closure of the valves by springs, but the springs were dispensed with after tests had revealed them to be unnecessary. All that was required was an ultra-small clearance and pressure inside the cylinder did the rest. This was how simply one of the original problems was overcome!

Whereas the cam track principle described earlier is easy to understand, the double-cam arrangement requires a brief explanation. The opening cam is of conventional form, while the closing cam is, in effect, an inversion of the opener: it begins to drop from its base circle when the opening cam lifts from its base circle; the peak on the opener coincides with the lowest point on the closer, and the closer lifts from its lowest point as the opener comes off its open dwell on to the return flank.

Besides Mercedes the motorcycle sphere had also seen several designers show a distinct interest in desmodromic valve operation around that time, most notably Joe Craig (race supremo at Norton in the early 1950s) and more significantly in the Desmo story, Ing. Fabio Taglioni. In a country with as proud an engineering heritage as Italy it is men such as Taglioni who have made it so. And, unlike Craig, Taglioni was able to transform his ideas from the drawing-board into

hard metal. Whilst studying as a young man at Bologna University Taglioni first put pen to paper to conceive his initial motorcycle engine designs—which included desmodromics and a 90-degree, L-shaped four!

But it was not until he joined Ducati in 1954 that he was able to exploit his true potential as a design engineer, or the potential of positive-valve operation. First with his specialized works racers, then in the late 1960s came the world's first *production* engines with desmodromic cylinder heads, and by 1980 perhaps his crowning glory was that all Ducati production motorcycles had desmodromic valve operation. This is, in fact, the picture today with Ducati, now owned by Cagiva, still exclusively marketing a range of bikes with one feature that no other producer in the world offers—and that magical word, Desmo. This sales success is surely lasting proof of an idea which had its roots firmly in the veteran and vintage days of motorcycling, but even today is viewed by many as being amongst the very vanguard of two-wheel progress—a rare achievement indeed.

This was not because others didn't try after Ducati came on to the scene. During the period 1958–61, for example, many others tried unsuccessfully to emulate Taglioni's success. Firstly, Mondial would probably have raced a desmodromic 250 in 1958 had they continued racing. Benelli experimented but gave up. A desmodromic version of the Manx Norton was built, but this did not proceed. Even private concerns such as Velocette specialists BMG of Ilford, Essex, converted a 500 Venom to desmodromic valve operation, but none were anywhere near as successful as Taglioni and Ducati.

In the succeeding chapters is the full story of just how all this came about, the men and the machines and the chain of events which brought about the fact that today the word Desmo is as important to the Ducati enthusiast, as the name Ducati itself.

3

From drawing-board to tarmac

It was not, as many may have thought, the automobile giant Mercedes-Benz's successful foray into the world of desmodromics with their W196 racing car, which had given Ing. Fabio Taglioni the idea of applying the principle to a motorcycle engine.

He had, in fact, first realized its possibilities as far back as 1948, but was unable to put his ideas into practice until after he joined Ducati in 1954. And in any case, as the previous chapter has already catalogued, there had been many attempts previously to perfect the use of positive-valve operation—as far back as the dawn of the 20th century.

But it was to be the gifted Bologna University engineering graduate who was the first person to successfully harness the full potential of desmodromics in a motorcycle engine, at first for racing and later for standard production machinery.

But none of this would, or could, have happened without Dott. Giuseppe Montano, who had been appointed as the governing managing director of the Ducati motorcycle side, when the Bologna concern had been split into two separate companies in early 1954.

To understand this move it is necessary to trace Ducati's involvement with two wheels from the end of the Second World War, when they had begun production of the *Cucciolo* (little puppy dog), a 48 cc 'Clip-on' (or auxilliary) engine unit, with pullrod operated valves. From this humble beginning the Bologna company had rapidly expanded, until in 1950 it had begun building complete motorcycles. Not only

98 cc single overhead-cam Gran Sport—Ing. Taglioni's first design for his new employers following his appointment in May 1954

Ducati hero Degli Antoni with his class winning Gran Sport during the 1955 Giro d'Italia

this but the other sections, notably the one making electrical components, had also steadily forged ahead. So, at the end of 1953 it had been decided to split the business into two totally separate organizations, each with its own title.

The mechanical side, which included not only the two wheels but also stationary industrial and small marine engines, was to trade as Ducati Meccanica S.p.A., whilst the non mechanical sections—radio, electrical, as well as an excellent miniature camera, would come under the wing of a separate company, Ducati Electronica S.p.A., with its own management team. Luckily for Ducati Meccanica, Dott. Montano was a motorcycle enthusiast and it was to be under his leadership that the company began to take a serious interest in sporting events for the first time.

First this was restricted to assisting local competitors in off-road events. But soon, realizing the importance of successful results on sales, Montano authorized the factory's official participation in the 1954 International Six Day Trial, held in Wales that September.

Specially prepared versions of the production 98 Sport ohv model were built, and not only did the two factory entries both gain silver medals, but as the smallest machines in the event created a lot of interest—and publicity.

Dott. Montano also realized that to achieve *real* success in sporting events, including road racing, it would be necessary to recruit a new designer—a man who could create legends, that man was Ing. Fabio Taglioni.

Recruited from rivals, FB Mondial, Taglioni's first task was to provide a motorcycle which could not only get the road racing programme under way but also act as a development vehicle for a totally new range of production roadsters. This was not easy, other companies such as MV Agusta, Gilera and Moto Guzzi employed totally separate designs for each purpose. But Montano's instructions were clear: 'the racing programme must benefit the production line'.

So, Taglioni was forced into building a concept which could achieve success on both road and track. And this integral roadster/racer concept led to the 100 Gran Sport. The GS, soon nicknamed the *Marianna*, was announced publicly in March 1955. And when one considers that Taglioni had only joined Ducati a few short months previously, it was a remarkable achievement—as the Gran Sport owed absolutely *nothing* to the earlier pushrod models. Not only this, but the design was to spawn a whole range of racers and roadsters over the next two decades, up to 436 cc!

Gran Sport engine details—note exposed hairpin valve springs, straight-cut primary gears and full circle crankshaft

With a capacity of 98 cc (49.4 × 52 mm) the original Gran Sport was able to take part in the 100 cc sports racing class which was highly popular at the time in Italy. Hitherto this category had been dominated by either two-stroke models from firms such as Benelli and Motobi, or more recently the Laverda ohv sportster. Hardly anyone had even considered an ohc design, except Taglioni of course!

Turning out some 9 bhp at 9000 rpm, the engine was a supremely neat and compact full unit construction device with single overhead-camshaft, featuring exposed rockers and hairpin valve springs. The light-alloy cylinder, with cast-iron liner, was inclined 10 degrees forward, there was an alloy cylinder head with 80-degree valve angles and a separate cambox (unlike later models) and vertically split crankcases. The straight out primary drive and wet multi-plate clutch were on the nearside, transmitting power to a four-speed close ratio gearbox. The crankshaft, with full-circle flywheels, carried a flywheel-mounted generator on its drive side extremity, supplying current for the 6-volt battery of the coil ignition system; and at the opposite end, outside the

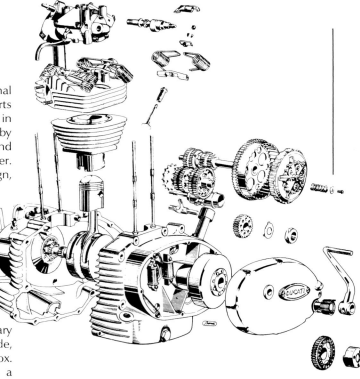

Below **From the smaller Gran Sport, Taglioni then developed a 125 version. This acted as a basis for both the Grand Prix and Desmo 8-litre racers**

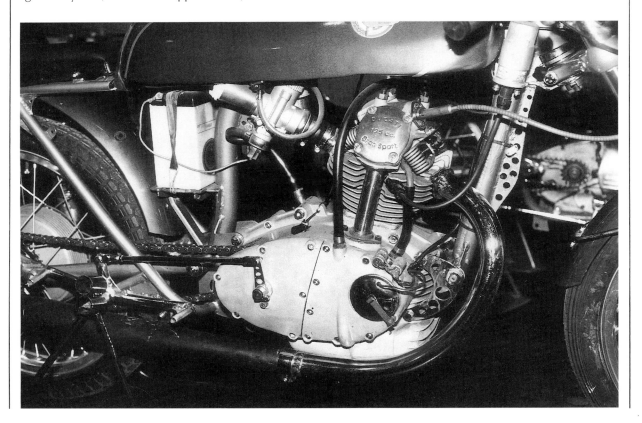

125 Grand Prix, essentially a double knocker GS, it was first tested during the winter of 1955–6

timing bevel, a gear with straight-cut teeth provided the drive for the oil pump and also for the contact breaker. Adjustment of the points could be made through a spring retained inspection cap at the front of the crankcase timing cover.

Drive to the overhead-camshaft was effected by vertical drive shafts and bevel gears—with a split Oldhams coupling half-way up the side of the cylinder barrel.

The crankshaft was equipped with a replaceable connecting rod, which featured a caged roller bearing big-end and phosphor-bronze bush small-end. There was wet sump lubrication and a particularly high quality of castings and specification of materials for the whole engine unit.

If anything the 100 Gran Sport was over engineered, not only making it entirely suitable for such classic long-distance events such as the Giro d'Italia and Milano-Taranto, but the basis of ever increasing capacity enlargements as time went by. Except for the obviously pure racing components such as double webbed con-rod, straight-cut primary gears, high compression

piston, separate cambox, exposed valve gear and a few smaller details it was essentially the same as the later singles which followed it.

Likewise, the frame and the rest of the running gear acted as a prototype of what was to come later. The frame consisted of an open-cradle, single downtube design with the engine acting as an integral stress member.

Other details of this first Taglioni Ducati included a 20 mm Dell'Orto racing carburettor, fully enclosed front and rear suspension, single-leading-shoe conical brake hubs, laced to 17 in. alloy wheel rims, an 18-litre alloy petrol tank, single bum stop racing saddle, and an overall red finish.

Importantly, although the maximum speed was limited to 80 mph (later with more power it was boosted to 87 mph), the fuel consumption—under full racing conditions—averaged an amazing 100 mpg, providing a range of some 420 miles!

After a period of extensive (and successful) testing of the new model at Modena Autodrome during the early spring of 1955, the Gran Sport was ready for its competitive debut—the famous Giro d'Italia. The Giro had first been held in 1953. Limited to machines of not more than 175 cc, it was an ultimate test with its spectacular point-to-point stages run over nine days and covering some 2000 miles of ordinary Italian roads (remember that this was before the motorway network was constructed), which varied from a mere 50 miles to almost 300 miles in a day.

The other challenge was the weather, as it took place in April this could invariably mean several days of unfavourable conditions, and the Giro's claim to have been the toughest, if not the most difficult, of motorcycle road races ever conceived has to be taken seriously.

The bikes taking part fell into two categories: the standard production models, often *very* specially prepared and the so-called sports class (including the Gran Sport), which in effect meant pukka racing machines limited only by certain legal requirements.

In all, there were a total of 37 Ducatis entered for the 1955 Giro. If Taglioni and his team were satisfied with the results of their testing with the Gran Sport, they could have been less sure of their riders—most were totally inexperienced locals from the Bologna area. Ranged against them were some of the country's most experienced racers. The 'unknowns' included Gianni Degli Antoni, Italo Fantuzzi, Leopoldo Tartarini, Giuliano Maoggi and Francesco Villa. Team leader was a certain Bruno Spaggiari. Most, including Spaggiari, were having their first taste of a major event. . . .

Four of the Ducati entries are of particular note: the most gifted was probably Degli Antoni, and it was he who was to prove to be the factory's first star—and the man destined to give Ducati its first ever grand prix victory. Spaggiari needs little introduction to any serious Ducati buff as for almost two decades he raced not only for Taglioni, but also for Benelli and MV Agusta in the 1960s. Later, as the 1970s dawned, he finished second twice in the Imola 200-miler on Ducati V-twins, before finally retiring to become a successful car dealer, first with Peugeot and later Fiat.

Francesco Villa, after a racing career which included works rides with Ducati, Mondial and Montesa, went on to establish himself as one of Italy's leading two-stroke specialists, not only founding the Villa motorcycle factory, with his four times world champion brother Walter, but in 1987 playing a leading role in the rebirth of the Mondial marque.

Finally, Tartarini was to achieve fame together with fellow traveller Monetti when the pair travelled around the world over a 12-month period from September 1957 to September 1958, on a couple of the new 175T ohc roadsters. Later in the mid 1960s he founded the Italjet marque, a company he still controls to this very day.

Ducati were very much the dark horse with their new, unknown motorcycles and equally raw and inexperienced riders, who were not taken too seriously by some of the other factories with several years' racing under their belts. But what transpired rocked the Italian racing fraternity—from a line-up of 37 starters, only

Bevel shaft and series of gears to drive cams on GP engine

nine Ducatis retired and of these eight were the pushrod 98S model!

From the second stage onwards, Degli Antoni roared away from the rest of the bunch to lead his class. After nine stages he comfortably cruised home to record an impressive winning debut for the ohc Ducati single at an average speed of 98.90 kph (61.5 mph). Not only that, he finished 5th overall, and in the process beat a number of larger machines, including some 250s! He even got home in front of the Benelli-mounted 125 cc class winner. The final results saw all the top six in the class Ducati mounted: Degli Antoni, Villa, Fantuzzi, Spaggiari, Maoggi and Scamandri.

Following this highly successful and impressive debut, the Gran Sport went on to pile up a truly amazing run of successes over the next three seasons, not only in the Giro d'Italia, but also in the Milano-Taranto.

Unlike the Giro, the Milano-Taranto was open to machines of up to 500 cc capacity, sidecars and at one time even scooters were included in a history which stretched back to 1919. Then it was called the Milano-Napoli, and the first event was won by a 350 cc two-stroke Garelli at just 24 mph. From then till 1936, it was won by a variety of machines: the American Harley-Davidson and Indian, and the Italian Frera, Bianchi and Moto Guzzi.

The Mandello concern continued their winning run with the first race on the new, full-length Milano-Taranto course in 1937. From then on the famous event became almost the reserve of Guzzi and Gilera—at least so far as the outright winner was concerned. But in 1954 a smaller machine, an FB Mondial ridden by Remo Venturi won, after all the leading Guzzis and Gileras, one by one, blew up or otherwise fell by the wayside.

Ducati machines had previously taken part in the Milano-Taranto, but had been noted for their total lack

Cambox details of GP. Note external oil lines

of success, so for the 1955 event—even though the team had taken the first six places in their class in the Giro, they paid particular attention to the preparation for the event.

They were rewarded with another outstanding performance in the 100 cc category. Degli Antoni led for almost the entire distance at an average speed of 103.172 kph (64.08 mph) for the 1400 kilometre single-stage event, and finally finished 16th overall. This particular achievement should be viewed in the light that unlike the Giro, the Milano-Taranto not only had machines of *five* times the capacity of the diminutive Ducatis, but some were fully fledged grand prix machines, such as Bruno Francisci's winning four-cylinder Gilera!

Once again Degli Antoni led home the 125 cc winner but surprise, surprise, this was also a Ducati, ridden by Giuliano Maoggi.

Working with great speed, Taglioni and his team had burnt much midnight oil in striving to get the larger model ready. When first announcing the 100 Gran Sport, he had made no secret of the fact that the next step would be 125 cc and 175 cc versions.

In reality the 125 had been a relatively easy task, achieved by boring out the cylinder by 5.85 mm, the resulting 55.25 × 52 mm measurement made it the first oversquare Ducati design—a trend which Taglioni was to follow in future years. Although not by any means the first engine where the bore exceeded the stroke, the 125 Gran Sport none the less flew very much in the face of a motorcycle world dominated at the time by the more traditional long-stroke concept.

The appearance of the larger Gran Sport was significant—if only because it was the vital link in the development of a purpose-built circuit racer known as the Grand Prix, which first appeared in early 1956. This featured dohc, but was otherwise mechanically similar to the Gran Sport design.

After extensive development and track-testing at venues such as Modena and Monza, the prototype Grand Prix was given its baptism under fire not only in Italy, but at events throughout Europe including the Saar GP, Dutch TT and Belgian GP, ridden by various riders including the West German Willi Scheidhauser.

However, although it proved a generally competent and reliable performer, the Grand Prix simply couldn't compete on speed with the likes of the MV Agustas, FB Mondials and the new Gilera twin, let alone the two-stroke DKW and Montesa machines. The Gilera, for example, lapped the Spa Francorchamps circuit in Belgium at over 100 mph, fully displaying just what Ducati were up against.

But Taglioni and Ducati had an ace up their sleeve. Through the winter their gifted engineer had been working on his secret weapon: positive-valve operation. Known as the desmodromic system, the earlier history of this has been explained in detail in the preceding chapter. The purpose was to eliminate one of the major restrictions of valve operation at high rpm—the phenomenon of valve float, or bounce! This happened when the valve springs were unable to respond quickly enough to close the valve back on to their seats. The desmodromic idea was to replace the troublesome springs with a mechanical closing system much like that used to open them, thus giving a positive action. Eliminate the springs and you eliminate the bounce and get a higher revving engine, well that was the theory....

Many other men in the two-wheel world had tried but none, until Taglioni, made it work totally successfully. Using the cylinder head of the valve-spring Grand Prix model as a base—although of course there were differences in size and detail—Taglioni drastically cut down development time *and* cost by utilizing the remainder of the dohc from the cylinder barrel downwards, including the 55.25 × 52 mm bore and stroke measurements. This left him free to concentrate his total efforts on the cylinder head and its desmo system.

Like the GP, the front and rear shafts carrying the valve opening cams worked very much the same way as those in the twin overhead-camshaft model. The difference was that on the Desmo these cams actuated the valves through the medium of levers which pivoted inboard of the shafts and not through sliding tappets; the hardened valve caps used on the Grand Prix were used on the valve stems. The cam lobes were extensively hollowed for lightness, a principle used throughout the engine wherever possible—such as gears and the like.

Underneath the lever pivots were two rocker pivots. The inner arms of the rockers bore on the underside of the closing cams (which were mounted on the central shaft), while the outer ends were forked to embrace the valve stems and operated them through flanged collars located by split-wire half rings retained in matching grooves on the valve stem. The closing cams had lobes with longer dwell periods than those of the opening ones. All the cams were a taper fit on their shafts. And the rocker pivots were mounted in fully floating phosphor-bronze bushes. The valve adjusting caps and top collars were made in a variety of thicknesses for adjustment purposes.

To compensate for greater reciprocating weight and the need for ultimate performance Taglioni provided the Desmo with much fiercer cam lifts, although the actual valve opening and closing points were identical to those on the Grand Prix. These higher lifts for the Desmo engine were: inlet 8.1 mm (against 7.5 mm) and exhaust 7.4 mm (against 7 mm).

Taglioni also discovered that it was necessary to close the valves mechanically to only 0.300 mm (0.012 in.) from their seats and relied on valve inertia and gas pressure to achieve the rest. In his early experiments lightweight springs were employed to ensure that the valves returned to their seats. However, these were soon discarded as they were found to be unnecessary.

Each valve was inclined 40 degrees, and the seating material was aluminium-bronze. Valve size remained as the GP—31 mm inlet, 27 mm exhaust with a choice of carburettor sizes, between 22 mm and 29 mm, depending on the circuit.

Fuel consumption, compared to the majority of the desmo's competitors, was truly excellent—up to 50 mpg under racing conditions.

Pistons proved somewhat of a problem. The type used were essentially the same as in the Grand Prix, but varied in compression ratio and supplier. All were forged three-ring affairs, the most common ratio being 10:1. The main problem proved to be hairline cracks around the skirt, even though full skirt, rather than slipper types, were used. Also the top piston ring was

The Grand Prix proved incapable of providing enough power to challenge the MVs, Mondials and Gileras, so Taglioni produced his ace card—the Desmo. Here is how it worked on the 125 Ducati single

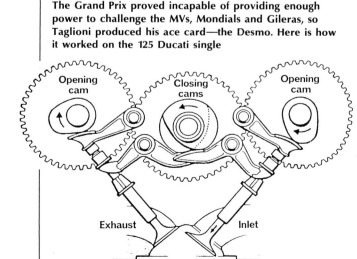

Opening cam   Closing cams   Opening cam

Exhaust   Inlet

prone to breakage. The other problem was that with extra power and higher engine revolutions there was a drastically shortened big-end lift, needing replacement after a single GP or $\frac{2}{3}$ shorter races to ensure total reliability.

The big-end featured a steel cage with 19 steel rollers, each of 3.5 mm diameter and a 30 mm crankpin bearing and diameter—25 mm on the portion pressed into the crankshaft flywheels.

The connecting rod, which also formed the outer race for the big-end, was machined from a solid billet and was, like the Gran Sport and Grand Prix, heavily webbed at both top and bottom for additional strength. The small-end, a simple phosphor-bronze bush affair ran in a 16 mm diameter, taper-bored gudgeon pin which was located into the piston by wire circlips.

Unlike the valve-spring racing models, or for that matter the production single-cylinder models, the main bearings were of the axial-thrust type and spring-loaded outward by a large star washer on the drive side of the fly-wheels. This arrangement was designed to eliminate vibration experienced at maximum rpm with roller bearings owing to the inevitable, however slight, radial running clearance.

Otherwise, the bottom end was an almost exact replica of the Grand Prix, including straight-cut primary drive gears and wet multi-plate clutch. But Taglioni had provided for the choice of five- or six-gear ratios. In either case, four pairs of pinions were situated inside the main crankcase walls, whilst the other pair (or two pairs) were in the primary-drive compartment inboard of the clutch.

With such a high revving single, the SAE20 grade castor oil was preheated before filling the sump and firing up the engine from a cold start. This method had been used earlier by NSU, in particular, who went to great lengths—even employing blowers to ensure that their race engines on the Rennfox and Rennmax models were sufficiently warm before they were run from cold.

It is worth noting that a bonus of the desmo system was its lack of compression—compared to the conventional valve spring layout—in fact the engine could be started whilst the machine was mounted on its paddock stand by simply spinning the rear wheel sharply and dropping the clutch!

Ignition was taken care of by a 6-volt battery and a pair of 3-volt coils. These fed a conventional 14 mm plug on the nearside of the cylinder head and a smaller 10 mm item on the offside—situated at the front of the camshaft vertical drive-shaft housing. Taglioni confirmed recently that, unlike the modern engine of today, dual ignition was needed in the 1950s and 1960s, 'because combustion shape was not of the level it is now'.

Taglioni's first prototype Desmo was in fact a standard dohc Grand Prix, but modified to positive-valve operation. Soon, other more specialized units

July 1956, the Desmo single made its stunning race winning debut at the Swedish Grand Prix—lapping the entire field in the process. The fully faired streamliner was piloted by Degli Antoni

followed—but still with the real secrets confined to the cylinder head.

Much of this early testing was carried out on the bench. Then, when the basic principle had been proved to work further extensive development followed over several months in the spring of 1956, on both bench and track. Power output was found to be some 17 bhp at 12,500 rpm, and most significant of all the desmo valve gear passed all these tests with flying colours. Hundred-hour bench tests on full throttle caused no drop in the engine's performance. And no ill effects resulted from over-revving, even though track-testers were at times letting the revs soar to over 15,000 rpm— a fantastic figure at that time.

By early summer, Taglioni deemed his new brainchild ready for action and the chosen venue for its competitive debut was none other than the Swedish Grand Prix, to be staged at the Hedemora circuit on Saturday and Sunday 14/15 July.

With Geoff Duke and his mighty 500 Gilera four billed as the star attraction, some 40,000 eager spectators from all over Scandinavia and beyond converged on the popular 4.51-mile circuit, hoping to witness a true feast of speed and sound.

As an additional bonus the weather was truly superb—both days' racing were run in dry weather and unusually brilliant hot sunshine. This, unfortunately, brought its own problems, with melting tar at Vasterby hairpin requiring emergency treatment by trackside marshalls.

The first day's racing consisted of various national events and the 350 GP, with Sunday reserved for the main menu, the 500 cc and 125 cc classics. Sunday dawned under a cloudless sky, and at 1 pm the racing got under way with the remaining national event, for 350 cc machines. This was followed by the 125 GP. And as the tiddlers came out on to the starting grid for their race some welcome clouds had taken the edge off the sun's searing heat.

As the flag fell, the two works Desmo singles, with their distinctively white and red fully streamlined front and rear alloy shells, streaked into an instant lead. Piloting the sweet sounding machines were Swedish champion, Olle Nygren and Ducati team leader, Degli Antoni—the latter fresh from his successes earlier that year in the Giro d'Italia and Milano-Taranto events.

Nygren led briefly but by the end of lap 1 it was Degli Antoni who screamed past the start and finish line with a 3-second lead over his team-mate. Nygren, in turn, was 5 seconds ahead of the third place MV Agusta.

When Willi Scheidhauser climbed into fifth place on

his dohc Grand Prix there were *five* Ducatis on the leader-board at the end of lap 2, although only the leading pair were on Desmos. Nygren got back in front on lap 3, but it didn't last as the Italian was first again a lap later. On lap 11, of the 15-lap 67.73-mile event, Nygren retired with a sick engine, leaving Degli Antoni some 2½ *minutes* in front of the next man. And all but the first four men were a lap behind. But even this was not good enough for Degli Antoni, as he put the finishing touches to one of the most sensational grand prix debuts ever by calmly lapping the entire field by the end of the 14th lap! At the finish the Desmo rider had not only set a new race record in a time of 48 min. 8.1 sec., a speed of 84.45 mph—but also a new lap record at 87.56 mph.

Quite simply, the remainder of the field, including MV Agustas, Mondials and Rumis, were completely overwhelmed by this breathtaking performance by machine and rider. For Taglioni it was a very special moment, against all odds he had been vindicated, his Desmo proving beyond all doubt that positive-valve operation could work on a motorcycle engine—and win races too. It was a happy and elated team who celebrated afterwards and prepared to make the long journey southwards.

The Desmo's next race outing was scheduled to be at Monza, the venue for the 1956 Italian Grand Prix just

A few weeks later at the German Grand Prix in August, ex Guzzi rider Alano Montanari took another Desmo to seventh spot

under two months later in September. To prepare for this, Degli Antoni embarked on a programme of preparation which included track-testing at Monza during August. And it was during one of these outings that tragedy struck. Rounding the infamous Lesmo curve, the 26-year-old team leader lost control and crashed heavily, succumbing to his injuries—7 August 1956 was a sad day indeed for Ducati Meccanica S.p.A. Not only had Taglioni and his team lost a true friend and dashing rider, but also with his mechanical skills he had played a vital role in the Desmo's development, Without Degli Antoni the whole programme suffered a major blow.

But with honour at stake the show had to go on, the Grand Prix Des Nations that year was vitally important to any marque striving for recognition in the hotbed of the sales war in the mid 1950s. So hurriedly, newcomer Alberto Gandossi was drafted into the squad to back up Artusi and Nygren.

Monza on 9 September 1956 was at the very height of what today is rightly regarded as the 'Golden Era' of grand prix racing. A massive array of mouthwatering machinery greeted the vast number of spectators who had gathered around Monza to view the spectacle.

It was the 125 cc race which got the proceedings under way. As *Motor Cycling* reported: 'Really I'm not so sure that the 'tiddlers' aren't the noisiest class of all, for conversation is impossible as they line up on the grid revving away with but five minutes to go for the 9.30 am start'. There were 26 of them including Gilera twins, MVs, Mondials, Montesas, DKWs, and the three Desmo Ducatis.

As the field screamed away from the start of the 18-lap, 64.31-mile race in an ear-splitting crescendo of noise, World Champion Carlo Ubbiali (MV) and

In November 1956 this 98 Gran Sport powered streamliner, piloted by Mario Carini and Sandro Cireri, set 44 new speed records at Monza

Gandossi led off the grid. But soon Romolo Ferri, on one of the Gilera twins, had taken over and in the process pushed the lap record to over 100 mph, before being forced out with faulty ignition.

Thereafter, Tarquinio Provini set the pace on a Mondial, but after going even faster than Ferri and setting a new lap record of 101.92 mph even he had to accept second best to that master track craftsman Carlo Ubbiali—the MV star won by a mere 0.4 seconds. Meanwhile, the Ducati trio finished in 5th, 7th and 9th positions (Artusi, Gandossi and Nygren respectively), and at least displayed reliability.

So, as 1956 drew to a close the Ducati team had proved that the desmo concept really did work—even though in a short space of time it had experienced the ultimate in highs and lows of top class racing.

4

Grand Prix challenge

After the highs and lows of 1956, and with a team of 14 riders, 1957 could reasonably have been expected to be a real year of progress for Ducati on the race circuit. But as events were to transpire, it was destined to be just the opposite—for a number of differing reasons.

The death of Degli Antoni at Monza the previous August had cast a shadow over the magnificent desmodromic winning Swedish debut performance. Robbed of their leader, the Ducati race team just couldn't get their act together for the rest of the season. And 1957 was to prove even more of a see-saw— with hindsight these reasons are easy to see.

The pursuit of simply too many goals at the same time proved too much. Formula racing in Italy, the long-distance road events of the Giro d'Italia and Milano-

Taranto (the latter event aborted at the last moment), endurance racing in Spain, and selected grand prix events were just too much for an overstretched design team, who were already busy with the introduction of the new ohc roadsters.

The ultimate result, certainly as regards world championship aspirations, was a management which soon realized that another year would have to pass before a serious effort could be mounted.

This was not to say that there was no success, in fact, many factories would have been highly delighted with

124 cc (55.25 × 52 mm) Desmo single—the first engine design to win Ducati, and Taglioni, truly worldwide acclaim. It was a technical masterpiece

the victories which included the Giro d'Italia (Graziano) Italian F2 and F3 championships, taking the Italian Junior title (Farnè) and the Barcelona 24 Hours (Spaggiari and Gandossi). The F2 championship is significant to this book, because it was gained by a 125 Desmo Sport ridden by Spaggiari.

At GP level, several of the over-the-counter Grand Prix valve-spring models were in action, including ones ridden by the German Scheidhauser and the Dutchman Van Bockel (8th and 10th respectively at Assen in early July). Two weeks later, on Sunday 14 July, a year after their winning debut with the Desmo, the Ducati racing effort returned to Hedemora, for the Swedish GP.

After wet conditions for the 350 cc event the previous day, which had also seen a Ducati victory in a local Nordic-only 125 cc race by the Finn Rauno Aaltonen, the main race day had ideal conditions for racing. The cloud had lifted, fanned by a light breeze, and the edges of the sun-dappled 4.51-mile course were thronged by a crowd of some 50,000 spectators.

Olle Nygren (later to win world acclaim as a speedway rider), who had just won a 15-lap Inter Nordic 350 cc event on his AJS 7R, was on the line with one of six 125 Scandinavian piloted Ducatis for the mixed 15-lap 125 and 250 GP. And in a show of speed and reliability all six Ducatis finished, occupying the first six places! They were won in the following order: Aaltonen, Nygren, Söderström, Nicklasson, Bohlin and Eriksson. The fastest lap, by the winner, was at a speed of 86.18 mph. This was well down on Degli Antoni's 1956 fastest lap of 97.56 mph. But it should be noted that none of the 1957 Swedish bikes had desmodromic heads.

The only grand prix to feature desmo models that year was the home round at Monza on Sunday 1 September. It was the 125s which got the programme under way, with superb weather the crowds had been streaming into the circuit along every road. And although there were rumours circulating regarding various factories quitting racing, the local fans were their usual enthusiastic selves.

Twenty riders were waiting for the starter's flag to fall. A patter of feet and the tiny machines snarled and roared into action with a crescendo of noise. Leading the pack off the line was new Ducati team leader Alberto Gandossi on a desmo single. But this state of affairs was only to last until the Lesmo curve, when Gandossi threw his mount away in spectacular fashion and in the process brought down a third of the field— including Mondial's Cecil Sandford and MV's Tarquinio Provini. And so Ducati's season was over for another year.

During the close season Ing. Taglioni, now with more time available, got down to the serious business of further improving his most cherished creation—the 125

125 Desmo single produced in 1957. Note the change from the 1956 model referred to in Chapter 3, to rear streamlining. By the end of the year full enclosure was banned from world championship events

Romolo Ferri's 125 Desmo single pictured at the 1958 IoM TT in June that year. Unlike the other machines the factory entered, this one featured a lower steering-head and shortened front forks

Desmo single-cylinder Grand Prix racer. He was spurred on by the realization that it would be a straight fight with MV Agusta, as rivals FB Mondial, together with Moto Guzzi and Gilera, had announced their retirement from competition after Monza.

Taglioni was helped in his quest for grand prix glory, because Ducati badly needed the publicity to assist their sales push into overseas markets, which was just getting under way. And in analysing Italian racing strength in the 28 May 1958 issue of *Motor Cycle News*, Italian correspondent, Carlo Perelli, highlighted the desmodromic Ducati as 'the machine most likely to challenge the mighty MV team for honours'.

Not only had detail improvements taken place within the engine, but a new double cradle, tubular frame had been designed—in fact there were two types, one for 'fast grounds' and the other for 'twisty circuits', as Ing. Taglioni put it. There was also a choice of five- or six-speed gearboxes, whilst the brakes had redesigned side plates with repositioned air scoops, front and rear.

In early April, it was announced that the factory would be fielding a full grand prix effort. Riders for the first classic, the Isle of Man TT, were nominated as Romolo Ferri, Luigi Taveri and Sammy Miller, whilst in the Italian championship events riders would be Gandossi, Farnè, Francesco Villa and Spaggiari, amongst others.

Again, besides the open classics the F2 category would have desmodromic entries with Farnè selected to lead a team of *six* other Ducatis in an attempt to retain that particular title.

Before the world championship series got under way in June, Ducati had already established themselves in the leading position at home, in both the F2 and Senior championships classes. On his unfaired Desmo Sport, Farnè clearly led the F2 hunt. But even more important, things were going Ducati's way in the Italian Senior Championships. At the first round, staged at Modena on 25 April, Gandossi had won easily and in the process staked his name for inclusion in the full grand prix line-up. In this race were MV Agusta stars Ubbiali and Provini. . . . Then on 11 May at the Marinadi Ravenna circuit Ducati scored an impressive 1–2 victory. Spaggiari led Romolo Ferri home and in the process set new lap and race records. Meanwhile, Gandossi was unfortunately side-lined due to an accident on his road bike.

Taveri had scored his first victory for a Ducati a week earlier at the Saar GP, a round-the-houses, non-

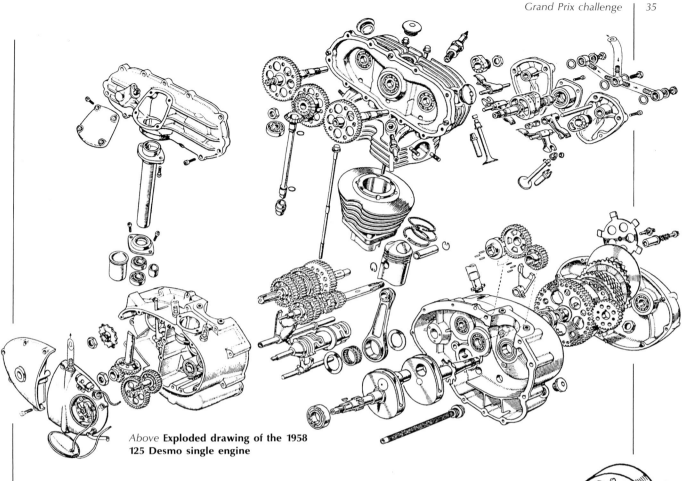

Above **Exploded drawing of the 1958 125 Desmo single engine**

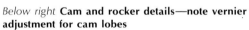

Below right **Cam and rocker details—note vernier adjustment for cam lobes**

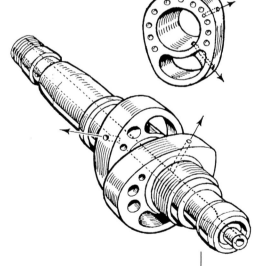

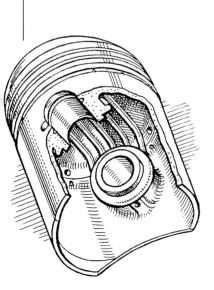

Left **Pistons were forged. Even though they had strengthening ribs they were still prone to breaking up at the extremely high revs of which the single-cylinder Desmo was capable**

Ducati's only really 'class' rider for its 1958 GP campaign was the talented Swiss lightweight star, Luigi Taveri

championship event staged near St Wendel in West Germany, on Sunday 4 May—his 125 Desmo single beating the factory MZs of Ernst Degner and Horst Fugner.

But the little Swiss star's debut for the factory had come at the Austrian GP the previous Thursday, 1 May. Originally billed as the fourth Rupert Hollaus Memorial event (after the famous Austrian NSU works rider killed at the Italian GP in 1954), the meeting over the 3.17-mile *autobahn* circuit near Salzburg, was staged in brilliant spring weather against a background of snow-capped mountains and a huge crowd. Throughout what was the opening race, Taveri held a safe second place behind MV team leader Ubbiali.

And so to the Isle of Man. This was to be staged over the shorter 10.79-mile Clypse circuit and comprised 10 laps (107.9 miles). The original trio had been joined in the official entry list by Gandossi. But in reality he had not fully recovered from his accident and was therefore a non-starter. The only other Ducati out of the 30 entries for the Ultra Lightweight TT was Englishman Fron Purslow with his conventional valve-spring Grand Prix model. Had Gandossi actually raced in the TT, the final outcome at the end of the season might well have been very different—but that is how even world titles are won and lost. . . .

Wednesday 4 June, and the earlier 250 race had hardly finished before most of the riders were back in the paddock to collect their smaller mounts. Gandossi's place in the team had been taken by the experienced English rider Dave Chadwick, so it was four works desmo riders who lined up on the front grid with the MVs of Ubbiali and Provini. The Clypse circuit featured a massed start, rather than the pairs system employed for the longer $37\frac{3}{4}$-mile mountain course. Besides the machines mentioned there were several other entries to make matters interesting, including three works Montesas, a pair of MZs, a Mondial, a Paton (ridden by one S. M. B. Hailwood!), several private MVs and a couple of British specials, the LEF and EMC.

The start got under way at 12.30 precisely and the air was rent with, as the *Motor Cycling* reporter put it, 'an hysterical crackle', as the flag fell. Straight into the lead shot Taveri, followed by Miller, Jim Baughn on the EMC, Provini and Ferri.

By the time Willaston was reached, Ubbiali had moved up to second place behind Taveri with Provini, Chadwick, Miller and Ferri on his tail, but at Creg-ny-Baa, the MVs were already through to the front and everyone imagined a repeat performance of their runaway 1–2 in the 250 race.

But the pundits were to be proved wrong, because as they rounded the Governor's Bridge dip Ubbiali was only a few yards in front of Taveri who was back to second, with Provini on his heels, and rocketing down the Glencrutchery road past the massed grandstands the Ducati screamed up to its maximum revs to blunt the MVs. Chadwick, on the only Desmo without full streamlining, lay a close fourth, followed by Ferri and Miller, with the rest of the pack already well behind.

As the second lap began it was easy to see that the MVs were not going to have it all their own way this time, for Taveri sensationally snatched the lead from Ubbiali before they reached Willaston and as he came through he started his third lap with a 50-yard lead over the Italian, whose team-mate Provini was close behind and some 15 seconds ahead of Chadwick.

The Ducati seemed to have a distinct advantage, but by the time they reached Cronk-y-Garroo Ubbiali was again in front. At Old Hall Corner Provini had displaced Taveri from second and Taveri gave a definite 'thumbs down' as he sped past the start and finish line to complete his third circuit. Taveri's race proved to be over on the sixth (the cause later found to be broken piston rings), but even before this happened Provini, who was by this time in the lead, fell at Onchan on the fourth lap after striking gearbox trouble. So, at the end of the sixth lap Ubbiali led, with Chadwick second, Ferri third and Miller fourth, followed by the MZs of Degner and Fugner.

By the start of the eighth lap most of the fire seemed to have gone out of the race, though Ferri was gradually overhauling Chadwick, apparently with little hope of catching him. But by the end of this lap, drama, as Ferri came through over a minute up on Chadwick, who pulled into his pit without losing any more places to straighten out the gear lever which he had bent when he clipped a kerb. Inspired by his good fortune Ferri then set off in pursuit of Ubbiali. He started his final lap barely 16 seconds adrift of the leader. This was cut to 15 seconds at Hillberry; 14.5 seconds at Creg-ny-Baa; and 10 seconds at Ballacoar. Was a real shock on the cards?

But the MV team had a signalling station out on the course and by the Manx Arms Ubbiali had regained a 16-second advantage, which he held to the end. Even so Ferri's second spot was an outstanding result considering his lack of course knowledge. Chadwick was third and Miller fourth.

Of the two Ducatis which finished second and third, Ferri's was in much the better condition, there being absolutely no trace of oil leakage anywhere on the machine. The desmo cylinder head was lifted free by the machine examiner (a ritual carried out for the first three finishers) and it was then discovered that the piston had a crack on the inlet valve facing side. Ferri's frame was a one-off job specially constructed to accommodate the 29-year-old Italian's extra small stature. All the vital parts of his machine (except the aforementioned piston!) were in excellent order, but it was noticed that his rear tyre (both machines were equipped with Avons) was very much more worn than that of Chadwick whose frame was like that of Taveri and Miller's machines. Chadwick's engine stripped well and did not display the piston problem on Ferri's example.

In reviewing the 1958 TT, in his 'Talking Technically' feature, Graham Walker wrote for *Motor Cycling*: 'From the purely technical angle it was the two Lightweight (125 cc and 250 cc) classes which provided the major interest. Pride of place in novelty was taken by the 125 cc Ducatis with their ingenious desmodromic valve layout'.

At around the same time certain information was revealed about the actual desmos which had been used by the team members in the Isle of Man. Ferri, who had finished second behind Ubbiali's MV, used shorter front forks than his Ducati team-mates; each top stanchion cap was fitted with an interior baffle and an exterior breather nipple equipped with a long length of plastic piping to prevent any risk of oil mist getting on to the rider's goggles. It had been found that without such breathers air compressed in the short, upper fork chambers and tended to stiffen up the springing unduly. It was confirmed that Taveri had a six-speed gearbox, whereas Miller and Ferri had only five cogs, the same for Dave Chadwick. All the four machines employed dual ignition. Finally, as mentioned in the post-race strip examination, Ferri's machine also had a different frame. This was not only shorter than the others but had a lower steering head with heavy

gusseting. The alloy dolphin fairing was also a closer fit, and cut away to clear the exhaust pipe.

Some ten days after the Isle of Man race the next round of the Senior Italian Championship took place at Alessandria on 15 June. This was a battle royal between Ducati Desmo-mounted Bruno Spaggiari and Carlo Ubbiali's MV. Spaggiari led for 13 laps until he crashed, but within two laps had regained the lead and went on to win by one second. He collapsed at the finish and was subsequently found to have sustained a broken collarbone and was rushed to hospital! Provini was third on another MV.

A fortnight later, on Saturday 28 June, the Dutch TT took place over the 4.75-mile Assen circuit. The *Motor Cycling* headline summed things up nicely: 'Tiddler's Day at Assen—MV and Ducati battle in 125 cc class highlight of the Dutch GP'.

The other events by comparison were 'processional'. But then came the 'race of the day' with 'one of the cleanest starts ever'. From the grid, Alberto Gandossi led, as *Motor Cycling* put it 'by the paint on his Ducati's fairing from team-mate Taveri'. But MV team leader Ubbiali was trying everything he knew and slotted into third spot, with Ferri (Ducati) and Provini (MV) close behind.

By lap 4 the watch could not separate the leaders— Taveri, Gandossi, Provini and Ubbiali. Dave Chadwick, also Ducati mounted, lay fifth and 36 seconds in arrears, Ernst Degner on an MZ lay sixth.

Two laps later Gandossi's mount had tired and Provini led with Ubbiali second. But showing the Ducati's potential to the full Taveri was back in front on

Romolo Ferri aboard his 125 Desmo in the 1958 125 TT in which he finished second. He is shown at Onchan on the Clypse circuit

the next lap. Mike Hailwood, having his first ever ride on a Ducati—a production Grand Prix model—lay ninth, two places behind Sammy Miller, which put a total of six Ducatis in the top ten!

Ubbiali, yapping at the heels of the desmodromic Ducati, started to scratch in earnest. He broke the lap record, almost caught Taveri and left Provini's shadow for the first time, 20 yards astern. Thrill upon thrill. By three-quarters distance in the 14-lap, 66.98-mile race Taveri had the lead back again—and the lap record into the bargain. On lap 12 Ubbiali and Taveri duelled side by side! And they stayed that way—exciting stuff.

With the penultimate lap in progress, any advantage was purely a technical one for the timekeepers' books. And back in third spot Provini hung determinedly on to his unaccustomed third spot.

As Ubbiali willed himself towards the chequered flag, Taveri breathed down his neck. The crowd held its breath, the only noise coming from the scream of the high-revving battlers out on the circuit.

Right at the finish Taveri pulled out of the MV's slipstream, closed and just failed to snatch the lead over the line. Thus ended what had been the best race of not only the day but, some would say, of the entire 1958 championship series.

A week later the Belgian GP took place. Held over the ultra-fast 8.774-mile Spa Francorchamps circuit, nestling in the beautiful, heavily forested Ardennes mountains near to the German border in the southern part of the country.

It was here that Ducati notched their first ever classic win, when Gandossi not only set the fastest lap at 99.06 mph, but took victory in the 8-lap race, with team-mate Ferri second. With Provini third and Ubbiali fifth the previously unbeatable MV Agustas were well and truly humbled. Chadwick on another Ducati was fourth and Taveri sixth, thus making Ducati's day complete.

Next round in the world championship series was the German event at the Nürburgring. Held over the difficult tree-lined 14.17-mile circuit, everyone hoped for a repeat of the Ducati–MV battles of the first three rounds. True to form Gandossi overtook early leader Ubbiali on the first lap and as they started their second circuit, led him by four lengths with Provini third.

Displaying superior speed Gandossi piled on the steam and steadily pulled away at the front. Then, disaster struck. First, Ferri crashed breaking a leg and

A trio of 125 Desmo singles at the 1958 Belgian GP. Each one was different in detail

suffered, in addition, badly cracked ribs after he had run out of road. Almost straight after, Taveri's engine went off song and, finally, Gandossi's motor blew up. With all the works Ducatis out, MV took an easy 1–2.

The fifth round of the championship trail was that happy hunting-ground for the Bologna marque, the Swedish GP at Hedemora. And 1958 was the first year it counted towards the world championship series.

The fast 4.51-mile circuit, as in Belgium, proved to the desmos' liking, with the Ducatis again proving more than a match for their MV rivals. Try as they might, Ubbiali and Provini couldn't stop another Ducati victory.

The 15-lap 125 cc race was held in brilliant sunshine at 4 o'clock in the afternoon on Saturday 26 July. At the start, Gandossi and Taveri shot ahead, swapping places occasionally, and only once did either of the MV pair get ahead of them, and then this was for less than a lap before the Ducati duo steamed back in front to take the flag—with Gandossi taking victory.

In his 'Continental Comment', writing for *Motor Cycling*, former world champion Geoff Duke commented, 'only the appearance of the fantastic desmodromic Ducati in the 125 cc class has cramped the style of the all-conquering MV équipe'. Geoff said what everyone, who was lucky enough to witness the 1958 Grand Prix series, was seeing with their own eyes. . . .

From the sunshine of Sweden, the team's next stop was at Dundrod for the Ulster Grand Prix two weeks later on Saturday 10 August. And in contrast to conditions at the Swedish round, the outlook that greeted the 125 cc race which started the proceedings in Ireland was cold and bleak, with heavy mist and cloud enveloping much of the 7-mile, 732-yard natural road course.

The original race entry of 17 had been reduced by non-arrivals and non-qualifiers to 11—four Ducatis, three MVs, two MZs and one apiece for Mondial and Montesa.

At the start East German Horst Fugner streaked away on his MZ two-stroke, hotly pursued by Taveri and Gandossi with Ubbiali close behind. At Leathemstown the three Italians had passed the German and at Jordon's Cross Ubbiali, anxious for world championship points, had forced his way to the front.

At the end of lap 2 Gandossi, the only man who could challenge Ubbiali for the title, was ahead but at the end of the next lap Ubbiali led Gandossi. Dave Chadwick, back on a Ducati and riding brilliantly, was just in front of Provini. However, Provini was shortly to make an error and take the slip road at Leathemstown, followed by terminal gearbox trouble.

On the eighth of the ten laps Gandossi was back in front and he, together with Ubbiali, had drawn clear of the pack. But Gandossi was trying too hard—first he was reported over the loudspeakers as having touched

Fourth placeman Alberto Gandossi cranks his Bologna single through a fast curve at the 1958 Belgian event

the bank at the Hairpin but then came a real blow to Ducati's championship hopes when he crashed at Leathemstown Bridge. Even though he pluckily restarted he could only limp home to finish fourth, his chance of the world title gone—Ubbiali was the new champion. The only consolation for the Bologna team was that Gandossi had made the fastest lap at 79.03 mph.

At the end of August came news that following his accident at the German GP Romolo Ferri would unfortunately not be fit to contest the final round in Italy.

With national pride at stake, if not the world championship, the Ducati and MV teams prepared to do battle for the final time that year. Billed as the *Gran Premio delle Nazioni* (the Grand Prix of Nations), it was held over 18 laps of the 3.59-mile Monza circuit, just outside Milan.

This final chapter in what had been an incredible season was also to be one of Ducati's greatest moments ever as they slaughtered literally everyone—including the mighty MV Agusta team to take the first *five* places!

The final finishing order was Spaggiari (his first GP!), Gandossi, Francesco Villa, Chadwick and Taveri. All were mounted on the desmo singles—which at last seemed totally reliable, except third place Villa, who was giving a brand new twin-cylinder Desmo its debut race. Spaggiari had also made the fastest lap with a speed of 98.04 mph.

When interviewed after the race, Ing. Taglioni said that his new twin was 'practically a prototype and there was every intention of developing it'. This machine, of which only two others were ever constructed, is probably the real Desmo racer which Ing. Taglioni would have conceived, had he not been instructed to work around the basis of the single-cylinder Gran Sport design.

The heart of the twin was, of course, its engine, with triple ohc (and desmodromic valve operation of course!). This was driven by a central train of gears, which ran up between the cylinders in their own compartment. The lubrication system followed that of the successful single, with a gear type pump and separate external oil pipes which fed the top end of the engine. Each camshaft having its own oil line and roller bearing, with return being made through the central gear-drive compartment back to the deeply finned wet sump at the base of the full unit construction crankcases.

Unlike the Desmo single, the twin relied on only a single (10 mm) spark plug per cylinder—for the simple reason there was no room in the combustion chamber for anything larger! The two crankshaft flywheels were clamped to the central take-off gear by Hirth couplings (like the earlier German NSU Rennmax twin).

Other details included special 10.2:1 German Mahle three-ring pistons, equally specially commissioned Dell'Orto 23 mm carburettors with integrally cast oblong float chambers and a close ratio six-speed gear cluster. All six of these ratios were housed with the central crankcase compartment, unlike the single.

Power output of the original twin used at Monza was a claimed 20 bhp at 15,000 rpm. This was later upped to 22.5 bhp for the 1959 season. But its real failing, compared to the single, was an ultra-narrow power-band, making it a real pig to ride.

At the end of November, Ducati announced their racing plans for the forthcoming season. Officially, the factory would be entering all the 125 cc world and Italian championship races in 1959 with both the single-cylinder Desmo model and the new twin. The team was stated to be Taveri, Ferri, Gandossi and Spaggiari. There was also said to be a distinct possibility that Emilio Mendogni, surprise winner of the 1958 250 cc Italian GP on a Morini single, might leave Morini and join the Ducati team. His existing factory seemed to have no intention of participating in all the 1959 world championship events, preferring courses like Monza to the Isle of Man and the Ulster GP. In any case, Morini was a much smaller concern than Ducati and far less able to back a full challenge for grand prix honours.

But perhaps the biggest news, certainly as regards British fans, was the very strong rumour that Mike Hailwood was to be loaned a pukka works 125 cc Ducati. This news was soon to become a reality and is fully related in the next chapter.

When *Motor Cycling*'s Norman Sharpe visited various Italian factories to bring readers the latest race news at the beginning of 1959, he included the Borgo Panigale factory.

At Ducati Meccanica the company's general secretary, Dott. Cosimo Calcagnile, told Sharpe that besides Hailwood 'there would be works 125s for Bruno Spaggiari who was to be found working in the race shop during his visit, and Alberto Gandossi. But the factory was now 'only *thinking* of possibly supplying a machine for Switzerland's Luigi Taveri'.

In fact, the Ducati race shop was, Sharpe commented, 'little smaller than the entire Morini factory'. He met Ing. Taglioni and saw the complete range of 1959 Ducati racers, which not only included the 125 single and twin Desmos, but the latest batch of Grand Prix valve-spring models. Up to the end of 1958 some 30 of these had been produced. They had mainly been sold in Italy and South America. Another 15 had been built that winter, one of which was being readied for despatch to Australian entrant Jack Walters during Sharpe's visit. At that time Ducati had some 700 employees who produced around 20,000 motorcycles a year.

Calcagnile revealed to Sharpe that the design of a 250 Four existed. And though he said there was no intention of producing it at present it was a 'possibility' for the future. This was, in fact, a development of the L-shaped 90-degree vee engine which Taglioni had first become interested in back in 1948—when it had been decided to build a 125 twin, it had been enough to 'remove' the front two cylinders!

The new racing season got under way in Italy during March with the first round of the Senior Italian Championships taking place at Modena on Easter Monday.

A colossal struggle ensued in the 125 class between Gandossi, on a Desmo single, Provini (MV), Spaggiari on a Desmo twin and world champion Ubbiali (MV). The struggle was finally resolved when Provini retired at the pits and Ubbiali passed Spaggiari, who had been plagued by gearbox trouble, with victory finally going to Gandossi. After this excellent result, everyone imagined that the 1959 Grand Prix circus would be a repeat performance of the previous year with a straight fight between MV and Ducati. But it was not to be, only new boy Hailwood making any really consistent impact and by the end of the season the Ducati management had decided to pull out of racing, selling off their works 125s—after first converting them to conventional valve-spring operation. . . .

And so the first chapter of the Desmo saga had come to an end as the 1950s drew to a close.

Besides taking the first five places in that year's final 125 GP at Monza, Ducati rider Francesco Villa also won the Formula 3 race at the same meeting with his 175 FIII Duke on 14 September 1958—a great day for Taglioni and his team

5

Mike-the-Bike

Stanley Michael Bailey Hailwood was born on 2 April 1940, the son of a self-made millionaire motorcycle dealer. Father Stan had taken part in sprints and hillclimbs until 1925, and grass-tracking (as a sidecar man) in the late 1920s when an accident ended his motorcycling and he took up car racing. His four-wheel achievements included finishing fifth in the 500-mile race at Brooklands in 1931.

But Hailwood Senior's real success had been in the business world. He had worked in partnership with Howard King to build up the largest grouping of motorcycle dealerships ever seen in Britain, which had branches in most major cities and towns from its original base in Oxford. He was also a successful player of the stock market and it is perhaps this latter field which contributed greatly to his personal wealth.

All this had meant that Stan was able to enjoy a life-style which few could match, but this in itself was to create a few special problems as will become apparent.

The family home was at High Moor Hall, Nettlebed, on the Oxfordshire/Berkshire border between Walling-ford and Henley-on-Thames, in the Chiltern hills.

Even though his family were affluent, this didn't mean that Mike had an easy, undisciplined existence as a child, far from it. At the tender age of four he was packed off to a kindergarten. At the age of six he was sent to a boarding school (which he hated), followed by the Pangbourne Nautical College. So his upbringing was very much within the British public school system. His sister Chris thinks it made him more independent, even though at the time he was often very unhappy.

Mike's first real contact with motorcycles came at the age of seven, when he rode a specially-built 98 cc Royal Enfield powered mini bike, pottering around the lawn and, later, a chalk pit on his father's estate. Soon, with Geoff Duke as his hero, our youngster became deeply interested in road racing. He was soon to get first-hand experience. . . .

Just after his 17th birthday Mike entered, or to be more precise his father entered him, in his first race at Oulton Park on 22 April 1957. At the famous Cheshire circuit he rode a 125 MV Agusta sohc Sport Competizione, loaned by Bill Webster, to 11th place. Unknown to our hero, father Stan and *Websterini* conspired to keep the newcomer out of mischief by ensuring that the machine was overgeared and over-jetted for the circuit.

This relatively insignificant debut was followed by a whole string of ever improving results over the following months. 'Meteoric' was the term most used to describe his progress! And not only racing, as he even rode a Triumph Cub in the 1957 Scottish Six Day Trial. In many ways it was really his father who created and carved out Mike's competitive riding career. One has to realize that Stan Hailwood was a truly 'awesome personality', as close friend Ted Macaulay once described him, and a man who was *always* used to getting what he wanted in life. And with Mike this meant that the youngster had to be successful out on the track.

John Surtees described it another way: 'I remember feeling rather sorry for Mike, because if ever anybody set out to manufacture a world champion, Stan set out to make Mike one, and fed him relentlessly into a

A young Mike Hailwood riding around the family's Nettlebed, Oxfordshire estate, aged around eight years

starmaking machine fuelled by his money and his overwhelming personality.'

I came across this state of affairs, when as the Cagiva importer in 1980, my company was importing the WMX125 motocrosser. As the world's first *production* water-cooled dirt racer the little Italian bike attracted considerable publicity appearing as it did bang in the middle of the motocross season. Ranged against the air-cooled Japanese machines it was a race winner in the highly competitive schoolboy motocross events. A feature of the schoolboy dirtbike racing scene were the Stan Hailwood type characters, men who had made their own way in life and had succeeded in the dog-eat-dog world of commercial life. These men were in a position to provide the very best equipment for their sons. Unfortunately, quite often these youngsters were just not talented enough to take advantage or didn't want to race anyway. More often than not the father just couldn't see this, or accept it. The result was that the son could be seen in tears, sometimes even before the race started!

Mike, therefore, *had* to succeed. A more difficult task than one might think. It's one thing to do it entirely off your own back, with no pressure. Just stop a minute and think if *you* would have been able to race—and win, with a millionaire father breathing down your neck!

From day 1 the Hailwood équipe had nothing but the best—even going as far as transporting the bikes to

Mentor and father, Stan Hailwood

meetings in a vast transporter with the words 'For the love of the sport' emblazoned on its sides in enormous letters.

John Surtees again: 'That was typical of Stan, and certainly in those days when you thought of Hailwood you thought of Stan first, and Mike second, trailing along behind Dad, dominated.'

The press soon began to run stories with titles such as 'The Golden Boy; The fastest Teenager on Earth; The Lad born with a Silver Clutch Lever in his Hand,' and many others.

But strangely this father–son relationship seemed to be the reason why Mike made the grade. The only place where he himself was in charge was when he was alone out on the track. And perhaps, even without realizing it a motivation to win developed more and more. Incidentally, Mike always referred to his father as Stan—or 'Stan the wallet'.

Certainly in that first year the big brash arrival on the scene by the Hailwood équipe created as many enemies as it did friends. Many objected to this, as they saw it as 'money speaks' success. This was another problem which the young Mike had to put up with. Many disliked the name Hailwood, not because of the son who was doing the riding out on the track, but the team's creator, father Stan.

By August 1957, Mike had qualified for an international licence, having scored four wins, three seconds, three thirds and three fourth places in just 18 races.

But his international debut at Oulton Park didn't get off to the best of starts. After finishing second in the 50 cc race and third in the 125 cc category he made a mistake and took a tumble after running out of road in the 250 cc race, on his double-knocker 203 cc MV, when chasing John Surtees' NSU Sportmax and finished up with a broken collarbone.

In typical fashion Stan then bought the NSU from Surtees for Mike! And it was the machine with which he undertook his first overseas racing when, with Dave Chadwick, he wintered in South Africa. Without a doubt this was a major reason why he was able to mount such a challenge in 1958. In Chadwick, Mike had the advantage of a travelling companion who was able to pass on much useful experience, and therefore greatly shorten the Hailwood learning curve time.

The South African racing season took place from December to March and far from being a backwater and a way of gaining easy victories it was highly competitive. This was helped by the fact that several of the world's leading riders had originated from that part of the world over the years, and the local race machinery was allowed to run on alcohol, making machines such as the 250 Velocette competitive.

From his race winning debut in the Port Elizabeth 200 on 1 January, where he set an eyebrow-raising lap record of 92.87 mph, to the final meeting at Cape Town

Tuner Bill Lacey (left), Mike and Stan. The combination was not always a harmonious one

on 29 March, Mike put together a string of impressive results—and at all but two meetings set new lap records!

'South Africa did me a world of good', recalled Mike afterwards. 'Dave Chadwick taught me a lot.'

He flew back, having his first meeting of the new British season on 4 April at Brands Hatch. At the Kentish circuit he won the 200 cc class on his MV and finished second on the NSU in the 250 cc.

In *Motor Cycling*, dated 1 May 1958, Geoff Duke commented: 'If the results in South Africa and various British circuits are anything to go by, the name Mike Hailwood should appear on many leader-boards.' The former world champion couldn't have been more accurate in his forecast. . . .

At the very beginning of the 1958 British season, *Ecurie Sportive*, as the Hailwood équipe was now called, boasted MV Agustas for the 125 and 200 classes and the NSU for the 250 cc. By May those had been joined by a pair of Manx Nortons for the 350 and 500 cc categories. To maintain this vast array of machinery, which often included spare bikes and engines, the services of top tuner Bill Lacey were acquired. In a recent interview Lacey revealed that his time with *Ecurie Sportive* was not always entirely harmonious—

the problem being the overbearing manner of Stan Hailwood. In fact, had it not been for Mike, Bill Lacey wouldn't have returned to the fold under any circumstances following one big bust-up.

Besides his racing, Mike somehow found time for his other big interest, music—jazz and playing the piano at his parents' Nettlebed home.

The purpose of obtaining the Nortons had been to enable him to compete in all four classes of the Isle of Man TT that June. The usual route to the TT had been through the Manx grand prix races in September. But Stan wanted Mike in the TT without serving any 'apprenticeship' in the amateur races.

His TT mounts were a 125 Paton, the ex-Surtees NSU Sportmax and the brace of Nortons for the larger classes. Mike finished in all four races—no mean achievement in itself—7th in the 125 cc, 12th in the 350 cc, 13th in the 500 cc and a superb 3rd in the 250 cc.

Third place in a TT, for a rider who had only just celebrated his 18th birthday, was an outstanding result. And proved that his ability was for real.

Next came the Thruxton 500-mile endurance race

on 21 June, where he and co-rider Dan Shorey shared a 650 Triumph T110. Both riders worked at that time at the Triumph factory (a job which Mike didn't like). In addition they had the same oil company, BP, which was as good a reason for sharing the bike as anything else.

There were other connections too, Dan Shorey's father, Bert, ran a motorcycle business, North Bar Garage in Banbury, and had quite often dealt with Stan Hailwood's Oxford branch. The pair showed a clean pair of heels to all the other teams to score a popular win. Later, when Mike had full factory support from Ducati, Dan raced Mike's old valve-spring GP model, on which he gained considerable success in 1959 and 1960, before it passed on again, this time to Jim Curry.

Dan Shorey recalls Hailwood Senior as someone who was 'not afraid to call a spade a spade—and a shrewd businessman'. He also said he could get on with him, although he realized that many couldn't.

Having seen the performance of the Desmo Ducatis in the Ultra-lightweight TT, and after consultation with old friend Dave Chadwick, Stan Hailwood purchased an ex-Fron Purslow valve-spring dohc Grand Prix model. Mike's first race on the Ducati was at the Dutch TT—his European debut.

As mentioned briefly in the preceding chapter Mike finished 10th in the 125 cc race at Assen. He also came

One of Mike's 125 Desmo singles, with which he scored so many victories over a two-year period

4th on the NSU and 5th in the 350 on his smaller Norton. This, combined with his IoM success, at last silenced the critics who had said his success was entirely due to the financial backing of his father.

The following weekend the *Motor Cycling* headline read: 'Four Victories for Mike Hailwood.' The setting was the Wiltshire circuit of Castle Combe. Not only did he gain his first Ducati victory, but he also broke the class lap record for good measure.

Then came the next round in the world championships—the German GP at the Nürburgring. He didn't have an entry in the 125, but took fourth in the 350—behind Dave Chadwick, also Norton mounted, and the two front-runners, Surtees and Hartle, on works MV Fours. In the 250 race he was out of luck when he was forced to retire on the first lap after his NSU developed brake trouble.

On August Bank Holiday Monday, some 15,000 spectators flooded into the famous Crystal Palace circuit in south-east London to see some excellent racing over a period of 4 hours. The 1.39-mile circuit gained Mike more victories for his Ducati and NSU, but in the 500 his Norton went sick.

Whilst the Ducati factory were staging their famous 'first five performance' at Monza on Sunday 14 September, Mike was at Silverstone the day before for the Hutchinson 100 meeting, scoring yet more victory 'benefits', as the press termed them, with his Ducati and NSU machines in the two lightweight races.

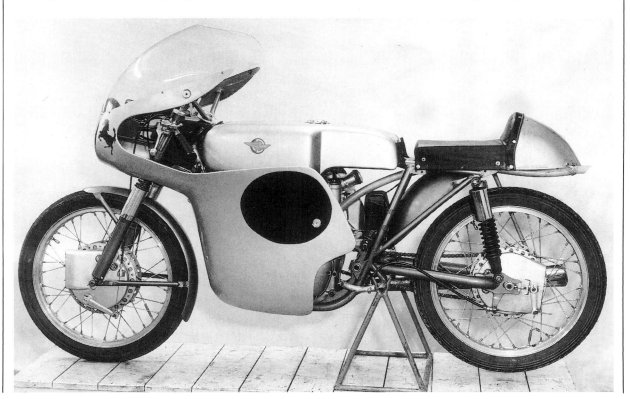

After Silverstone came Aintree on 27 September, which brought the season to a close with yet another Ducati triumph.

November saw the young star, as he now most surely was, awarded the coveted Pinhard Trophy (the most notable contribution to motorcycling by anyone under 21), to add to his 125, 250 and 350 ACU road-racing stars (British championships).

If the South African results are counted, the 1958 season had seen Mike Hailwood win a total of 29 races of national or international status, plus numerous more minor events.

The next major event—and certainly one very relevant to this book—was in January 1959 when a new company, Ducati Concessionaries Ltd of 80 Burleigh Road, Stretford, Manchester, was formed.

By now the motorcycle dealerships controlled by Stan Hailwood, mainly operating under the King's label, had risen to over 20 outlets, making it the largest such grouping in Britain. This commercial muscle had enabled Hailwood Senior to take full advantage of the situation which had arisen when the former British Ducati distributors, S. D. Sullam Ltd, had ceased importing the machines in September 1958. Ducati

Concessionaires Ltd was, in fact, an offshoot of the King's of Manchester dealership and was run by sales director Alan Mullee.

Many observers saw this as an ideal bargaining chip for Stan to further Mike's racing career—and they were to be proved correct. The very first transaction by the new company was to obtain a pair of pukka works Desmo 125 singles and the full-time services of a factory mechanic, Oscar Folesani.

They also obtained the services of a couple of British mechanics, Jim Adams and John Dudley. The latter pair worked mainly on the non-Ducati machinery in the Hailwood team.

Whilst at the factory Stan agreed to purchase one of the race 175 valve-spring F2 twins. Although at the time this attracted considerable attention in the British press it proved a total flop. The man most affected by its failure was leading privateer Arthur Wheeler, who had also ordered a 125 Grand Prix model. Wheeler was none too pleased, and subsequently forced Stan Hailwood to buy it back. As recounted in my book, *Ducati Twins*

Hailwood race mechanic Jim Adams working on a 125 Desmo with fellow spannerman, John Dadley

Mike (centre), with Gary Hocking (seated on bike) and Dr Joe Ehrlich, before the start of the 1959 Ulster GP

(Osprey), this machine then sat around the factory for many months gathering dust before eventually being converted into a full 250.

The curtain raiser to what promised to be an exciting season for the Hailwoods kicked off at the end of March, with a full programme over the Easter weekend: at Brands Hatch (Friday), Snetterton (Sunday) and Thruxton (Monday).

At Brands Hatch, a 3-lap opening 50 cc race was followed by one for up to 200 cc. Mike and his 125 desmo were pitted against Dave Chadwick's MV. His old travelling companion won the closely-fought duel, but Hailwood was close behind on a wet track. In the 250 class the NSU was replaced by an ex-works FB Mondial.

At Snetterton the *Motor Cycling* race report headline read: 'Two Men Share Five Wins—Mike Hailwood and Pip Harris dominate'. It went on to say 'Three solo races in a row fell to young Mike Hailwood at Norfolk's

Snetterton last Sunday. Only a brilliant ride by Bob Anderson in the Senior event robbed him of a clean sweep of the solo part of the programme.'

The first of the day's races was the 125 cc 4-lap event. Astride his works Desmo single Hailwood was away like a rocket at the drop of the flag. By the end of the first lap of the 2.71-mile airfield circuit he had built up a fantastic lead of well over half a mile! And by the finish he had broken the lap record by over 5 mph, with a new speed of 77.73 mph.

The following day at Thruxton was acclaimed: 'A Hailwood Benefit'. Winning all his races, Mike totally dominated the national, solo-only meeting. Torrential showers made the broken surface of the 2.275-mile course hazardous, but Mike piloted his Ducati, Mondial and pair of Nortons with a skill which belied his lack of years.

And this, at least in the smaller classes, was a taste of what was to be repeated time after time on British short circuits that summer.

Then it was to the Isle of Man for the 1959 TT, once again the first classic of the year. Mike had the distinction of being the first man away during

Mike, Aberdare Park, 15 August 1959, a week after his first grand prix success. He won every race he started including the 125 event

practising, when he pushed his 499 cc Manx Norton into action on Saturday evening 23 May.

But it was not until Monday evening 25 May that the opening 125 cc session got under way. Press interest centred around the debut of the Japanese Honda team, which although appearing fast, none the less failed to achieve leader-board places.

There were two riders on works 125 Ducatis—Mike Hailwood and Bruno Spaggiari, who was making his TT debut and was reported by *Motor Cycling* to have 'shown splendid form on a desmo single', while Mike rode one of the twin-cylinder models—the first time he had used it in anger. Spaggiari was third fastest at 71.25 mph, Hailwood fifth at 69.54 mph. In the race on his trusty single, Mike came home averaging 72.15 mph. But after a promising start Spaggiari retired on lap 3 of the 10-lap race.

Second place went to ex-Ducati teamster Taveri who had become an MZ rider.

The next classic was the German GP at Hockenheim. Here Ducati fielded three works bikes—with Hailwood, Spaggiari and Francesco Villa. Gandossi was absent, he had been seriously injured whilst practising at Modena

Right **Mike (7) on his way to his first GP victory ahead of MZ rider Gary Hocking; 125 cc Ulster GP, 8 August 1959**

The British importers produced this range brochure showing Mike winning the 1959 Ulster GP on his Desmo single

in early May. It was Mike's spirited attempt, when piloting his Desmo single in the 125 race, to break up the MV pairing of Ubbiali and Provini which was the highlight of the meeting. In this race the leadership changed hands no fewer than *ten* times. Although never having ridden at Hockenheim before, Hailwood gave the two experienced MV stars something to think about, and at the end was not far astern of the Gallerate duo. Mike's average race speed was 97.62 mph (against Ubbiali's 97.74 mph). Villa came next and then Spaggiari, giving the Bologna team third, fourth and fifth places.

The Dutch TT at Assen on 27 June saw Spaggiari turn the tables by finishing second to winner Ubbiali, with Mike in third spot. But the following weekend on 5 July at Spa Francorchamps for the Belgian round Spaggiari finished a lowly eighth, whilst Mike was a non-finisher.

Two weeks later over the weekend of 25–26 July, that happy hunting-ground for Ducati, the Swedish GP, for once failed the Bologna team. The first Ducati was Mike in fourth position behind winner Provini, Ubbiali (both MVs) and East German Walter Musiol (MZ).

But to make up for what had in the main been a disappointing season, after the great promise shown in 1958, relief was just around the corner. The Grand Prix circus then crossed the Irish Sea for the Ulster GP on Saturday 8 August. It was destined to be a day that two future world champions would never forget—and their first GP victories.

In both the 125 cc and 250 cc classes champion elect Carlo Ubbiali's lead was not entirely safe from attack from his own team-mate Tarquinio Provini. But the smaller factory MV Agustas failed to arrive, so Carlo was 1959 125 cc and 250 cc World Champion anyway.

This meant that southern Rhodesian Gary Hocking, with a pair of fleet East German MZs, and Mike, with his 125 desmo Ducati and 250 Mondial, were ready to do battle. Each was to wear a laurel wreath before the day was out.

On the hill-tops above Belfast, the 7.42-mile Dundrod circuit could be an unpleasant place on a rainy day (witnessed by the 1958 event!) But for once the

Right **The engine which promised so much, but delivered so little, the 1960 250 Desmo twin, commissioned by Stan Hailwood for son Mike to ride**

sun smiled, and thus guaranteed a large crowd and exciting racing. As the 125 race got under way to start the programme, Hocking hurtled into the lead, with our hero finding a niche just ahead of Ernst Degner (MZ). That order was not to change throughout the opening lap.

By lap 2 things were really hotting up, for Hailwood was hard on Hocking's tail. Degner held the second MZ in a solitary third position, in front of several private Ducatis and MVs, headed by ex Guzzi star Ken Kavanagh and young Alberto Pagani, son of the MV racing team manager.

At Cochranstown Mike slipped past Gary, but at the pits they were almost side by side, and Hocking passed

Below **250 Desmo twin, prior to its first test session at Silverstone, March 1960. The prancing horse motif on the fairing had exactly the same origin as Ferrari's—it was the emblem of World War 1 air ace Francesco Baracca's squadron, of which Taglioni's father was also a member**

on the long straight down towards Leathemstown. But with one circuit of the 12-lap, 74.16-mile race to go it was evident that Mike was pulling away from the Rhodesian, the MZ's engine having lost its edge. Still, it got him home to a safe second place with Hailwood in the end taking an easy victory—his first classic.

Later, in the 250 race Hocking turned the tables, with the MZ rider finishing ahead of the Hailwood Mondial.

When interviewed later, after the end of the 1959 racing season, Mike picked out his first ever GP win in Ulster as the main highlight of his career, up to that time.

Exactly seven days after that memorable milestone in the Hailwood story, Mike was back in short-circuit action. The location was the 1320-yard Aberdare Park course. Here, Welsh enthusiasts were treated to a feast of 'outstanding racing' as *Motor Cycling* put it. As the crowd left the venue, the name on everyone's lips was that of the native of Nettlebed, 'Mike-the-Bike' Hailwood, who won every race he started, which of course included the 125 event.

In quick succession there followed a whole host of Hailwood–Ducati triumphs, as race and lap records fell in the style of that summer 30 years ago.

'Mike's Mellano' shouted the press headlines following a record-breaking session aboard his 125 desmo at Silverstone on Saturday 22 August in the international Hutchinson 100 meeting. By leading the 125 Championship race at 84.54 mph—a *race* average of 2.4 mph faster than the previous *lap* record, Mike won the coveted Mellano Trophy. This award went to the rider whose average race speed exceeded the

existing lap record by the greatest margin, or approached it most closely if no lap record was broken. Held over the full 2.92-mile circuit the organizers, BMCRC (British Motor Cycle Racing Club), had attracted a truly star-studded line-up.

When the 125s came to the line it was no secret that Mike and his Desmo single, would set a sizzling pace to bid for the Mellano Trophy. Even so, few were prepared for the state of affairs at the end of the first lap, when his lead extended from Copse Corner to Woodcote— more than a quarter of a mile!

By the end of the 6-lap 17.52-mile race, not only had Mike smashed the old lap record from 82.14 mph to 86.60 mph, but was half a lap in front of second-place Dan Shorey on an ex Hailwood 125 valve-spring Grand Prix model, with Irishman Tommy Robb on another GP Ducati in third place.

But just to prove that no machine performs perfectly all the time, Hailwood's Desmo single was most decidedly off-colour at the Italian GP in Monza on 10 September and he could only finish a lowly eighth, just failing to be lapped by race-winner Ernst Degner's MZ. Even this was better than his 250 race result, when on a borrowed works MZ twin he only finished tenth.

Even so, in his first full GP season Hailwood had finished third in the World Championships on his Desmo single (and fifth on a Mondial in the 250).

Sunday 28 September saw the *Ecurie Sportive* équipe

250 Desmo without fairing. Note Norton forks and Girling rear shocks. Even these failed to cure its handling problems

back home in England, and in action at Snetterton. The 2.71-mile East Anglian airfield circuit witnessed brilliant sunshine and windless conditions for this its last meeting of 1959.

To an ear-splitting exhaust cacophony 25 125s left the grid to get the 11-race programme under way. Straight to the front went Mike, with his screaming Desmo single. He then gained an unassailable lead and steadily pulled away from the opposition.

Six days later, as he had done so many times throughout the season, Mike once again won the 125 race at the last British international meeting of the year, at Aintree on 26 September.

But the British racing season was not yet over and Mike scored a record-breaking *seven* wins in a single day at Biggin Hill, Kent—the famous Battle of Britain fighter airfield.

A week later came the first official news of a 250 Ducati twin which was being specially constructed in the Bologna race shop. Like his successful 125, this was a Desmo and the work of Ing. Taglioni. Though it followed the layout of the smaller twin-cylinder model, the new bike was to have a frame based on drawings supplied by Stan Hailwood. Much was expected of this new design. And the Hailwood camp expressed its great enthusiasm for the whole project. On the surface it appeared to have real potential, which can be understood when one looks at the achievements gained by the 125 Desmo single.

Mike had also been offered works MZs, but was reported to favour the new Ducati instead, such was his confidence in the factory's ability.

In October, as detailed in Chapter 1, Ing. Taglioni was rumoured to be joining MV Agusta and Ducati themselves rumoured to be in financial trouble. These press stories proved to be incorrect, although the racing programme—except for the new 250, was being pared back. In fact Dott. Montano, the general manager of Ducati, was so incensed by references to the factory's financial situation and internal affairs—which he flatly denied—that he was reported to be considering taking legal action against the offending parties.

If nothing else, these stories and counter-claims served to keep the Ducati name in the public eye—any publicity is good, or so the saying goes. . . .

A month later Taglioni said himself there was every possibility that valve-spring versions of the 250 Desmo twin engine would be made available to top privateers (but nothing was to come of this). And a new type of Mahle piston for 125 was reckoned to give an additional 2 bhp output. Finally, he repeated his denial of the rumour that he would join MV and added that if the Ducati racing department was made semi-independent he would take charge of it.

On 10 December Ducati's general manager Dott. Montano announced that Mike Hailwood and 'another British rider' would use the 250 Desmo twins in the following year's world series. But that the factory would only compete in the 125 championships if it promised 'to be particularly interesting'.

The machine, which *Motor Cycle News* referred to as 'that 250' finally arrived in England at the end of March, just in time for the new racing season. Taglioni had been working flat out all winter, not only building the 250 twin for Hailwood, but also working on another couple of designs for Australian veteran Ken Kavanagh.

Mike went straight to Silverstone for tests. It was, in fact, his first *real* chance to try the machine. He had ridden it at Modena but the track was, in his opinion, 'far too bumpy and too slow to genuinely assess its capabilities'. From Silverstone Mike reported that the Desmo twin 'had really got something and is capable of at least 130 mph'.

Timed by the press on varied laps it was found that as the day progressed his times came down from around 2 minutes 10 seconds to just over 2 minutes, representing a speed of between 86 and 87 mph.

Bore and stroke measurements of the engine were 55.25 × 52 mm, identical to the 125 single, giving a capacity of 249.7 cc. Power output was 37 bhp at the rear wheel, or 43.3 bhp at the crankshaft at 11,600 rpm—with maximum torque at 11,200 rpm. Transmission was via a six-speed gearbox built-in unit with

Except for several wins on the British short circuits, the best performances put up by Hailwood and his twin were a couple of fourth places in Holland and Ulster (pictured)

the engine following the line of the earlier Desmo racers. Of particular note was the engine porting arrangement, the carburation induction tracks were divergent and the exhaust ports were convergent.

Float chambers of the twin 30 mm Dell'Orto SS racing carburettors were of the flat type (as used on the period MV Fours) due to the limitation of space. These were similar to those fitted on the 125 twin—which on the smaller engine gave nothing but trouble, being prone to flooding the engine once the machine left the vertical position.

Oldani twin leading-shoe brakes were fitted to both wheels. The front component of 220 mm diameter and 200 mm at the rear.

Forks were shortened Manx Nortons (also used on the works MZs), whilst the frame was a twin duplex affair. Typical of the attention to detail which had gone into the design was the simple but effective arrangement used for the adjustment of the rear chain.

The wheel spindle was mounted eccentrically within two circles of metal, which in turn rotated with two clamps located at the extreme ends of the swinging arm. Years later a similar, although technically different, system was used in certain Ducati production models from the mid 1970s onwards. A pair of 6-volt 7-amp/hour batteries were used in series together with twin coils for the ignition.

Twin generously proportioned megaphones extended almost to the rear tyre and were swept upwards in a peculiar bend, this was not so much for engine efficiency but ground clearance reasons.

When it appeared, the 250 Desmo twin was without doubt the most powerful $\frac{1}{4}$-litre four-stroke racer in the world. Unfortunately, it had three major drawbacks. Firstly, it needed at least a season's development on the racetrack with the full support of the factory, it was at least 50 lb overweight and finally, to quote Mike, 'It was the fastest five-bar gate in the world'. Which meant that it didn't handle well.

These major failings were none too apparent to the world's press when the machine made a victorious debut at the Silverstone international BMCRC Championship meeting on Saturday 9 April 1960. Following his Mellano Trophy ride of the previous season, Mike was able to retain the coveted award with the brand new twin when he won the 250 race, and in the process set a new lap record at 91.43 mph. The deep note of the desmo engine could be heard all the way round the Northamptonshire circuit.

To conclude a successful day, Mike also won the 125 race on his Desmo single, and took second places in both the 350 and 500 races behind Bob McIntyre.

The 14 April issue of *Motor Cycle* carried the exciting news 'that Ken Kavanagh will ride a 350 Ducati desmodromic twin in the Junior TT'. *Motor Cycle* went on to say that he had been so pleased with the 125 and 220 cc dohc singles, on which he had scored seven wins

on his winter tour of Australia, that he had persuaded Ing. Taglioni to increase the bore and stroke of the 250 Desmo twin. Kavanagh was reported to be giving the 350 its baptism at Imola on Sunday 24 April, meanwhile Taglioni was striving to get a sister model ready for Hailwood to ride in the Isle of Man.

The new engine had a bore and stroke of 64 × 54 mm (against 55.25 × 52 mm for the 250) and maximum power, measured at the rear wheel, was claimed to be 48 bhp at 11,000 rpm. As the bike was in all other respects identical with the 250, it was expected that its performance would be impressive, in particular its acceleration with a much superior power to weight ratio.

The double act of the Desmos continued when on Good Friday 15 April Mike took his 125 single and 250 twin to easy victories at Brands Hatch. But, two days later, Mike's Easter racing which had started so well at Brands Hatch, ended abruptly at Snetterton on Sunday. Shortly after notching up a new 250 lap record, the Oxfordshire ace swung his Ducati into the second bend of the Esses, when a Velocette rider, whom he was about to lap dropped his machine almost under the twin's front wheel and Mike had to lay the model down and slide to a halt to avoid collision.

The unfortunate Velo rider was taken to hospital with concussion and suspected head injuries but Mike escaped with a severe shaking and a badly gashed heel, though that was enough to put him out of action for the rest of the weekend.

Gearbox, crankshaft and cam drive details of 125 Desmo twin

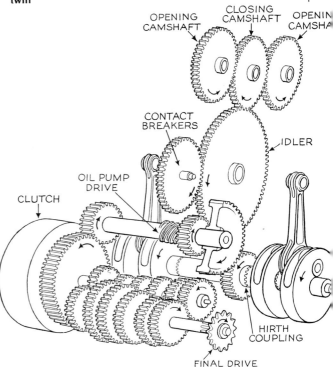

The 125 Desmo twin proved even less successful. Although Hailwood Senior purchased the factory's stock of three bikes, they were soon sold off to Southampton rider/agent Syd Lawton, whose son Barry is shown piloting one (79) at Mallory Park, 31 March 1963

But although the new 250 twin had not been beaten, some questioned even at this early stage just how successful it would prove. Typical comments were those of Mick Woollett writing in *Motor Cycle News'* Paddock Gossip dated 4 May: 'Although Mike Hailwood's 250 cc "desmo" Ducati proved fast enough to win the class quite easily in our races I wasn't very impressed by the speeds put up—to stand a chance in the world championship series these days you have to have a "250" considerably faster than standard production 350 cc Manx Nortons and 7R AJSs.'

With that in mind, Woollett called round to see Mike and his mechanic Jim Adams at their Nettlebed workshop. When questioned about the 250's maximum speed (claimed by the factory to be 135 mph) Mike replied, 'I don't know. The roadholding and general handling were so bad that I never had it flat out.'

The 250 Desmo twin was back in Italy, supposedly to have a new frame fitted.

By the end of May, Stan Hailwood was able to announce that he'd bought all three of the works 125 Desmo twins complete with spares. However, from later events when Bruno Spaggiari raced one in Spain during 1963 this is debatable.

But Stan realized that roadholding was not as good as the singles and they were still plagued with carburation problems. At that time he was not quite sure what to do. He might decide to keep all three and run a team or he might sell two and keep one for Mike. (In the event, the two known to have reached England were sold to Southampton dealer Syd Lawton and were ultimately raced by his son Barry.)

The new 350 Desmo twin for Mike (as opposed to the one for Kavanagh) arrived in England by air on the morning of Thursday 26 May. Mike tried it at Silverstone that afternoon but in his opinion the roadholding just wasn't good enough for that weekend's big Silverstone Saturday meeting, so he rode his AJS 7R.

But perhaps most serious was that the 250 model didn't seem to have benefited from its trip back to

Italy—in fact Mike couldn't equal his lap times of earlier in the year, even though he still won the 250 race.

Once again, the faithful Desmo single proved the best bet when he not only won the 125 race, but broke his own lap record with a speed of 87.22 mph!

Then came the annual visit to the Isle of Man for the TT. And unlike some riders Mike thoroughly enjoyed racing over natural road conditions like those to be found in Mona's Isle. He entered three classes on Ducatis in 1960. His 125 (and Ken Kavanagh who was also down to ride a 350 Desmo twin) now sported single downtube frames for their ultra-lightweight mounts. Strangely, it had been found that the original single downtube design of 1956/57 was superior to the double downtube type used in 1958/59! Both front and rear surfaces of the front member were reinforced by welded-on strip. And all acute angles were gusseted for extra strength.

On his 250 Mike's fastest practice lap was 82.04 mph, whilst on the 125 he got round in 78.47 mph.

But the races, as far as the Ducatis were concerned, turned out to be a nightmare. First Kavanagh's 350 Desmo twin seized a valve early on in practice and the desmodromic valve gear was damaged beyond repair. Then in the first event of the 1960 series, the 3-lap Ultra-Lightweight (125), held over the 37¾-mile Mountain Circuit for the first time since 1953, saw Mike and Hocking (MV) get the racing under way. But Hailwood's ride ended less than a third of the way round the first lap at Glenhelen: the rear wheel stepped out on the left-hander and Mike stepped off. With a broken windscreen as evidence of his tumble, Mike toured slowly round to retire. Then holding 12th place Ken Kavanagh was forced out when his rear wheel collapsed at Quarter Bridge at the end of lap 2. Things were no better in the Lightweight (250) TT as Mike was forced to retire with a broken throttle cable early in the race.

In the Junior (350) he chose to race his AJS rather than the larger Desmo twin, only to again notch up yet another retirement. But he made up for all the disappointment by finishing third in the Senior (500) on his Manx Norton behind the MV Fours of Surtees and Hartle.

The next round in the world championships was the Dutch TT at Assen, there Mike rode his 125 single to eighth spot—by now there were not only the MVs but also the emerging MZs and Honda twins to contend with. Added to all this was the fact that Ducati themselves had all but stopped their direct involvement.

In the 250 Mike rode his Mondial even though it was slower, because of the handling problems on the twin, finishing fifth in front of Jan Huberts and Jim Redman (having his first ride for the Japanese factory) on Honda Fours. In fact Redman only got the ride because Tom Phillis had broken a collarbone, Naomi Taniguchi had

Above and opposite **Various parts of 125 Desmo power unit**

sustained a broken wrist and financial reasons excluded John Hartle.

The following week in Belgium, on a much faster circuit, Hailwood chose to use the 250 Desmo twin and came fourth—its best GP performance. His average race speed was 108.16 mph, against 113.46 mph of winner Carlo Ubbiali's MV twin (which had 5 bhp less!)

In the 125 event against stiff opposition Mike came sixth.

A week later and the Hailwood équipe were back on British short-circuit duty to score an impressive array of wins at the first meeting on the lengthened 2.65-mile Brands Hatch GP circuit. The *Motor Cycle* headline spat: 'Master Mariner Hailwood'.

Wet roads for this inaugural international status event proved that by now Mike was not only skilled, but shrewd into the bargain. In scooping all four solo races he blended dash and restraint so wisely that he stayed afloat while rasher men slid off, yet went so fast that none who slithered round behind him had a ghost of a chance.

In winning the 125 race *Motor Cycle* commented, 'The superiority of Hailwood and his desmodromic Ducati single was so overwhelming that he lapped the third finisher'. And on his Desmo twin Mike showed a clean pair of heels to second place Alan Shepherd on Geoff Monty's GMS.

The German GP was given a miss as there was no 125 race and the 250 twin was having more attention in the navigation department. Fast as it may have proved, the machine's handling had not been in the same field as its speed potential.

Therefore, Birmingham engineer Ernie Earles was commissioned by Stan Hailwood to build a new frame, which if successful would also be fitted to Mike's other 250 twin, plus one for the 350.

The main aim was to lengthen the wheelbase from the original 51¾ in. to 54 in. (similar to a Manx Norton), and the opportunity was also taken to lower the engine by 1½ in. and move it forward to improve weight distribution. Earles estimated that, as originally constructed, the original design carried 75 per cent of the engine weight above the wheel spindle height.

Tubes of the new frame were in Reynolds 531, 1¾ in. × 16 gauge. A layout was adopted, with the top and engine loop tubes crossed at the steering head. From the base of the head the twin top tubes ran horizontally rearward at a diverging angle to afford a triangular

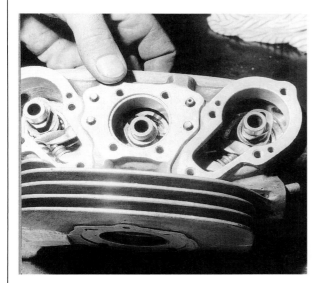

structure resistant to whip. Cross-members braced the triangle and from the forward cross-tube there was a bracing strut to the top of the steering head. A loop to support the rear mudguard engaged with the top tube open ends.

The engine-loop tubes descended from the top of the steering head and these, too, were at first at a diverging angle, with a cross-member ahead of the engine so that the construction was triangulated. They then ran parallel, sweeping beneath the power unit and rising to meet the top tubes under the seat. Rear suspension was by an orthodox pivoted fork fabricated from tubing. The frame was of welded construction throughout.

Finally, a notable feature of the new design meant that the megaphones were now straight, not kinked as on the original.

The race debut for the Earles chassis came at the Ulster GP in early August. Even though he came home fourth—in front of Takahashi (Honda Four) and Taveri (MV twin), Mike was still not happy with the handling, in spite of the frame change.

John Surtees, reflecting on the Ulster GP, commented in *Motor Cycle*: 'Mike Hailwood's Ducati twin was a bit disappointing. As with the MZs I think it is wrong to hang a Manx Norton front fork to a lightweight frame; it doesn't help the power-to-weight ratio even if it is a good stop-gap where handling is concerned. The Ducati has stacks of power but the machine as a whole is too bulky; it needs paring down to make better use of the power.'

After this showing, the 250, and for that matter the largely unraced 350, were not raced by Mike any more, eventually being sold off—going to John Surtees, who also bought Kavanagh's 350 twin, after the Australian veteran lost interest in the machine following a lack of help from the factory. (See Chapter 6.)

Mike raced his 125 single for the last time at the Senora de Pilar road races near Barcelona, Spain (his first appearance in that country) on Sunday, 16 October 1960. And unlike many of his British victories on the bike this was hard earned. For the first 15 laps of the mile long Zaragoza circuit, Jorge Sirera (Montesa) led, pursued by Marcelo Cama (Bultaco), with Hailwood third. For the next 18 laps Cama was in front, Sirera second. Then Mike slipped past and four laps from the end John Grace (Bultaco) took third place from Cama who had been repassed by Sirera.

And with this final victory in Spain an end came to 'Mike-the-Bike's' first Ducati chapter. In the years which followed he built on the foundations made over the first four years of his racing career.

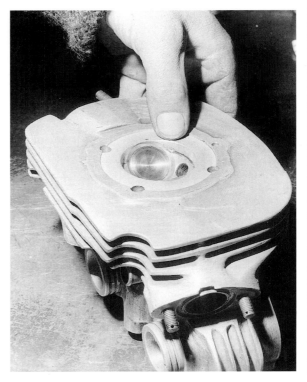

6

First production Desmos

In many ways Taglioni and Ducati were much more successful with their roadgoing Desmos than the racers. You may ask why, well read on and things will become clearer. . . .

First, it is necessary to recall that although the single-cylinder works Desmos managed to put up some remarkable performances, especially in 1958, they still didn't win a world title. Quite simply they were not consistent enough to successfully challenge their main rivals, MV Agusta, over a whole season. Some of this may be argued away—that MV had the best pilots, but the fact remains that Ducati just couldn't put a string of results together over a long enough period.

And as for the parallel twins. . . . The first of these, featuring valve-spring heads, was built by Taglioni in early 1956, but kept 'top secret' until the Milan Show that year. This was a dohc 175, mainly intended for sports class racing in Italy—including long-distance road events, such as the Giro d'Italia and Milano-Taranto classics.

This meant that it had to conform to the bizarre set of rules for such events drawn up by the Italian Federation, who on the one hand limited the size of carburettor/s and banned the use of streamlining, but on the other turned a blind eye to factories such as Gilera and MV using lightly modified works four-cylinder Grand Prix models!

Because of this one can believe Taglioni's claim that it 'would be easy to change the specification to make the twin suitable for Grand Prix racing'. And as early as Milan 1956, qualified observers were already talking about an overbored 250 version.

The power unit was of a particularly neat vertical twin design, with light alloy for both the cylinder heads and barrels, the latter featuring austenitic liners. Twin carburettors were fitted, each with a separate float chamber and with the choke diameter limited to the maximum permissible of 20 mm.

The crankcase was of die-cast light alloy and had two separate crankshafts, at 360 degrees, with a central Hirth coupling. The dohc were driven by spur gears set in a separate case in the middle of the cylinders, and these gears (no fewer than *seven* in number) also drove the contact breaker and oil pump. As was usual Ducati practice, the oil for the full unit-construction engine was contained in an integral finned sump at the base of the crankcase.

Innovative for its day, a six-speed gearbox was operated by a heel-and-toe lever on the offside, whilst the multi-plate clutch, of the dry variety, and the straight-cut primary drive gears lived in the opposite side of the power-unit.

Valves were set at 80 degrees and controlled by hairpin springs. Bore and stroke were 49.4 × 45.6 mm respectively, giving a capacity of 174.7 cc. Running on a compression ratio of 10.2:1, maximum output was claimed to be near the 25 bhp mark at an ear-splitting 11,000 rpm, giving a top speed in the region of 105 mph.

Launched in a blaze of publicity, much was expected of the little twin, but in reality it was to achieve very little. Its only real claim to fame was that it heralded a whole range of similar twins—but all Desmo—from 125 cc to 350 cc over the next few years.

As 1957 dawned, circuits such as Monza and Modena reverberated with the intense wailing of the twins' shallow taper dual megaphones as it screamed out its war cry, whilst the development team prepared it for a baptism of fire in the new season's public road events.

The Giro d'Italia, in April, saw the debut of the new twin, but it was hardly a very successful one as rider Leopoldo Tartarini was forced to retire with electrical problems on the third of the eight stages, having failed to make any real impression on the leaders.

Of the two 175 twins built, one eventually found its way to Venezuela, the other was brought to England for a brief period in 1959, via Stan Hailwood for Arthur Wheeler. But the well-known Epsom rider/dealer was so disappointed by its performance that he forced Hailwood to take it back, from thence it was returned to Bologna where it lay until 1963, until Francesco Villa spotted it in a corner of the factory and converted it to a 250. To bring it up to a full 250, the 175 valve-spring twin was bored *and* stroked to 55.25 × 52 mm, the same measurements as those of the works 125 desmo singles.

We now retrace our steps back to the spring of 1957 and to the event which caused the 175 twin to be shelved in the first place. Quite simply, the loss of life caused by a car ploughing into a group of spectators during the Mille Miglia—a four-wheel version of the Milano-Taranto—caused the Italian government to ban *all* forms of mechanized competition over public roads. This killed off the very events for which the 175 twin had been created. There was no 1957 Milano-

Taranto or any other such event (including the Giro d'Italia) thereafter. But after so much work and not least expense, Taglioni and Ducati wished to salvage something from the twin project.

As related, rumours had already circulated regarding a 250 version and when Stan Hailwood—through King's of Manchester—became the British importer early in 1959 he not only purchased the remaining 175 valve-spring twin which he sold to Arthur Wheeler, but more importantly commissioned Taglioni to build a pair of 250s, but with desmo valve gear. This decision was influenced by a combination of not only seeing the 175, but of course the then new 125 version—which Taglioni had created to succeed the 125 single for the factory's GP effort in 1959 and 1960. But due to both financial and production needs, this was never really developed, as Ducati cut back heavily on their GP budget at the end of 1958 (although at the time factory boss Dott. Montano denied this was true).

Much of the saga surrounding the Desmo twins has been recorded in the previous chapter, but there is another angle, a vastly different view of events than any previously published. . . . Enter 1950s grand prix star and

Original twin, the 175 valve-spring Formula 2 which appeared at the end of 1956

ex Norton and Moto Guzzi teamster, Australian Ken Kavanagh.

At the twilight of a memorable career the Aussie, who by then was based in Italy, rode a 350 Manx Norton and 125 Grand Prix Ducati as a privateer during the 1959 season. On the Ducati he had gained some considerable results that year, including victory at the several non-classic GPs—including Helsinki, Turku and Ruisalon.

At the Swedish Grand Prix, on his Norton, Kavanagh had made an excellent start with Gary Hocking (also Norton mounted), and was close to John Surtees' MV for the first couple of laps. And although the MV rider gradually pulled away from the pair of British singles, Kavanagh noticed that the smaller MV multi was not all that much better than a good Manx.

With this in mind and with his good relationship at the time with the Bologna factory, following his run of successes in the 125 class, the Australian persuaded Taglioni to build a full 350 Desmo twin, based around the 250 which was being built for the Hailwood équipe.

This machine was to be financed by Kavanagh himself, but as he recalled recently, 'Stupidly I didn't have the foresight to block the project as far as others were concerned'. The 'others' were expressly the Hailwood équipe, or more accurately its leader and

Above **Factory mechanic Recchia working on Ken Kavanagh's 350 Ducati Desmo twin at the 1960 TT**

Below **Unfortunately, whilst in Kavanagh's hands the 350 twin spent a large amount of time on the work bench, rather than out on the race circuit**

chief financier, Stan Hailwood. It should be remembered that father Stan put an exclusive clause around his agreement with Ducati that the 250 twins should only be supplied to him, and him alone. And when tying up the 250 Desmo twin deal Hailwood Senior had not even considered the possibility of a larger Desmo—as Mike already had the use of some of the quickest Nortons around—in any case Stan Hailwood already had his eyes firmly on the four-cylinder MV Agustas at the earliest possible date for his son to ride.

Ken Kavanagh's deal with Ducati was finalized in September 1959, with a letter of intent and a price fixed by Ducati to supply one 350 Desmo twin at 3 million lire, complete with fairing and sprockets. On the strength of this Kavanagh negotiated a contract for the 1960 season with the oil giants Castrol during a visit to England that autumn, much of this centring around the 350 Ducati twin project. It was also agreed that he would not race his Norton anymore but dedicate his activities to promoting Ducati.

For example, this included acting as host to a large group of visiting North American dealers and the importer, Joe Berliner. Kavanagh, together with a publicity man, met the party in Rome and accompanied them as interpreters for the week or so they were in Bologna. In appreciation of these services Ducati prepared a special single-cylinder 220 for an Australian racing tour that winter, the full story of which is related in my book *Ducati Singles* (Osprey).

However, things began to get out of step, when after Kavanagh had left Italy for Australia in the middle of November, Ducati tried to back out of the contract to build the 350 Desmo twin—after a third of the price had already been paid up front. Kavanagh (who still has all the original correspondence relating to the transaction) cites the reason for this as being that by now Stan Hailwood had also ordered a 350. . . . But after an exchange of letters from both Kavanagh and his Italian lawyer, Ducati relented and agreed to still supply the machine.

Unfortunately, as events were to prove, Ducati were now not only a reluctant partner to the agreement but in practice Kavanagh would probably have been wiser (easily said, of course, with the benefit of hindsight) to have just asked for his money back.

When he arrived back from his Australian venture in March 1960, Kavanagh telephoned the factory and was informed that the machine would be ready for Imola on Easter Monday 23 April. The machine was duly tested at Imola in practice and was found to vibrate very badly and the gearchange would not select gears. . . . Stability, after some careful modifications to the suspension was, to quote its owner 'quite reasonable'. Taglioni told Kavanagh that he had only tested the engine on the test bench up to 9800 rpm and was afraid to run it to 11,500 rpm as 'this might cause the crankcase to fracture, as happened in the case of the first 250 prepared for Mr Hailwood'.

At Imola Kavanagh was unable to use the 350 because of an accident, caused when the crankcase plug came out (on his 125 Ducati) allowing some 3 litres of oil to go under the rear wheel—as the Australian was using one of the factory's desmo engines he was none too pleased.

Two days afterwards, still feeling the effects of his Imola spill and unable to ride, it was left to close friend Jim Redman to test the 350 on a road near the factory, whilst Ing. Taglioni assured its owner that it 'no longer vibrated or missed gears'.

During May a catalogue of problems surfaced mainly centring around a reluctance or inability to sort the bike out sufficiently to race in a grand prix. The machine spent almost the entire month at the factory, even though its owner should have been giving it its classic debut at Clermont-Ferrand—the French GP.

An extract of a letter from Kavanagh to factory boss Dott. Montano, dated 31 May 1960, is interesting and highlights the level of dissatisfaction: 'Unfortunately, regardless of my begging down at the works there has been nothing but outright obstruction in the last month or so towards making the machine raceworthy, and now I must miss the first two or three practice periods at the 'TT', a thing I can hardly afford. Yesterday as a sign of

Former works rider for Norton and Moto Guzzi, Australian Ken Kavanagh's experience with Taglioni's 350 Desmo twin was far from happy

good faith on my part, I gave to Dott. Calcagnile [Ducati's secretary], a cheque for the rest of the money outstanding. . . . I can do no more, but hope that Ducati will now try to be as prompt and as helpful towards me, as they were with the "350" for Hailwood. . . . !'

This letter, at least, had some effect. A 125 Desmo single was provided, the 350 twin handed back and Kavanagh, with factory mechanic Recchia—considered by the Australian to be probably the best, 'very modest and very capable', finally set out for the Isle of Man, where they duly booked into the Majestic Hotel in Douglas.

One of the first problems they discovered with the 350 was the front forks. These were (unlike Hailwood's bikes) fitted with standard touring Norton Roadholders. Unfortunately, these had no real damping, just a cone in the bottom to stop bottoming and as Kavanagh put it 'absolutely useless for racing'.

Fortunately, Alan Trow was able to provide a set of genuine ex works Norton legs, which he and Eric Hinton had 'acquired' from the Bracebridge Street Works.

The only spares provided with the 350, for what was the toughest road race in the world, had been a set of clutch plates. These, so Kavanagh says, were in aluminium, and Taglioni had copied this idea from the 250F Maserati car. Unfortunately it wasn't a very practical solution as the alloy discs tended to burn out far too easily—after about 20 miles—and then the clutch would no longer disengage!

In contrast to Mike Hailwood, Ken Kavanagh considered the handling of his 350 Desmo twin 'good enough'. What concerned him far more was 'the terrible vibration, poor gear selection and no clutch, which to put it mildly made it a very unpleasant bicycle to ride around the island'. However, the pair sorted it out the best they could and as the photograph on page 60 shows it used a lot of sponge rubber . . . not for the comfort of the rider, but to try and keep the fuel tank in one piece!

The final morning practice for the 1960 TT races was on Saturday and saw Kavanagh concentrating and trying hard. But the bike got slower and slower, then the engine rattled to a stop between Stone Breakers and the Verandah, 'I coasted on down to the Les Graham memorial shelter and waited in the cold mist till the end of practice'.

With the passing of the road's opening car, Kavanagh then pushed and coasted back to the Majestic. It was a long way and he was none too happy. . . .

Later that morning on closer inspection, it was discovered that one of the rockers for operating the

John Surtees purchased various Desmo twins from Hailwood and Kavanagh. Picture shows him (far left), with team mechanic, *Motor Cycling* **staffmen Bruce Main-Smith and kneeling John Hartle, early 1963**

desmodromic valve gear was broken. And as Kavanagh summed it up: 'We did not dismantle it . . . we had no spares and no idea if any existed.'

While still sitting there in the garage that morning mulling things over with Recchia, as to the possibility of calling Bologna to see if parts could be obtained within 24 hours (remember there were no jets in those days), the pair received a visit from two ACU (Auto Cycle Union) officials.

'Ken', they said, 'Just a little friendly advice, somebody has decided to put in a protest if you race the 350 Ducati, the exhaust pipes do not comply with TT regulations, so before coming to the weigh-in ceremony you'd be wise to have them modified'.

Kavanagh thanked them very much, and did not bother to tell them that the engine was broken. But that, in effect, was the final straw, with the problems they already had it was decided there and then not to race . . . and so the 350 was a non-starter for the Junior TT.

On his return to Italy, followed by a strongly worded letter to Ducati boss Dott. Montano, the factory eventually took the bike back for repair.

After this came Kavanagh's only other race on the machine, at Monza, for the Italian GP that September. But it took the help of fellow competitor Bob Anderson to finally get the bike at least raceworthy for the event, after many laps of practice. And as Kavanagh recalls, 'It vibrated terribly, had six gears and six neutrals and would lap about as good as a 350 Manx'.

In the race the Aussie got off to a bad start, way back down the field. On the second lap he caught Geoff Tanner on his Manx, following him into the second Lesmo curve, taken in 3rd gear on a Norton at between 90 and 100 mph. Tanner got into a big slide, hit the straw bales on the outside of the curve, managed to stay on but had to retire, he'd broken off the left-hand footrest and bent the rear shock absorber. With three or four straw bales rolling across the track he nearly brought Kavanagh off too. Only by desperate zigzagging measures did he stay aboard. But then it was back to business, chin on the tank, full bore around the Ascari curve then braking hard for the Parabolica, scratch it round the curve, then into the finishing straight.

Accelerating up the straight Kavanagh suddenly thought 'I've decided it will be my last race, I'm risking being hurt for peanuts, I'm in twelfth position, if I stop now or at the end of the race it won't change anything'. So he just rolled off the twistgrip and coasted gently to a stop at the pits. He'd finished his racing days, which had spanned well over a decade.

The Desmo twin was returned to Kavanagh's Bergamo home, where it sat until it was finally sold to John Surtees the following year for £1000—his brother Norman came over to Italy to pick it up.

Surtees had a few months earlier purchased the

Surtees commissioned a Reynolds frame and leading-link racing forks in an attempt to finally solve the problem of bad handling

entire Hailwood stock of 250 and 350 twins (which consisted of two 250s and a 350). With Kavanagh's machine this made a total of four bikes. A large amount of parts had come with the Hailwood deal, although it must be said that these were *development* items rather than real spares which would be needed to back up a serious racing effort.

Why did someone who had been double world champion for three consecutive years on the MV Fours by 1960 and then 'retired' to concentrate on four wheels purchase the Desmo twins?

The man best qualified to answer this is John Surtees himself: 'I had been impressed, when at Monza in 1960 the 350 Ducati appeared *faster* than my 350 MV. I felt the design had potential, the 350 was more promising, because it enjoyed a much superior power-to-weight ratio than the 250. The smaller machine was really too heavy.' Surtees also voiced the opinion that one has to appreciate the fact that as far as Ducati were concerned: 'It was purely a money thing they produced both the 250 and 350 Desmo twins for X amount of money and that was that'. He also agrees with my view that what the bikes needed most of all was an intensive development programme by the factory, which they never got. John also stated that he considered Taglioni

'a brilliant man who could create things, but who didn't have a consistent management behind him'.

The multi-world champion admits that his purchase of the machines was through his interest in motorcycles, rather than as a serious racing effort, although helping his brother Norman came into it.

The first thing he did was to instigate a new frame (for one of the 250s)—from Reynolds tubes. Funnily enough, it was not brother Norman who debuted the machine, but up-and-coming star Fred Neville, at Brands Hatch on 20 August 1961.

Motor Cycle magazine said: 'On a record-breaking day at Brands Hatch "King" Minter definitely relinquished his crown. And just as definitely Fred Neville emerged from the fray wearing it. For his performances last Sunday ripped that "up-and-coming" tag from his shoulder and established him as a genuine, dyed-in-the-wool star material'.

But it wasn't his win in the 1000 cc race or his places in the 350 and 500 cc events that gave him the title—it was his 250 performance, and he wasn't even in the top ten!

He went to the line, on John Surtees' ex-Hailwood Ducati, the only apparent challenger to Jim Redman's Honda Four. But straight from the off it was Redman who screamed away from the field with Neville puttering down to Paddock bend on one pot—disaster. Maybe, but a plug change put him back in the race, albeit two laps adrift.

Bruno Spaggiari on the factory 350 Desmo single, at Cesenático. Machines like this acted as development prototypes for the road-going Desmos

Meanwhile, Redman was strolling away from the field, with Norman Surtees (on Mike Hailwood's Mondial) and Dan Shorey (NSU) neck-and-neck in second and third spots. Then came the sensation. Neville started skittling the lap record and was whistling round overhauling the whole field, but 10 laps (of which he had already missed 2) just wasn't enough. Redman won comfortably from Surtees and Shorey.

Unfortunately, the combination of Neville and the desmo twin was not to be as the rider known as 'Fearless Fred' was killed a couple of weeks later whilst leading the Junior Manx Grand Prix on his AJS 7R.

Norman Surtees then rode the 250 twin to a whole host of leader-board positions during the final two months of the 1961 racing season—winning at Snetterton, coming third at the Cadwell Park international, second at Brands Hatch, second at Aintree and finally another second at Brands Hatch in late October.

During the winter more Reynolds frames were constructed. In 531 tubing, these were very similar in layout to the Featherbed Norton racing type, but with an important difference. There was no bottom right-hand frame tube. Instead, the right loop was bent across in front of the crankcase and was welded to the left-hand tube. Similar procedure was followed at the rear, with the right tube bent across to meet the left loop behind the gearbox. Main frame material was $1\frac{1}{4}$ in. diameter $\times$ 18-gauge tube, plus a rear sub-

frame in $\frac{3}{4}$ in. diameter $\times$ 17-gauge material.

In addition, a couple of the machines were fitted with a Reynolds leading-link fork of the type pioneered by Geoff Duke on his specials in the late 1950s. Wheels were 19 in.

The first outing for the revised machinery was planned for the North West 200 on 12 May, the riders were to be Norman Surtees and Phil Read. Much of the testing was carried out by John Surtees himself at Silverstone, *Motor Cycle News* even carried a large front page photograph of the former world champion flat out on the 350 Desmo at the Northamptonshire circuit.

Entered as JSR (John Surtees Racing) Ducati's machines failed to make an appearance in Northern Ireland. The next appearance was scheduled to be at the TT, where Read was entered by John Surtees on a 500 Norton and the 350 Desmo twin. Brother Norman was down to ride a Bultaco in the Lightweight TT.

Read was destined to finish seventh in the Junior (350 cc) TT, but not on the JSR Ducati. After arriving late for practice week the Ducati was not considered suitable for the island. The main problems centred around the ones already catalogued by Kavanagh—vibration and gear selection. In addition, the central gear-drive train proved a problem over the bumpy section of the circuit where the rear wheel quite often left the ground. 'Although alright on the 250, the 350', said Surtees, 'was marginal in this area'.

The final and most serious problem of all was the power curve. For example, on a fast, flat circuit like Monza or Spa the requirement was for performance at sustained high revolutions. And at circuits like this John Surtees thought the 350 was at its best. But on more demanding courses where there was a mixture of racing conditions the Ducati displayed its under-developed nature. Quite simply, at anything below near maximum revs it was extremely demanding to ride, because the engine response was not constant throughout the power curve.

For the rest of 1962 the 350 was put to one side, whilst Norman rode the 250, although not with the same level of success he had enjoyed the previous year.

For 1963, it was planned that John Hartle should ride both the 250 and 350 twins, but in the event a combination of things prevented this. First, Hartle was signed up by Geoff Duke for the reborn Gilera team and subsequently, John Surtees was to find that his growing commitments with four wheels, namely Ferrari, were to mean that he had no time to spare.

Except for a couple of appearances at the beginning of the year when Derek Minter rode a 250, including a victory at Mallory Park, the Desmo twins didn't move. Then later that year, after some gentle arm twisting, John agreed to sell the 250s to Pullins Motors of East

Cylinder head from the factory development racing Desmo single. . .

. . . and massive 42 mm Dell'Orto SS1 carb

Dulwich, the sponsors of Jim Russell who also had a 125 Grand Prix valve-spring model.

After a couple of relatively successful seasons with the 250s the $\frac{1}{4}$-litre Desmos passed on again, this time to enthusiast Dr Peter Bothwell, where they have been ever since.

John Surtees retained the pair of 350s until 1982, when they were finally sold to West German Alfa Romeo dealer Manfred Hartung.

So, in the end the Desmo twins which promised so much, ended up delivering very little. In retrospect they were sentenced from birth by being created as a business deal, not as a serious race programme by the factory. Starved of development they were never to exploit their true potential. They were not really bad bikes, just that they were constructed for all the wrong reasons.

Except for the débâcle of the parallel twins, desmodromics took very much a back seat in the motorcycling world during the early 1960s as first Honda beat the valve-float bogey with their four-valve layout, while MZ, Suzuki and later Yamaha got speed to spare from the humble two-stroke. And Ducati themselves, except for successes in the Barcelona 24 Hour race, took very little direct interest in racing—and certainly not with Desmos.

During this period Taglioni was forced to concentrate the majority of his efforts on the production side of things creating several new models, including a 250, which later became the Mach 1 and Mark 3, a 350, the Sebring and several two-strokes, although these were delegated to other development staff.

However, he still managed to design and build the valve-spring four-cylinder 125 and the Mach 1/S heavyweight single-cylinder production racers in both 250 and 350 engine sizes. It was these latter machines which were to act as prototypes for the later wide-case singles. Sold only in 1965, the Mach 1/S racers were not related to the Mach 1 sports roadster, but more to the special 285 cc constructed for the 1964 Barcelona 24 Hour race, which was ridden to victory by Spaggiari and Mandolini.

Although a few Mach 1/S models were offered for sale, the vast majority of Ducatis to be seen on the race circuits during the 1960s were home-built, race-kitted roadsters. Unpublished at the time, Taglioni converted a 250 Mach 1/S to positive(desmodromic!)-valve operation during the winter of 1965, and this was given its debut by Franco Farnè at Modena in March 1966.

But it was Gilberto Parlotti (later a works rider for Morbidelli) and Roberto Gallina (to win fame as a development engineer and team manager for Suzuki amongst others), who Taglioni entrusted with much of the race testing for his new baby.

It was Gallina who rode the first purpose-built prototype Desmo (a 350) during its inaugural outing at Modena in March 1967, finishing well up in both the 350

and 500 classes. Soon, Taglioni had also built a 250 version. Both engine's capacities shared their respective standard production roadster bore and stroke measurements (Mach 1/Mark 3 and Sebring 350)—although at that time the roadsters used valve-spring heads and narrow-case crankcases.

Taglioni had also been authorized to proceed on a semi-official basis and therefore was able to construct a specially built 250 Desmo for Farnè to ride in North America. The venue was Daytona and the race, the 100-mile Experts Lightweight event in March 1967. However, because of some quaint rules which allowed machines such as Yamaha's TD1 twin but banned Ducati's non-standard single, Farnè was not allowed to start and the Ducati team, which included a couple of factory mechanics, had an altogether futile and wasted journey.

Back home, Parlotti and Gallina were putting together some excellent results, in particular at the tight and twisting street circuits which were popular in Italy. Soon the pair were to be joined by former Benelli, MV and Ducati works star Bruno Spaggiari.

All this development had a much more important purpose than purely flying the Ducati flag at a racing circuit again—it was for the launch of the world's first desmodromic street bike! The next stage towards this came in September 1967, when the factory displayed a prototype 350 *wide*-case roadster, the Mark 3, at the international Cologne Show in West Germany. At the time no one outside the factory knew it, but it was this machine which acted as the basis for a Desmo version, which was publicly revealed the following April.

First deliveries of the newcomer—in both 250 and 350 engine sizes—began in June 1968. Except for extra brightwork, and of course the desmo cylinder head, the desmo and valve-spring models were identical.

In Britain *Motor Cycle News* carried the first details of the new breed, the story going on to say: 'Two new single-cylinder roadsters from Ducati are the world's first production touring bikes to be equipped with desmodromically operated valve gear. The bikes—a 250 and 350—are aimed firmly at the sporting rider. The specifications include single overhead-camshaft engines, five-speed gearboxes, racy looks and improved frames that offer remarkable cornering powers. But the unique feature of the Ducatis is their desmodromic valve gear, a luxury usually reserved for racing machinery.'

Although the basic principal of the desmo system was very similar to the one Taglioni had devised on his various racing machines, the roadsters had their valve closing assisted by lightweight springs. This was

Rimini, 24 March 1968. Roberto Gallina on his Desmo single leads a stream of contenders in the 350 race, including Dave Simmonds' Kawasaki. (Gallina later won fame as a top Suzuki tuner)

350 Mark 3 D
DESMO

Above **First ever road-going motorcycle with positive (desmo) valve operation, the 1968 Ducati Mark 3D. The factory brochure shot compares it with an American jet fighter**

Below **The so-called 'wide-case' frame introduced with the Desmo roadster line in 1968. This featured a much stronger rear frame section, with engine mounts some four times wider than at the front**

450 MARK 3 "D"

MOTORE: 4 tempi · cilindrata cc. 435,7 · Distribuzione a valvole in testa inclinate a 80 gradi, comandate da un albero a camme in testa · Cambio in blocco con il motore, a 5 rapporti · Velocità massima circa Km/h 167 con silenziatore. Km/h 182 con tromboncino · Consumo per 100 Km. lt. 5,7	ENGINE: 4 stroke · Displacement cc. 435,7 (26.578 cu.in) · Timing by O.H.C. valves inclined 80° · Gearbox in unit with the engine, 5 speeds · Maximum speed approx. Kms/h 167 (M/h 104) with silencer · Kms/h 182 (M/h 113) with megaphone. Fuel consumption for 100 Kms. lt. 5,7 (41 M/U.S. gal. = 49 M/imp. gal.)	MOTEUR: à 4 temps · Cylindrée 435,7 cm³ · Distribution par soupapes en tête inclinées de 80° et commandées par un arbre à cames en tête · Boîte de vitesses dans bloc moteur, à 5 rapports · Vitesse maximum approximative Km/h 167 avec silencieux; Km/h. 182 avec mégaphone · Consommation pour 100 Kms. lts. 5,7.	MOTOR · 4 Takt Motor · Zylinderinhalt c.cm. 435,7 · Steuerung durch 80° geneigten Ventile mittelst Nockenwelle eingebauter im Zylinderkopf · Wechselgetriebe im Motorgehäuse eingebaut und besteht aus 5 Gängen · Höchstgeschwindigkeit 167 Km/St. mit Schalldämpfer, 182 Km/St. mit Megaphon. Brennstoffverbrauch: 5,7 Liter je 100 Km.	MOTOR · 4 tiempos · Cilindrada c.c. 435'7 · Distribución con válvulas en la culata, inclinadas a 80° y accionadas por un eje de levas también en la culata · El cambio, que forma bloque con el motor. es de 5 velocidades · Velocidad máxima Km/h 167 con silencioso. Km/h 182 con megáfono. Consumo cada 100 Kms. lt. 5'7.

The 450 was introduced in 1969. Here factory racer and tester Bruno Spaggiari (left) and two other employees pose with the new big-bore MK 3D

necessary to forestall problems which could otherwise have caused owners mechanical failure, had something—even a piece of grit—become trapped, even for an instant, between the valve seat and valve face. In typical fashion, Taglioni chose to use existing springs—the hairpin type previously used on the 125 and 160 ohc models.

Valve seat wear was greatly reduced over the conventional Ducati ohc motors—seat pressure was a mere 8 lb/sq. in. on the Desmo, against 80 on the other models, resulting in a *ten*-fold reduction!

The above is perhaps the greatest benefit of the system for roadgoing use, and one which has not been highlighted significantly in the past.

The disadvantage, of course, was cost but in creating the street Desmo Taglioni kept this down to an absolute minimum, in fact the only really additional parts were the extra pair of rockers and rocker shafts, two more lobes on the camshaft, method of valve retention, design of guides and minor items such as shims. This simple solution not only kept costs to a minimum, but also meant that except for the nearside cam end cover the valve-spring desmo heads were externally identical.

In service, although setting up the desmo head called for patience and technical knowledge it was not as difficult as is generally believed. A definite plus—again largely previously ignored—is that with a 90 per cent reduction in seat pressure, valve adjustment is not needed anywhere as often as on the conventional valve-spring head.

The cylinder-head internals were not the only new features of the engine. Compared to the older Ducati roadsters, the wide-case models had new crankcases with a larger capacity (5½-pint) sumps. The drive-side main bearing had been enlarged, the bottom end strengthened, including a new crankshaft with larger crankpin and the electrical system, although still 6 volts, was uprated, including a larger 80-watt alternator.

As *MCN* said: 'The new Ducatis carry the mark of individuality about them. They offer a different style of motorcycling than the two- and four-stroke twins that now dominate the market.'

Both the 250 and 350 were identical externally—there was only a 2 lb weight difference between them.

A major mistake in my opinion was that Ducati did not choose at the time to make the Desmo and Mark 3 models different from a styling point of view, as they did so successfully later.

The *real* advantage which the Desmo had over its less glamorous brother was the word 'desmo'—so why didn't the factory give its more expensive models new clothes and new colour. . . . Yes, this was a serious marketing error.

Relatively few machines were produced in 1968, serious production commencing with the introduction of the 1969 models. The differences between the two years was confined to carburettors, tank filler caps and silencers. In 1968: Dell'Orto SS1 29D, twin filler caps (a styling exercise shared with the SL/1 two-stroke) and Silentium round-end cone muffler; in 1969: Dell'Orto VHB29 square slide, single filler cap and Silentium slashed-end cone muffler.

In 1969 a totally new engine size was introduced— the 450. Actually, the capacity was 436 cc (86 × 75 mm). On paper this might appear to have been a simple increase in bore size by 10 mm with the same stroke as the 350. In reality, it was quite a major redesign. In addition to the increase in bore size, the larger single (made in valve-spring as well as desmo format) had new crankcases, crankshaft assembly, primary drive gears, bevel gears, wider $\frac{3}{8} \times \frac{5}{8}$ in. (530) rear-drive chain (and therefore sprockets), and additional bracing of the top frame tube. As the cylinder barrel was taller, a deeper exhaust pipe was needed. Strangely, a shorter silencer, still of the slashed end cone variety, was fitted.

In its dimensions and appearance the 450 Desmo shared certain aspects with its smaller brothers. As a 250 the bike was by no means the largest and heaviest in its class, as a 350 it was small, and the 450, well it was positively tiny! One could conclude from this that the largest capacity Desmo would have been the best, and from a power-to-weight ratio it was. But in almost every other area, except for engine torque, it was *inferior*. The 450 vibrated which didn't affect the other two. It was only marginally faster. It had no more room, so it couldn't make use of the extra torque for carrying a passenger and it was more expensive to buy, tax, insure and it consumed more fuel. Even in racing its power-to-weight ratio didn't make it as competitive as the other two in their respective classes.

But the biggest question has to be why not a full 500? To answer this fully we look at how the '450' was created.

It first appeared as a racer, ridden by Spaggiari, with a capacity of 386 cc (81 × 75 mm), in this form as simply an overbored 350. This was then developed into the 436 cc engine but with the changes previously catalogued.

And the reason why it stayed at this strange capacity was two-fold—firstly, because it was still hoped to develop the abortive pushrod 500 parallel twin and, secondly, because the existing single-cylinder design had reached its zenith of development and could not be taken out any further as the throw of the crankshaft only just missed the gears.

Ducati felt that with the twin it could not also justify (or afford) to redesign and retool the single-cylinder to create a full 500. Again, with the death of the twin shortly afterwards, this, in retrospect, can be seen as yet another management mistake.

Interestingly, Taglioni, always at least one step in front of his colleagues, had prepared all the necessary drawings for the 500 single . . . he also had on the stocks a four-valve desmo head for the 450 racer, but again this did not go ahead. And instead of making full use of the Desmo roadster concept, the factory back-pedalled and instead centred their single-cylinder marketing around, of all things, the valve-spring Street Scrambler models! This leads nicely on to the next stage in our story of the Desmo production singles—the R/T.

Based around an idea born from a prototype 450 motocross which the Berliner brothers (the American importers) had commissioned in the late 1960s when the 450 first appeared, the R/T was essentially a general purpose dirtbike powered by a 450 desmo engine with a specially designed chassis intended for off-road use in the United States.

First offered in 1971, *Cycle World* described the R/T in the following way: 'A set-it-up-the-way-you-like-it charger', going on to say 'for those of us who still appreciate the vibrant throb of a Rota-Rooter, its single power pulse traction, and torque from practically zero rpm, there are only two machines. The BSA 500 (Victor) and the Desmo Ducati 450 R/T. BSA offers its single in three models; motocross, dual-purpose and roadster. The Italian Ducati goes a slightly different route, offering you a sparse basic package with a lighting kit, then leaving you to puzzle out how to make the package fit your needs'.

The R/T Desmo. Not a serious motocrosser, but a 'backwoods' bike largely intended for the North American leisure market

DESMO DUCATI R/T 450

THE THOROUGHBRED OF MOTORCYCLES

A unique, desmodromic engine for special torque; smooth, unit-construction five-speed box; special frame; seven-inch travel front fork; fully-adjustable swing arm rear; 9.5 inch clearance; plenty of smooth, even power; chrome headlight and brackets and taillight assembly for instant connection or detachment. The new Ducati Desmo R/T 450 is bred for action, on and off the road.
See the new R/T 450 today, with all the true sports features for any type of terrain. One test ride will convince you. It's the thoroughbred of motorcycles.

BERLINER MOTOR CORP. / Hasbrouck Heights, N.J. 07604 / Sole U.S. Distributor
A Member of the Berliner Group: Norton, AJS, Moto Guzzi, Ducati, BeBe & Metzeler Tires

An advertisement showing the 450 R/T, from the American *Cycle World*, **dated May 1972**

Somehow the R/T was a bike which didn't fit any niche. As delivered, it looked similar in style to one of the big British scramblers but it wasn't a serious racing iron. And, except for what the Americans referred to as a 'woods bike', it needed modifying to participate in off-road competition such as desert racing, or short-track TT (American oval dirt-track) events. It wasn't strictly a dual-purpose trail bike either, for the simple reason that it wasn't completely street legal in several states when its lighting kit was installed.

The kit, which consisted of a headlamp, tail light and wiring and handlebar switches, did not conform, however, to most American federal licencing standards, the notable problem areas being the lack of a brake light switch, horn and street legal silencer. The kit was typical of the R/T as a whole and is best summed up by the single word, incomplete!

Besides the obvious attraction of its desmo engine, which *CW* described as its 'biggest drawing card', the R/T had one dominant feature which made it unique—its frame. Unlike the valve-spring Street Scrambler, the desmo R/T featured a specially designed, strictly one-off chassis. It could be argued that while the frame

geometry, and appearance, were radically different, the design was similar to the standard production models because the engine was still used as a structural member of the frame.

If this was true, the rest certainly wasn't. The steering head of the R/T was very much like that of a Featherbed Norton. But with the Ducati, there were *three* top frame tubes incorporated—the centre tube running from the top of the steering column back to the braced centre section of the twin outer tubes. These then continued to run all the way back to the top rear suspension mountings. At this point, there was a curved hoop connecting the two acting as rear mudguard support.

The single front downtube terminated at, and was bolted to, the crankcases, under which there was a substantial steel sump bash plate. Two parallel tubes passed downwards at the rear of the frame to the swinging-arm pivot, to provide effective rear subframe support. In an effort to ensure a range of rear shock positions there were four upper mount shock points.

The most rearward position, which placed the units practically vertical, raised the rear of the machine slightly transferring the weight forward. Moving the upper mount progressively forward angled the shock more, giving increased swinging arm leverage and hence a softer ride.

Up front were a set of super comfortable long-stroke Marzocchi motocross type forks. The spring rate was well suited to the bike and damping was variable by substituting oils of varying viscosity. The ride was very soft, and well suited to off-road use.

So, with its torquey 38 bhp (claimed) desmo engine, well-made frame and efficient suspension things looked good. Unfortunately, in typical Ducati fashion, there were also a number of faults.

The standard 'as supplied' Marzocchi rear shocks didn't work too well when hot, suggesting that they were really standard roadgoing units. The only solution was for the customer to fit aftermarket Konis or similar.

Both brakes were, in the opinion of the majority, considered too large for the bike—at least in its off-road role, tending to grab and lock up far too easily.

The Borrani alloy rims, although looking good, just weren't practical for the rigours of dirt use, high-tensile steel would have been much superior, and in any case they didn't feature security bolts. . . .

A similar problem was the various fibreglass components such as the tank, seat, panels and mudguards. These looked fine but unfortunately were not very flexible. The worst affected items were the mudguards which were liable to break all too easily, even though they were rubber mounted. And as *Cycle World* discovered: 'The high-mounted front fender presents no clearance problems, but the same cannot be said of the rear unit which isn't wide enough to cover the tyre and rubs frequently.'

Stateside dealers were, in fact, recommended to advise their customers to substitute the stock 'guards' with Preston Petty unbreakable plastic components, as this would solve both the clearance and breakage problems.

Cycle World also found that after some 100 miles of trail riding, stress fractures appeared in the gel coat of the tank. They, (CW), thought these were probably caused by vibration, and careful mounting of the tank was advised.

My own experience with Ducati models employing fibreglass components confirms that whatever else they could achieve, Ducati's ability to produce fibreglass ware was minimal. Not only was the quality poor but the cost of replacements expensive, when compared with other spares from the company, hence a thriving trade in 'pattern' mouldings.

Although the North American importer, the Berliner Motor Corporation, claimed the R/T to be a 'true sports machine for any type of terrain, on or off-road', it was as a trail mount in which it truly excelled. *CW* again: 'It is particularly suitable for Northern California or East Coast terrain where trees, gullies and mud bogs keep the speed down. Steering is quick and light, allowing excellent control at slow speeds. Bars, too, are comfortable when the rider is standing, and they are sufficiently wide for good leverage. Ground clearance is

a generous 9 in., and rocks and logs can easily be cleared. And while the ultra-low gearing is useless for the street, or in high-speed, off-road situations, it is handy when riding in close quarters. Quite simply, the R/T is a climber. Hills present no problem—either going up or coming down. Brakes are seldom needed, due to the engine's good braking characteristics, and, of course, the bike's low gearing.'

Unfortunately, all of these traits—low gearing, high ground clearance, quick steering—which made the R/T excel for low-speed off-road work, contrived to work against it for high-speed use, either on- or off-road.

Aided by a relatively quick throttle action and low gearing, the engine reacted rapidly, without displaying much flywheel effect. Wheelspin was excessive, almost akin to a powerful twin.

In their test *Cycle World* concluded that the R/T showed a lot of potential and, even with its faults, its 'as delivered' soft ride and broad powerband would endear it to trail riders who spend long hours in the saddle.

Add a speedometer and spark arrester (tail silencer), then 'dial in' the handling and they considered the desmo dirtbike would be competitive in enduros as well. The factory obviously thought this too. The 1971 International Six Day Trial, held in the Isle of Man, saw a total of seven Italian riders aboard lightly modified R/Ts. Four rode the normal 450 versions, the other three machines had the 350 motor fitted. All seven sported additional equipment such as a lighting set, centre stand, unbraced 'bars' and twin silencers branched from the single high-level R/T exhaust pipe. Six of the Ducati riders were official members of the national Trophy team, while the seventh represented the manufacturer's team.

Although reliable, the enduro kitted R/Ts proved no match for the purpose-built bikes from behind the Iron Curtain, such as Jawa and MZ.

A version for the Italian domestic market, known as the T/S was also offered. This was essentially a fully street-legal version, with low-level pipe, a quiet (at least compared to the R/T's open exhaust) Silentium silencer, full instrumentation, lighting equipment, horn, battery and chainguard. Both the R/T and T/S versions remained in production until late 1972.

By this time the roadgoing Desmo had been considerably updated and restyled. Unofficially nick-named the 'Silver Shotgun' the first of the new bikes had appeared in late 1971. The first engine size to appear was the 350, soon followed by the other two capacities. Although the engine remained unchanged, the same could not be said of the running gear or the appearance.

Previously, although using wide-case engines and suitably modified frames, the remainder of the machine was much as it had been on the earlier narrow-case models with old-fashioned 31.5 mm enclosed forks, and the 180/160 mm single-sided Grimeca SLS brakes—basically identical to the original ohc model, the 175, of the late 1950s.

As speeds had risen, these items had become that much less efficient. So with the Silver Shotgun, Ducati's objective was clear—not only to create a more modern appearance but also to rectify those shortcomings.

For a start, the colour—metal flake silver—hence the nick-name, was standard throughout the three engine capacities (valve-spring versions were also marketed with the same finish) extended to the tank, seat back, front mudguard and massive side panels. Except for the polished stainless steel rear guard and brightwork, the balance, such as the frame, chainguard, centre stand and rear light/number plate support were in black.

New for this model were the tank and seat, both of the racing variety, abbreviated front guard, the side panels, rearsets, clip-ons, 85 mm white face Veglia tach, Borrani alloy rims and much more robust 35 mm Marzocchi racing type front forks with polished alloy yokes and sliders, plus exposed chromed stanchions.

The Marzocchi rear shocks had stronger springs than those previously fitted to match the sturdier forks. Although the rear brake remained as before, the front

stopper was now a much more powered double-sided affair. Usefully, the rear brake pedal folded to allow the standard kick-starter to be used, thus avoiding the problems encountered when rearsets had been used on the earlier Mach 1.

With the new handlebar layout came new levers, although the infamous Aprilia horn/dipswitch was still used. And a new steering damper knob, of a smaller diameter graced the top of the steering column. The long serving oblong alloy-bodied CEV rear light seen on so many earlier models over the years had been finally ditched in favour of a less distinctive round assembly from the same source.

All in all, with its improved front end, racy lines and distinctive colour scheme the Silver Shotgun at last suceeded in creating the image of a sporting roadster, therefore capitalizing on the Desmo tag in a far more effective way than the earlier half-hearted measures. It not only looked right but performed better too, with its eager rider being able to make use of all the available performance—thanks to the improved 'earholing ability' and safer stopping power from the new front end.

Continued until the end of 1972 the Silver Shotgun served as the spur for what many consider were the finest Ducati singles ever, the final striking yellow café racer style Desmos. The story of these much-loved machines is related in the next chapter.

Lovely 'Silver Shotgun' 350 Desmo sportster. 1972 model shown, with double-side Grimeca front brake and silver (hence nickname) metalflake finish

7

Yellow singles

In late 1972, after almost two decades of production, the classic bevel-driven ohc single was about to receive its last and final update. During this time it had been built in a vast array of engine capacities and in just about every conceivable guise that a potential owner could require.

But it is widely held that the ultimate singles were the best of the bunch, representing an excellent blend of reliability, style and speed—and none more so than the desmo versions. Together with the valve-spring Mark 3 and Street Scramblers these last of the line versions were offered in 248, 340 and 436 cc engine sizes, plus a special 239 cc 'tax beating' version for the French market.

A new era was ushered in for Ducati as a whole in 1973. Not only was a new factory being constructed on the site of the previous one (work had commenced some 12 months earlier), but there hadn't been such an abundance of new models since the mid 1960s or such an interest in modifications to the existing machines. Indeed, it was some years since a range of such size and diversity had been available all at the same time. For 1973 Ducati's model range included new versions of the 750 twins, the GT Sport and SS production racer, plus

updated singles in 250, 350 and 450 cc engine sizes.

The most instantly noticeable change was the colour schemes. While the blue and gold Mark 3s and Scramblers in various hues gave a fresh look, it was the orange-yellow finished Desmos which stood out from the crowd like beacons—representing as they did the ultimate Café Racer Duke singles.

But there were other none the less significant and worthwhile changes to the engines and the cycle parts. Chief among these was probably the adoption of the then very innovative electronic ignition system. This was energized by an additional pulse coil on the existing alternator unit and fired by a transducer and pick-up unit. On the Desmo (and the other singles, except the 250 Street Scrambler) the ignition system was either by Ducati Electronica or the Spanish Moloplat concerns. Most bikes were fitted with the former and in practice the Moloplat system produced a weaker spark. This meant that bikes that had this system often lacked the easy starting virtues of the Ducati ignition. Electrics were further improved with a Japanese Yuasa 6-volt 13-amp/hour battery. The alternator was rated at 80 watts,

A classic Ducati, the 1974 350 Desmo disc (also available with drum brake and Marzocchi forks). Its striking yellow and black finish made it stand out from the crowd

A 250 Desmo disc on display in the Mick Walker Motorcycles showroom during the mid 1970s

and had an electronic rectifier and regulator.

All the engine units were fundamentally much as before, but the compression ratio of the 250 models had been reduced to 9.7:1, while the 350's ratio remained at 10:1 and the 450's 9.3:1. All models retained the square slide Dell'Orto VHB carburettors of 29 mm choke size, but with different settings.

Another major difference was an option only on the Desmos which was an improved braking system. All three capacities were offered with a choice of either the original double-drum Grimeca front brakes, or a single 280 mm (11 inch) front disc. The disc, in cast iron, and the caliper were by Brembo, and the bikes to which these were fitted were also given Ceriani 35 mm front forks, rather than the original 35 mm Marzocchis. Unlike the Mark 3 and Street Scramblers the Desmos retained 18-inch rims, which were Borrani alloy, on both wheels.

Of course, there were numerous other detail changes. These extended to new fuel tanks (in steel) and seats and side panels (in fibreglass). They also gained new mudguards—a fibreglass front and steel rear. The

fuel tank now came with a quick action flip-up filler cap and larger bore fuel taps.

The general electrics saw minor revisions. The front brake light switch (on the drum brake model) was now incorporated in one of the front brake cables, which had its outer section in two pieces. Unlike the valve-spring models the Desmo versions had the oblong alloy bodied rear light used on many of the earlier narrow-case singles, such as the Mach 1. There was a 150 mm Aprilia headlamp with a chrome-plated shell, mounted on Verlicchi brackets that incorporated rubber shock-absorbing pads.

Instrumentation and controls were also new or borrowed from earlier models. The instrument's rubber surround came from the previous Silver Shotgun. The instruments themselves were most commonly British Smiths, although some machines had CEV. Drive to the rev-counter was from the top cam drive bevel cover which like the later V-twins was a combined casting, unlike the separate cover and drive of the earlier singles. This was introduced in a bid to cure oil leaks.

They shared the black plastic and nylon Verlicchi twistgrip and rubber handlebar grips from the same source. A choke lever was mounted on top of the clutch lever fitting (the opposite side from the valve-

Right **Control layout of the Desmo disc model. This is the author's own machine brought into Britain during early 1974—the very first one imported**

Opposite **35 mm Ceriani forks and Brembo hydraulically operated cast-iron disc**

spring models) and, on the 350 and 450 only, a valve lifter lever under the same control clamp.

The Desmo had full rearsets and clip-ons. The hand controls had separate lever clamps so that the rider could adjust them (unlike the Mark 3 with clip-ons which were welded) to the most comfortable position. The rearset footrests were parts that were also used on the Silver Shotgun and these had no rubbers.

The first time I came into contact with the yellow Desmo singles was in February 1974, at the factory in Borgo Panigale, Bologna. I was on a visit to sort out various parts problems, and with me were John Nutting of *Motor Cycle Weekly* and Ray Elliott of Coburn & Hughes. C & H had taken over the British Ducati concession from Vic Camp in November of the previous year, but at that time were only importing the Mark 3 and the 750 twins.

Below **Cylinder-head details, showing rev counter drive, bevel tube and square slide 29 mm Dell'Orto carb**

As soon as I saw the sleek, purposeful lines of that yellow Desmo masterpiece I simply knew that this was *the* Ducati and asked why Coburn & Hughes were not interested in the model. The reply was that there would be no market for them in Britain but there was at least one buyer, because along with the parts order I had gone to collect I also loaded up a 350 Desmo (disc brake) model for myself. My subsequent enthusiasm on the way back convinced Ray that he should be importing the yellow Desmos and that they would sell. Coburn & Hughes remained largely unconvinced until the bike's arrival in the dealer's showrooms, and then they could not get enough to satisfy the hunger of the bike buying public.

In August 1974 the British list price of the Desmo singles was £599 for the 250 and £699 for the 450 (apart from my own, only six other 350s were ever brought over by C & H). By comparison the Mark 3 valve-spring models were considerably cheaper, at £519 for the 250 and £549 for the 350, and it was no doubt this price differential that had made the Desmos look hard to sell.

But, as I recalled in my earlier book *Ducati Singles* (Osprey), there is always a market for a masterpiece. Looking back at all the Ducatis I have owned and ridden through the years that 350 was the best of all, with the exception of my first Ducati racer, the 175 Formula III. It was one of a rare handful of motorcycles capable of feeding a message back to the rider whilst being ridden, making man and machine one.

Above **Author's 350 Desmo disc being tested by John Robinson of** *Motorcycle Mechanics*, **May 1974. Following is his brother Rick's 750 GT**

Below **250 Desmo disc, entered by Sports Motorcycles in the ~~1975~~ IoM TT** Production Race. Roger Nicholls 1974 7ᵗʰ 250cc class 81.09 mph

Ducati Owners Club (GB) member with his immaculate 450 Desmo disc, a decade after it left the factory—non standard are the megaphone silencer, rear light and Lucas chrome headlamp

To a large extent the press of the day agreed with me—here's just a sample of their opinions:

'Taken as purely sporting motorcycles, no other small machine holds a candle to the Ducati singles for sheer road, or clubman's performance', *Motor Cyclist Illustrated Road Test Annual*;

'It's a scratcher's delight, because not only does it handle like a dream, but squeezing on that 11 inch front disc has almost the same efficiency as hitting a brick wall. With a gearbox that's so sweet you change gear when you needn't just for the hell of it, that all adds up to a permanent adrenalin high', *Bike*;

'What we mean by a good old-fashioned single! It remains a mystery to me why single-cylinder Ducatis are not more in evidence on our roads. For over 10 years they have been hailed as classic motorcycles and every time I ride one, which I must say is not nearly enough, I end up by telling myself that this is just the sort of motorcycle I enjoy. It really is a motorcyclist's motorcycle', *Motorcycle Sport*.

Dave Minton, during his test of a 250 Desmo in the May 9 1975 issue of *Motorcyclist Illustrated*, got things just about right with the following comment: 'All in all I am convinced that the 250 is the best sportster 250 available today by a long way despite its failings. It will take you to work each day, but such practice would be akin to taking family snapshots with a Leica or rat shooting with a Purdy. You can do it—but what a waste.'

Yes, the Desmo singles are not without their faults and although they can be used as ride-to-work transport, such usage is not to be recommended. In many ways, the majority of Ducati's singles and Desmos are more suited to racing than road use.

Perhaps the biggest criticism levelled at Ducati singles over the years, on the mechanical side (in particular the earlier narrow-case models), was big-end failure. Much of this centres around the design which, although suitable for racing use, wasn't always the best for many of the machine's owners. For example, two features definitely contributed to problems: lack of regular oil changes and riding in too high a gear. Both would occur when riders were new to the game, or looked upon their machines solely as a means of basic transport.

Above **A totally original restoration of a 350 Desmo, undertaken by Nigel Ball during 1987–8, transformed a neglected wreck into this superb machine**

Right **Engine details from Nigel Ball's machine**

As with all Ducati singles, it is vitally important to change the oil regularly (every 1500 miles is recommended) and use one of suitable quality and type. Here I've found that the best results came from either BP or Shell 20/50 multigrade, or a monograde oil such as Gulf 40 SAE summer and 30 SAE winter (for British weather conditions). Do *not* rely on the dipstick provided at the front of the wet sump. This can provide unreliable readings and in itself has contributed to a number of big-end failures through the years. The only safe method is to measure the correct amount of oil before putting it in.

The oil filter is primitive. It is simply a nylon gauze attached to the drain plug. When fitting it make absolutely sure its end is properly located, otherwise when tightening up the drain plug the filter will be distorted and become completely ineffective.

The big-end bearing itself consists of a crankpin, alloy cage, needle rollers and side plates, with the one piece con-rod forming the outer eye of the bearing. The small-end is a conventional pressed-in phosphor-bronze bush. Besides the importance of correct quality *and* quantity of lubricant, the other reason for big-end problems is the 1950s racing technology design and lubrication system. The latter features a gear-driven pump contained within the timing cover. When overhauling the engine or replacing the big-end don't

presume that the pump is all right—check it, with special attention to the gear teeth, bushes, gasket and even the tiny pressure ball and spring.

There are other equally important requirements for longer big-end life. One is the centrifugal sludge trap screw housed in the left-hand crankshaft flywheel. This should be removed and cleaned out every time the engine is stripped and always following big-end failure. The reason is quite simple—once full the trap will let in particles it is designed to keep out!

Testing the con-rod for up-and-down movement in the time-honoured way is largely a waste of time with a

Previous page above **1958 125 Desmo single with the laurel wreath of victory**

Previous page below **Staschel 450 Desmo was a German special that used 450 Desmo power and a spine-type chassis**

Above **The 1971 450 R/T Desmo, a specialized bike originally intended for Stateside use. It appeared on the home market with lighting equipment and a low-level exhaust**

Superb orange/yellow 1973–4 Desmo single, which was
available in 250, 350 and 450 engine sizes, plus a 239
version for the French market. It came with the option of
double-drum (illustrated) or disc front brake

Opposite **The legendary Mike Hailwood en route to his history-making 1978 Formula 1 TT victory**

Right **A jubilant Mike Hailwood (centre) after his IoM Formula 1 TT success**
John Williams left 2nd, Tan Richards 3rd
Below **Mike Hailwood Replica, which first appeared in 1979 as a limited production run, but by 1982 (as shown), it was mass produced and Ducati's best-seller**

Above **1984 900S2, very much a watered-down example of the original 900SS**

Opposite above **Mid 1970s 750SS seen in action at Daytona in 1984**

Opposite below **Fogarty's and Eddie Roberts' 900 Desmos, both entered by Sports Motorcycles**

Above **American Pete Johnson hurls his Cagiva 650 Alazurra around Daytona during the 1987 Battle of the Twins race. He finished second**

Right **'Lucky' Lucchinelli, former Grand Prix star and World Champion, pictured at Daytona in 1986**

Ducati single because by then it will be too late. As a matter of course, during a major engine overhaul (or restoration project) split the crankshaft and inspect each individual big-end bearing roller. Flaking on just one of these is the first sign of impending problems and can only be detected by actually inspecting as described.

Also, inspect the con-rod side shims for wear. Finally, check the condition of both the right-hand (offside) end of the crankshaft to ensure that neither it, or the matching phosphor-bronze bush in the timing cover is worn. Any noticeable wear will mean lower oil pressure to the big-end bearing and can again spell trouble. The con-rod itself is only really a problem when pattern assemblies are used. I strongly recommend that only genuine parts are used—otherwise the rider risks a broken rod—certainly if used for racing. The same applies to pistons.

Classic racing took off in the early 1980s. Here John Wittman shows his form with a 350 Desmo in 1982. Ducati machines now make up a considerable portion of any entry

Genuine Ducati pistons are forged and will often last an extremely long time. In fact, it is often cheaper to fit a new liner and set of rings, than rebore the cylinder and buy a new piston.

Besides those points already mentioned the Desmo single engine unit is relatively trouble-free. And unlike the Desmo V-twin the singles gearbox is robust and not prone to problems. Unfortunately, the same cannot be said of some of the ancillary equipment.

Except for steering head races, swinging-arm bushes and pins, the frame is not a real problem, nor for that matter are the suspension or wheels. The real weakness centres, as on all the Ducati singles for that matter, around items such as the instruments and electrics. Both the speedo and tacho were not only small but largely undamped and not only inaccurate but suffered wildly swinging needles—in particular the Smith's clocks. I for one wondered how a British made instrument could be so inaccurate, and it was not until some years later that I found the real reason. Smith's had supplied Ducati kph instruments with mph faces—in other words these were at least 5/8th out!

Electrics: this is without doubt the Desmo single's

weakest point. I'm sure in my own mind that if Ducati had been able (or wanted) to have a decent 12-volt system fitted the production life of the single could have been extended for several years. As it was, they were saddled with a poor 6-volt system which, except for the electronic ignition, belonged to a bygone age. And it has become a fairly standard practice amongst owners to convert to 12 volts and/or with the Lucas Rita system.

Finally, there is the finish, or lack of it, as regards items such as paintwork and chrome plate, the latter in particular, and those dreadful silver-painted spokes! In contrast, the alloy castings were some of the best ever found on a production motorcycle, both in polished 'as cast' forms.

Besides the roadholding, smooth power (except the 450), handling, braking and general reliability, the Desmo single had the advantage of being a machine on which the averagely mechanically-inclined owner could work.

Most Desmo owners are probably put off at first by what *seems* like a complex engine design. In fact, not only is it quite simple to work on, but virtually no special tools are needed. The only one which is absolutely vital is the generator flywheel extractor. Others, such as the clutch holding tool, rocker-pin extractor and exhaust cooling ring spanner, can all be easily fabricated.

To remove the cylinder head and barrel, for example, the piston is raised to tdc, with both valves closed and the top bevel gear dots lined up. Then, simply remove

Laurie Parson with his almost original 250 Desmo during practice for the Classic Manx GP, August 1985; captured on film at the Gooseneck on the famous 37¾-mile Mountain Circuit

Typical Desmo single as raced at classic events. This is a 450 version at Knockhill, Scotland, August 1986

the exhaust pipe and undo the four long cylinder head/barrel through bolts—it's that easy.

It should also be realized that to do this task it is not necessary to remove the three oilway bolts on the right-hand side of the engine as these, together with the alloy bevel-shaft tower, will come off in one unit with the cylinder-head assembly. If the head is difficult to get off, a slight tap with a hide hammer underneath the central oilway bolt will usually be all that is needed. *Do not* on any account try to lever the head off, or in any other way put pressure on the fins of either the barrel or head.

Perhaps the one single most important statement to make is that unlike the majority of motorcycle engines the Ducati overhead-cam singles, in both desmo and valve-spring forms, were truly hand built. Each one used an amazing amount of shims. When dismantling or rebuilding, it is absolutely vital that each shim is kept with its respective shaft or gear.

As for modifications, whilst in production during the final two years there was only one 'new' model in the range of Desmo singles, this was the 239. This first appeared in early 1974 and was intended for the French market, to beat the tax penalties, which placed a much higher level of duty on motorcycles over 240 cc. It was made in both Desmo and Mark 3 form and, in my opinion, was probably the best of all the final models for its size. The 239 was quite different from the normal 248 cc '250'—not only was it faster and crisper but had a superior state of engine tune with a number of important changes. The cylinder head, barrel and valves were all different, and a new 72.5 mm slipper type piston was used. The 239 had a round slide Dell'Orto PHF 30 carburettor with a special manifold and a silencer based on the 860 GT type manufactured by Lafranconi. The only other point regarding the final machines off the line is that Ducati used up older components—such as 1969–71 side panels to complete the quota of bikes!

In 1974, the final year of production, the diameter of the big-end increased to a 32 mm crankpin. Originally when launched the wide-case 250/350 Desmos had a 27 mm pin, later upped to 30 mm.

If you are considering buying a Ducati single you will have noticed that prices have risen sharply over the last few years and the most sought after is the 1973–4 disc-braked Desmo (though some were actually sold in 1975 and even 1976). Prices tend to fluctuate fairly widely and it's still possible to pick one up cheaply but in need of restoration. In my opinion it is best to pay a higher price for a really nice example than to attempt to save a few pounds (dollars, deutschmarks, lira or yen!) and then find out too late that it's going to cost a fortune to carry out the necessary work to get the required result.

A definite plus to owning one of the Bologna singles is that even today, well over a decade since they ceased production, virtually every spare is still available for the engine, and a good majority of the cycle parts too—even such small items as decals—providing you know who stocks parts for older Ducati models.

In all honesty, the Desmo single is not the motorcycle for someone without other means of everyday transport. It is a machine built for the sole purpose of providing its rider with a unique motorcycling experience, which it does, providing its limitations are

understood. The Desmos' ideal backdrop is either the main trunk road or better minor roads, where traffic runs thinly and the bends are open, where only natural boundaries (and speed restrictions) discipline a right fist. Under such conditions, a rider will find that nothing grounds under the hardest cornering (for really hard riding remove the centre stand) and soon he will discover himself falling back into the classic riding style of the 1950s and 1960s, like that employed by masters such as Surtees and Duke, long before Smart and Sheene brought in the trends of hanging their knees and elbows out.

Tucked in hard, hugging the shapely fuel tank, feeling every inch of the tarmac, and line changing by mere thought alone, a Ducati Desmo single pilot enjoys the experience that only riders of cammy Velos and Inter Nortons understood, and what builders of the modern racer replica can only dream about.

West German Ducati tuner Hans Staschel with his very special 500 Desmo single. Also visible are some of the special goodies he manufactures, including crankshaft, dry clutch and barrel/piston assembly. Snetterton, June 1988

8

Imola

Some 20 miles east of Bologna, the town of Imola is situated near the point where the *autostrada* and the River Santerno cross and lies close to the rolling hills of the same name. Carry on along the *autostrada* eastwards and after another 40 miles you hit the Adriatic and the coastal resort of Rimini.

Both Rimini and Imola, together with names such as Riccione and Cesenático, were veritable hotbeds of road racing in the Italian calendar until the early 1970s, with only Imola surviving to become a permanent modern circuit for a full range of amenities. Unlike the others Imola went on to greater things including the first choice venue for the national grand prix on both two *and* four wheels and also Europe's richest road race, the Imola 200.

The first race to be staged on the 3.1-mile *Circuito Dino Ferrari* (named in honour of the *Commendatore's* son, who died at a young age in the 1950s), took place on 25 April 1953, before a crowd of over 40,000 spectators. The following year this became the Coppa d'Oro Shell [Shell Gold Cup] which was also run in April and eventually led to the subject of this chapter—the Imola 200, still sponsored, by the Shell Oil Company.

However, when charting Imola's place in the story of motorcycle sport, it is often overlooked that motocross also played an important role. For example, Imola was the location for the very first 500 cc Italian Moto Cross Grand Prix, counting towards the European Series, staged near the town on 1 June 1952. Watched by vast crowds it was dominated by Belgian riders, including the legendary Aguste Mingels, who took victory on a British Matchless.

Throughout the rest of the decade and well into the 1960s the town became associated with both on- and off-road two-wheel sport with many of the world's top competitors taking part.

But the most famous day in Imola's motorcycling history came on Sunday 23 April 1972, with the staging of the inaugural *200 Miglia di Imola—La Daytona d'Europa*.

This was the brainchild of Dott. Francesco Costa, a man of never-ending ideas. He was the one who had imported motocross into Italy and staged that first grand prix at Imola back in 1952, and the same person who had conceived the annual Coppa d'Oro Shell races and was once again the man behind the Daytona of Europe.

Costa, through the auspices of the Moto Club Santerno, had gambled heavily on staging Europe's first ever American type 200-mile event—with a then world record prize fund of £24,000. It was also destined to be one of the greatest days in Ducati's history and certainly one which must rate as one of the most unexpected and unusual victories ever seen at a major road race.

The *Motor Cycle* headline read: 'Outsider Smart Cleans Up'. Going on to say, 'Short of fuel and one gear adrift, Paul Smart ended a stop-gap ride in a blaze of glory at Imola on Sunday. For his flying trip from America to race a works V-twin 750 cc Ducati paid off in the most unexpected and sensational way.' But what made it even more remarkable was that without his wife's insistence on a promise she had made, Smart wouldn't have even been there!

Our story would have had quite a different ending if Paul's wife Maggie (Barry Sheene's sister) hadn't been a lady who stuck to her guns. While Paul was away in America, contracted to Bob Hansen and Kawasaki and resident in Santa Ana, Orange County, California, a phone call came through to the Smart family home which was to trigger a piece of racing folklore. With Ducati boss Fredmano Spairani on the other end of the line—waiting for a decision there and then, Maggie said '"yes", well the money they were offering was excellent'. But when Paul found out his first reaction was 'I'm not riding that old thing—you'll just have to phone them back and say the deal's off'. 'I'm not doing anything of the sort', retorted Maggie. 'I've given my word, so you're riding'.

I bet the whole incident has given Mr and Mrs Smart quite a few chuckles over the years. . . . Unknown to Maggie at the time, the Ducati boss must have been hugely relieved—he had already been turned down by Jarno Saarinen, Renzo Pasolini and brother Barry.

Today things are slightly different and Paul freely admits that his Ducati ride at Imola was something special: 'Although I won more money at Ontario in 1973, Imola was more satisfying because I hadn't gone there expecting to win.'

A magic moment—Bruno Spaggiari tips a bottle of champagne over Paul Smart's head on the victor's rostrum after the pair had scored a sensational 1-2 on their Desmo 750 V-twins at Imola, 23 April 1972

Line-up of works Ducati 750 V-twins, left to right, Spaggiari, Smart, Dunscombe and Giuliano

Originally, Smart had intended to ride at Imola for Triumph, whom he had left two months earlier to join Kawasaki's Team Hansen in America. But it is highly unlikely that this would have come about in the light of subsequent events, with the British company facing serious financial problems.

And no one outside Ducati, least of all Paul Smart himself, believed that Ducati's challenge would be anything other than a big flop. His American sponsor Bob Hansen simply laughed when he was told, saying 'they can't be serious'. But Ducati paid for his air ticket and flew him via Heathrow, where he spent half an hour with Maggie, and then on to Milan—where a chauffeur-driven black limousine, with window curtains, blasted him straight to Modena for testing.

This was the Thursday morning before the race meeting, and bleary-eyed and jet-lagged after a marathon 23-hour journey he was being asked to straddle a bike he had never seen before and rush around a circuit which was equally new. 'I must be mad', he thought.

But the sight which greeted him revived him with a start, there was a line of shining brand new silver-faired 750s to greet him. Smart tested three of them and selected one, which felt better than the others so he concentrated on that particular machine.

He had this to say about that first test session at Modena: 'The circuit was too tight for this long wheelbase bike and with its Dunlop TT100 tyres pretty difficult. It just didn't feel quick, but I found that after 20 laps that there were ten things I wanted altered and that I had broken Ago's lap record!'

Although he didn't speak a word of Italian, Paul soon felt 'part of my own "team within a team", just as I had at Triumph. I had two bikes left to me and two mechanics.'

Once at Imola, Ducati soon showed that they meant business. In the first official practice session veteran factory tester Bruno Spaggiari, the Percy Tait of Italy, as Paul described him, set the pace. The second session, scheduled for late on Friday, was rained off.

On Saturday, the sun came out after early rain, and again the Ducati men were flying. Spaggiari and Smart were fastest, ahead of Agostini, Dave Simmonds on a 508 cc Kawasaki, Roberto Gallina (Honda) and Walter Villa with an Italian prepared ex-factory 750 Triumph triple. Peter Williams and Phil Read on Nortons came next. But several of the other British stars were already in trouble—including Ray Pickrell, who suffered gearbox and clutch troubles.

After the first practice session Smart realized just how serious a challenge Ducati were going to pose for the opposition. The circuit was quick—remember that this was before chicanes were introduced the following year—and most of the way round was flat out on the Duke.

The Ducati organization was good with fuel consumption checks, pit signalling, refuelling procedure and so on.

Race day dawned, and although the weather was dull, the atmosphere was anything but. Not only had a record crowd of some 70,000 crammed into the 3.1-mile vineyard-bordered circuit, but there was also a total of 21 works or semi-works machines ready to come to the line. These included Norton and Moto Guzzi, who fielded full works teams for the first time since the golden era of the 1950s on continental European soil. Besides these two factories (and of course Ducati) there were also works entries from MV Agusta, BSA, Triumph and Honda, plus semi-works machines from BMW, Laverda, Suzuki and Kawasaki.

This really promised to be a clash of the giants—not to be overawed by this show of strength Ducati had *ten* 750 Desmo V-twins and four riders. Each of the quartet (joining Smart and Spaggiari were Ermanno Giuliano and Englishman Alan Dunscombe—sponsored by importer Vic Camp) had two machines and there were two spares. All ten machines had been transported to the circuit in the team's impressive glass-sided transporter.

After a nostalgic parade of ex-champions, including Stanley Woods, Geoff Duke, Bill Lomas, Ralph Bryans, Bruno Ruffo, Nello Pagani, Carlo Bandirola, Umberto Masetti and Benedicto Caldarella, the competitors set off on a warming-up lap.

Rain had fallen again and it was spitting as the riders reappeared. Inevitably, some were already in trouble. Peter Williams (Norton) had to change plugs, whilst John Cooper (BSA) discovered that his throttle was jamming. The start was delayed to enable these two enough time to make the grid. However, soon several riders were complaining that their engines were overheating.

Down went the flag and away went Agostini with Smart, Gallina and Spaggiari in hot pursuit. At the beginning of lap 4, Smart, followed by his team-mate, had passed the MV star on the fastest section of the course, the stretch past the start/finish line—much to the annoyance of the MV pit. Agostini then had to fight off a fierce challenge from Percy Tait.

At the 20-lap stage, Smart led Spaggiari but Ago still had the pair in his sights and was really trying. In fact, Smart, Spaggiari and Agostini all eventually shared the

Race winner Paul Smart—but it was a twist of fate which saw him ride for Ducati at all

Final stages of the race and Smart leads Spaggiari with victory in Ducati's grasp either way

fastest lap in 1 min. 52.1 sec., a speed of 100.1 mph.

By this time Tait had dropped back but held his place ahead of Read, whose Norton had slowed mysteriously, with Villa and Pickrell in attendance.

The two leading Ducati riders were enjoying life, circulating together as regularly as clockwork. But Agostini, however hard he tried, couldn't make an impression on them. On lap 42, the MV cried enough at the Acque Minerali curves. The cause of the retirement, although not admitted at the time, was due to rear drive problems—remember that the rules of the 750 called for certain 'standard' parts—so the MV was stuck with shaft rear drive.

Soon Tait was in trouble too. His rear wheel—an experimental one with a magnesium hub—had collapsed. So the hard riding Villa, who had overtaken Read on the ailing Norton, moved into third spot. Pickrell was now fifth, ahead of Jefferies and John Williams on the leading Honda.

Meanwhile, Dunscombe had fallen at the Tamburello, which is a fast left-hander after the pits, breaking a collar bone, and so sidelining the fourth Ducati.

Five laps from the end, following an agreement which Spairani had made with his riders—that team orders would prevail until that time, it was every man for himself. Effectively this meant a free-for-all at the front between Smart and Spaggiari.

Smart commented recently: 'As soon as Bruno passed the start line when the 5-lap board was shown, he tried everything to get past. Eventually, in do-or-die effort he ran out of road, with dust flying he was lucky not to drop it. After this I was home and dry.' And so it was, even though Bruno claimed afterwards that he had run out of petrol (well at least that was what the Italian press said!). But whatever the competition out on the track, the fact remained that Ducati had scored a famous 1–2 victory.

As Paul mounted the winner's rostrum after the race he said: 'I just can't believe it's happened'. Then he revealed that 'I lost first gear early in the race and ran out of petrol on the last lap.' (This was not strictly true as he later admitted!)

It was also the biggest birthday present he was ever to receive—he had not only won the then record European prize money totalling some £4500 but, in addition, Spairani kept a promise he had made earlier

After the race, Smart (right) with the winner's cup, whilst Spaggiari seems to be unconcerned at all the attention

'that I will give the winning bike to the rider who wins the race for Ducati'. So Paul also became the proud owner of one race-winning Imola 750 Desmo V-twin.

Smart and Ducati were not the only happy people that day—organizer Francesco Costa and the Moto Club Santerno were overjoyed at their success too. Later, there was a celebratory dinner in Bologna attended by about 100 guests. After that, Smart and Spaggiari were put on the roof of Ducati's glass-sided transporter outside the town's railway station in front of some 20,000 cheering fans.

For Paul it was then back to Heathrow and on to California immediately afterwards. The winning bike was despatched to England via importer Vic Camp, where it was handed over to Paul during one of his visits to Britain. He rode it at a few short circuit events that year, including the Hutchinson 100 at Brands Hatch which he won, but this wasn't without a piece of drama—a valve dropped in during practice and the Smart team (two works mechanics, Joe Caley and Don Godden) worked all night 'machining parts from blanks', as Paul said in the foreword he wrote for my earlier book, *Ducati Twins* (Osprey).

The ridiculous thing was that Ducati had made Smart promise 'not to look inside the engine' before handing it over . . . as if he was taking delivery of something other than, however good, a highly-strung racing machine.

At both Silverstone and Snetterton it went on to one cylinder after showing considerable speed. Following this, the Imola winner spent a couple of years on show in my Wisbech showrooms, before going back to its owner—who still has the machine to this very day—akin to a famous racehorse which lives in retirement at the family estate!

Paul admits to having a soft spot for 'that old thing—the 750 Duke was such a deceptive bike, faster than the works Kawasakis and everything that year, even though it hardly seemed to be firing more than every other lamp post!'

Except for his exploits on the 1972 Imola winner the Kent rider rode for Ducati only twice more. Once was at the Italian GP a month after his win, where he managed to hold second spot on one of the factory's 500 V-twins to Ago's MV, until he hit a problem with one of the machine's throttle cables, eventually coming in fourth. Paul admits that he was disappointed with the smaller vee reckoning 'although incredibly quick, it was also juddery—making me think it was both under-developed and overbored'!

Then, finally, in 1975 Ducati invited Paul to ride again at Imola on one of the later short-stroke dry clutch 750s in the 200-miler. But it wasn't the same. For a start he was still on crutches after breaking both thighs and it was his first race since the accident. In eighth place he brought the bike into the pits—it had lost 200 or 300 revs and was jingling 'just like it was going to explode. Franco Farnè revved it hard, said it was OK, and sent me

Ducati's glass-sided luxury race transporter, very much in the big spend policy of the then boss Fredmano Spairani

out again. Heeled over in second gear on the overrun it seized and threw me down the road. The next thing I knew was some nuns covering everything up in plaster—thought I'd broken it again—but luckily it was just bruising and pulled ligaments'.

Except for the incidents recorded above Paul never rode for Ducati again. And in any case the *serious* racing effort was whilst Fredmano Spairani and Arnaldo Milvio were in charge, which ended at the beginning of 1973. The rebirth of a full-blooded return to big time racing, rather than merely as an aid to a roadster development programme, as with the desmo singles in the late 1960s, began shortly after Spairani and Milvio took over the reins of power at Ducati in 1969.

The first racer they authorized was not the 750 that many might expect, but a 500 designed exclusively with competition in mind. During October 1970, with work well advanced on the new 750 V-twin roadster, it was decided to instruct Ing. Taglioni to work on a pure racing version of the concept. This was, however, to be for use in 500 cc class grand prix racing and made its inaugural appearance at Modena on 21 March 1971.

But the smaller V-twin was never destined to make a real impression, even though considerable development—and money—was lavished on it.

Besides several experiments using both Ducati and British Seeley frames and a whole array of technical changes to the engine, including at various times two- and four-valve heads, bevel and toothed belt-drive to the overhead-cams, contact breakers and electronic ignition and either carburettors or fuel injection the project was finally shelved in early 1973.

Left **Maggie (far right) and other** *Motor Cycle News* **glamour girls. Centre is brother Barry Sheene, circa 1971**

There was also *another* design around this time for GP honours, although not the work of Taglioni, which was the three-cylinder 350. The engine, which Spairani and his henchman Milvio had commissioned in 1971, was designed by the British based Ricardo Engineering concern.

At a press conference staged in Italy at the time of the Italian GP, during May 1972, Ducati managing director Spairani told journalists that the company was making good progress with their now water-cooled 350 three. 'The three-fifty has been designed to beat the out-dated MV Agusta and the engine has topped 16,000 rpm on the bench. We are using all the most advanced techniques to make it competitive', boasted Spairani. He added that the factory hoped to start track-testing within a month and to have the machine racing before the end of the year. Specifications included dohc, with four-valve heads, fuel injection and a seven-speed gearbox.

In reality, much of this was wishful thinking. Maximum power of the 12-valve engine was never more than a claimed 50 bhp at 14,500 rpm and

accounts for why it was never even mounted in a frame. The standard production racing TD3 Yamaha two-stroke twin of the era was lighter, faster and more competitive—let alone a pukka works bike!

The amount of money spent on racing in the Spairani/Milvio era was probably the reason why they were 'removed' from office and their replacements far less inclined towards motorcycle sport, not to mention costly and ineffective efforts such as the 500 V-twin and 350 three-cylinder GP projects.

For all the expense, it had been the production based 750 Desmo which had actually achieved the results which the racing mad Spairani had so dearly wanted.

At the end of 1972, Ducati 'officially' announced that they were retiring from Formula 750. But in spite of this, when Imola came round once more in April 1973 Spaggiari was back in the saddle of a Ducati V-twin attempting to repeat the triumph of the previous year. Smart had by now left the Ducati camp and the Italian veteran was the only rider remaining from the quartet who had competed for the factory in the 1972 event.

Joining him, in a team entitled *Scuderia Spaggiari*, were Mick Grant and Bruno Kneubuhler, both riders who had been impressed with the speed and reliability of the 750 V-twin.

Grant, who had wintered in South Africa, had seen

Below left **The woman who made it all happen! Maggie and Paul Smart a few hours after their marriage, 31 December 1971**

Below **Smart thunders his Imola race winner around Brands Hatch during one of a handful of races he contested after the factory had given him the bike**

just how much potential the bike had when one of the Imola bikes entered by the South African importer and piloted by one of the locals had outsped the Yorkshireman and his ultra-quick 350 Yamaha. This was enough to persuade Grant to visit the Bologna factory—and arrange a works ride in early 1973.

The bikes the trio were to use were brand new, not rehashed 1972 models, which was in stark contrast to Ducati's declared 'no racing' policy! At 155.5 kg (343 lb) they were much lighter than the previous year's racers, with considerably modified engines. Smart's victory had been achieved on a bike not dissimilar to the one being sold to the public, and even closer to the so-called Imola Replica, the superb 750SS Desmo which was ridden on the streets and raced during the mid 1970s by the few lucky enthusiasts who were able to buy one.

But in their need to repeat their Imola 200 success the Bologna based team, headed by Ing. Taglioni, came up with a very much more specialized design to defend the 1972 result. Unlike the previous year's model, this didn't have the roadster frame with lugs for the centre-stand and other fitments. Instead, the chrome-moly chassis was a special factory item used not only for the 1973 Imola effort, but also to house the prototype 860 engine of the 1973 Barcelona 24 Hour winner.

The most notable feature of the new frame was the eccentric swinging-arm pivot adjustment and choice of three different locations for the rear-wheel spindle, allowing the wheelbase to be varied. Another notable change was the use of central axle Marzocchi forks (used on the production 750SS) in place of the leading axle type. Less obvious were the mechanical changes. Here the biggest news was the short-stroke 86 × 64.5 mm bore and stroke measurements (compared to the previous standard production 80 × 74.4 mm). Readers will note that the short-stroke 750's 86 mm bore is the same as the 860 . . . once again displaying Taglioni's liking for utilizing something more than once.

With fiercer cam profiles the shorter stroke resulted not only in higher engine revolutions but also a narrower power-band. This meant in practice that whilst power was bumped up from 84 to 89 bhp, at a higher 10,000 rpm, it was also more difficult to ride. The new lighter chassis, engine tuning and revised fairing gave an increase in maximum speed by some 5–6 mph to around 160 mph, but at the expense of low to mid range punch. Although the carburettors remained

Bruno Spaggiari on the ill-fated 500 GP Desmo V-twin at the Italian GP, 21 May 1972

Above **Spaggiari finished second overall at the 1973 Imola 200 on an updated version of the V-twin**

unchanged 40 mm pumper Dell'Ortos, the exhaust system saw high-level pipes on both sides, against the strange low, offside, high nearside, of the original Imola racers.

The biggest problem was a higher level of opposition—what a difference a mere 12 months had made! Although after their less than impressive showing in the inaugural event Honda had opted out the other three Japanese manufacturers were at Imola 1973 in force. Yamaha, Suzuki and Kawasaki all fielded strong works teams, as did Harley-Davidson. Amongst the riders which the Ducati trio would have to beat were such formidable opponents as Barry Sheene, American hero Cal Rayborn and the 1972 winner, now Suzuki mounted, Paul Smart. Also present was the man currently in top form in the shape of the Flying Finn, Jarno Saarinen, who only a month earlier had become the first European to win the Daytona 200, America's most prestigious race.

However, Giacomo Agostini was not at Imola. Strikes and work on the grand prix machines at MV had seen to this—as had the retirement of the Gallerate team's F750 bike the previous year. . . .

Mirroring the huge success of the 1972 event, the organizers—once again the Moto Club Santerno—had

Right **British star Mick Grant, one of three works riders for Ducati at the 1973 Imola event**

Smart's 1972 winner on display during the mid 1970s at a show in Britain

been overwhelmed by entries. They had finally accepted 90 and decreed that only the fastest 45 would start the race.

The 1973 200 Miglia Shell di Imola was scheduled to be staged on Sunday 15 April.

Practice over the preceding few days saw Guido Mandracci set the fastest lap at a scorching 1 min. 47.7 sec. (104.2 mph), which not only beat the previous year's fastest lap by over 4 mph but even the *outright* lap record held by none other than multi-world champion Giacomo Agostini and his 500 MV Agusta, established at the Italian GP the previous May.

With the second best practice lap of 1 min. 49.6 sec. Saarinen was quietly confident of repeating his Daytona triumph and Spaggiari and Villa made it four different makes of machine on the premier grid positions: Suzuki, Yamaha, Ducati and Kawasaki.

As fifth fastest, Hideo Kanaya swayed things in Yamaha's favour. And, despite still feeling weak following a crash at Daytona, Rayborn was sixth quickest and best of the Stateside contingent on his Harley V-twin.

A decision to split the race into two legs, each of 100 miles, was to play into the hands of the Yamahas, and against Ducati. To oblige television, the start of the first leg was delayed and, when the flag finally fell for the

clutch start, certain riders were soon in trouble—notably Mick Grant whose Ducati debut was marred when he burned the clutch out on the line and was unable to start. Practice leader Mandracci lasted only one lap before a piston disintegrated.

Up at the front French Canadian Kawasaki star Yvon du Hamel held Saarinen at bay for two laps. Then the Finn got ahead and pulled away, the small 350 Yamaha holding the 750s on acceleration. Soon, another Kawasaki rider, Art Baumann, took up the challenge while du Hamel was ousted from third spot by Smart. Both were soon sidelined, however, du Hamel with a broken con-rod and Smart with ignition troubles.

But by lap 10 the two remaining Ducatis were beginning to show, with Kneubuhler having his first ride on anything larger than a 350 Yamaha, closing in on second place man Baumann, with Spaggiari and Rayborn in his slipstream.

Soon, however, that wily old campaigner, Spaggiari, had grabbed second position and was opening a gap, after first overtaking Baumann and seeing Kneubuhler bite the dust. But even he was unable to make an impression on the leader. So, at the end of the first leg it was Saarinen from Spaggiari, with Kel Carruthers (350 Yamaha) in third place.

The survivors, and those whose bikes could be repaired, came to the line for the second 100-mile leg after an interval of $1\frac{1}{2}$ hours. After the warming-up lap Saarinen shot into an immediate lead but this time Spaggiari (and Rayborn) gave him a run for five laps. Thereafter, first Rayborn retired and then towards the end Spaggiari began to drop back eventually finishing third behind Walter Villa who had come up to claim second spot.

But with a second and a third, the Ducati team leader finished runner-up for the second year running—better than the 1972 hero Smart, whose Suzuki had not even started the second leg.

With Kneubuhler out of the meeting following his earlier crash, Mick Grant got some consolation for his early retirement in the first leg, by piloting his Bologna V-twin into seventh place.

But, unfortunately, the 1973 Imola 200 had shown that however good, the best four-strokes were no match for the even quicker 'strokers'. Saarinen's win on a machine with less than half the capacity proved the

writing was now well and truly on the wall for machines like the Ducati in Formula 750.

Not only the Desmo Duke, but Norton, Triumph, BSA, Moto Guzzi and Harley-Davidson—all had been made obsolete by the new breed of Japanese two-stroke. And without the charismatic four-stroke Formula 750 couldn't survive, so in the end no one gained.

In the event the following year, Spaggiari, who was Ducati's only entry, finished eighth in the first leg but retired in the second and therefore came nowhere in the overall result. His only consolation was finishing third behind Phil Read's works 500 MV and the 750 Suzuki of Roberto Gallina in the supporting race.

Even worse was 1975, with Smart crashing after his mount seized, as already recorded, and future world champion Franco Uncini unable to finish higher than a lowly 14th overall.

And so the Desmo V-twin ended its F750 Imola career and it was only many years later, with the introduction of the popular Battle of The Twins racing series on both sides of the Atlantic, that once again racegoers could witness a re-run of the original beauty of F750 racing—the sight *and* sound of large capacity four-strokes doing battle on the world's circuits.

In many ways the BOTT series is a present day replay of the magical day in April 1972 when Ducati ruled the racing world—as it's usually the Bologna V-twins which clean up.

The Smart family on holiday in Jerusalem, February 1988. With the proud parents are Scott (aged 13) and Paula (aged 9). By now Imola was all but a memory—but what a memory!

9

Bevel-driven vees

The sensation of the 1972 Imola 200 was the performance of Paul Smart and Bruno Spaggiari who had created one of the most unexpected results in racing history. Not only finishing first and second, but by dominating the race and in the process defeating the most outstanding machines of the era from the likes of Honda, Suzuki, Kawasaki, Moto Guzzi, BSA and Triumph, not to mention the combination of MV Agusta and multi-world champion Giacomo Agostini.

But perhaps most amazing of all, the machines they rode were not exotic multis, but V-twins. An engine configuration which could trace its history right back to the very dawn of motorcycling. Almost as long as there had been motorcycles—at least big motorcycles, there had been V-twins. Bikes such as Harley-Davidson, Indian, Brough, HRD and Matchless Silver Hawk, to name but a few.

Even though others tried in the pre-war and immediate post-war days to improve on the vee concept with either fours or parallel twins the vee held on—thanks mostly to the popularity of the Harley and Vincent (the successor to HRD), loved by many

Classic bevel-driven layout, loved by countless admirers of the Ducati marque around the world. A V-twin version first saw the light of day in 1970

enthusiasts for its relative simplicity and its raw 'real' (that is vintage) motorcycle looks.

Early fours were not too reliable and the vee scored in smoothness, even though in many ways it was little more than a pair of singles in a common crankcase, over the parallel twin which was renowned for its vibrations. In 90-degree configuration, the V-twin offered the promise of an almost total elimination of primary imbalance.

Always one to look for mechanical simplicity balanced with technical innovation and finesse, Ing. Taglioni was able to grasp the nettle and open up an entirely new era for the Bologna factory in 1969, when a management shake-up saw Arnaldo Milvio and Fredmano Spairani take over the hot seats at the top of Ducati Meccanica S.p.A, succeeding the man who had appointed Taglioni in 1954, Dott. Montano.

To give Milvio and Spairani credit it was they who had realized that the 1970s would see a move towards larger machines, and it was they who authorized Taglioni to produce a 750 as a matter of priority.

Taglioni's only real design experience with motorcycle engines of a capacity greater than 500 cc, were the ill-fated 1200 V4 Apollo and 800 ohc parallel twin projects of the mid 1960s. If nothing else these had provided Ducati's chief designer with much vital experience in two areas—large capacity and a 90-degree vee layout. So it should have come as no real shock to close observers of the Ducati marque, when the prototype 750 V-twin was unveiled in September 1970 at its press debut. In addition, the new design was unmistakably not only a Ducati, but clearly had Taglioni's stamp all over it—even though it was the company's first V-twin.

Skilled engineer as he was, Taglioni had opted to set the cylinders at 90 degrees, which not only endowed the engine with the optimum primary balance characteristics, but also meant that the rear cylinder, for so long a problem on narrower angle V-twins, could be cooled properly. A vee engine also ensured a bare minimal frontal area *and* a low centre of gravity. The only real drawback was an overlong wheelbase, but this was partly overcome by mounting the front pot through the frames' front downtubes.

Almost as soon as the new management team was in place, work had begun on the new design. By March 1970, the initial drawings had been completed and

The ultimate roadgoing Ducati V-twin, the 1974 750SS 'Imola Replica'

were ready to be transformed into metal. By mid July, the first engine was up and running on the test bed. With no serious problems encountered, the result was that the prototype could meet its September press launch towards the end of the month—in all an amazing six months from the drawing-board to the complete motorcycle, incredible!

Of course that original bike was very much a first effort and it was to be some months before it reached the form with which it was offered to the bike buying public. Even so the frame and engine remarkably remained almost intact, although ancillaries and styling differed considerably.

For example, in 1970 disc brakes were in their infancy as far as production machines were concerned—even most racers still sported drums. So when the prototype 750 was first shown, it was equipped with massive double-sided four leading-shoe front brake, complemented by a single leading-shoe drum at the rear— the latter was to be carried through into the production non-Desmo V-twins.

It was not until well into 1971, June to be exact, that the factory began to sell the first production examples of the 750 V-twin. This was the GT, and in this form it was to remain virtually unaltered until being taken out of production in favour of the larger capacity 860 GT in the mid 1970s.

A host of detail modifications meant that the new 750, weighed in at 185 kg (408 lb), 15 kg (34 lb) more than the prototype. But at its heart the V-twin engine was virtually identical to the original design which Taglioni had sketched out. Each cylinder had a bore of 80 mm and a stroke of 74.4 mm, giving an actual

capacity of 748 cc. Like the earlier Mach 1 single which had introduced five-speed gearboxes to production European motorcycles back in 1964, the new engine drove through a five-speed transmission.

Taglioni had put much thought into the inherent problems of what he termed the 'L-shaped' V-twin configuration. To counter these he incorporated several innovations which were to be of benefit for both road and track use. The front cylinder was inclined 15 degrees from vertical to provide sufficient ground clearance for the front exhaust pipe. And as the GT

On the bevel-driven Desmo V-twins, this lightweight spring assisted the positive-valve mechanism to return the valves to their seats

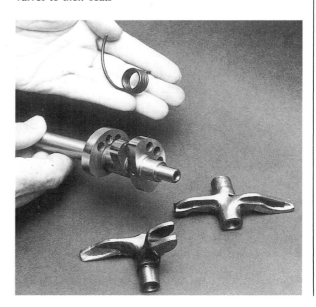

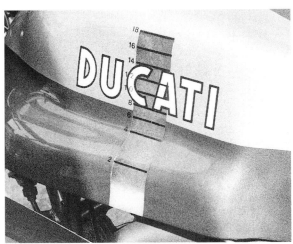

Top **The 750SS ridden by Charlie Sanby throughout Britain in 1974/5, including the Isle of Man TT**

Above **The 1974 750SS came with a large fibreglass tank, with a clear section which permitted the fuel level to be judged instantly**

used valve springs, rather than the desmo system Taglioni envisaged for the super sports or pure racing V-twins which were to follow, he chose to use coil springs, rather than the traditional hairpins found on singles. This was necessary to keep rocker-box width down to a bare minimum. The cylinders were staggered, with the single crankpin/dual con-rods on a front-to-left, rear-to-right basis, thus enabling both exhaust pipes to be mounted closer inboard. The gearbox layout had the layshaft mounted above the mainshaft which, although

Right **Mick Walker Motorcycles' 750SS was the first of 24 such machines imported into Britain in 1974. The bike was raced by Mike James then sold to journalist Mark Wigan**

Above **Massive 40 mm Dell'Orto PHM carb. One of these fed each cylinder on the SS models**

Below **Club rider Simon Morris with his 1974 750SS which can still be seen competing regularly in British classic events**

it meant a slight increase in height, reduced overall crankcase length. Combined with these features the front head neatly fitted between the two front-frame tubes. Thus, the problem of engine width and length was effectively minimized.

The 750 V-twin engine faithfully followed several important principles tested over many years in the factory's single-cylinder line, including unit construction, wet sump, bevel-drive overhead-camshaft, multi-plate clutch and geared primary drive.

The crankshaft used con-rods of the same specifications as the singles, with a 22 mm phosphor-bronze-bushed small-end and a single straight 36 mm crankpin, with hardened steel rollers retained by an alloy cage, and supporting thrust washers pressed into separate crankshaft flywheels. This crankpin size was retained for all the 750 models. The oil-feed to the big-end assembly was fed through the left-hand (nearside) crankshaft end (opposite to the singles) and there were two flywheel sludge-trap screws.

The crankshaft was supported by two massive $35 \times 80 \times 21$ mm main bearings, each with eleven 13.5 mm steel balls in a fibre cage. The reason for using this material instead of a conventional all steel bearing was simple—size and crankshaft speed. Each main bearing had its own steel sleeve, which was mounted directly into the crankcase. This proved a successful method of preventing the age-old problem of a bearing becoming loose and therefore damaging the casing. This method was used on all the subsequent bevel-driven V-twins.

Unlike later larger capacity versions, the 750 crankcases were sandcast, which often meant blow holes being sealed with Araldite by production staff!

The oil circulation and filtering system closely followed earlier Ducati design, with a gear-driven pump and a nylon sump gauze attached to the oil drain plug. But one change to this was a matching plug on the offside of the finned sump. This plug did not, however, have another filter but a detachable cylindrical piece of rubber held in place by an external grub screw. The purpose of this rubber was to give a better seal to the far end of the sump filter, which on the singles had proved a somewhat haphazard affair—quite often ending with a misformed filter which served no useful purpose at all and could soon lull the unsuspecting owner into an expensive engine rebuild.

Like the singles before, the 750s used three-ring Borgo pistons, which ran in alloy cylinder barrels with cast-iron liners, with oversizes available in a range of measurements. The front barrel had two oilways, the rear *three* (two drain, one feed) and all had their own O-

Spanish endurance star Benjamin Grau rode the prototype 860 V-twin to victory in the 1973 Barcelona 24-hour race. He is shown in the 1975 event—still Ducati mounted

ring seal. Like the singles no conventional head gasket was used, only paper ones for the base of each barrel. On no account should gasket cement be used as it will easily block the oilways with disastrous results!

On production engines, whether valve-spring or desmo—the valve head diameters were 36 mm exhaust and 40 mm inlet and were not only used throughout the 750's life but also for the later, larger capacity bevel-driven vees.

Both the clutch and gear selector mechanism followed very much the concept and design employed on the singles, so in some respects did the frame. This, like the smaller bikes, employed the engine unit very much as an integral stressed member. At first glance the 750 chassis gave the distinct impression of having been built around the engine, which in fact it was. In spite of the handicap of an overlong wheelbase, brought about by the 90-degree vee layout, Taglioni and his team of engineers managed to build a bike that not only had a comparable seat height and was one of the lightest machines in its class, but also one which handled superbly.

It is interesting to recall a statement which Taglioni made during an interview in the early 1970s: 'Frames are not designed. They evolve slowly and they are inseparable from the rest of the machine.'

So why did the V-twin handle so well? For a start it had the advantage of a low centre of gravity afforded by the oil sump and the nearly horizontal front cylinder and because of this it followed the same design thesis as such incredible 'earholers' as the grand prix Guzzi singles and Aermacchi-HD Sprint. Other help came from the Colin Seeley designed swinging-arm and rugged leading-axle Marzocchi 38 mm front forks and rear shocks from the same source. But somehow, however good the 750GT might have been, it didn't really set the world on fire, with its somewhat staid lines and unpretentious looks.

Next came a 'half-way house' to the real thing—the 750 Sport. The first pre-production 750 Sports appeared in the middle of 1971. Their striking yellow and black paint job and café racer styling certainly revised the machine's appearance. Gone were the touring bars and sit-up-and-beg rider stance of the GT to be replaced by clip-ons, rearsets, sculptured tank, single-bum stop saddle and racing styled top half fairing. But except for its 32 mm carburettors (30 mm on the GT) and forged slipper pistons (usually of Mondial manufacture), giving a 9.3:1 compression ratio, the Sport motor was completely standard.

It was to be left to Taglioni's 1972 Imola racers, with their desmo heads, to be responsible for the ultimate Ducati 750 V-twin, the Desmo Super Sport, known to enthusiasts of the Bologna marque around the world more generally as the 750SS. As recorded in the preceding chapter, racing bred the SS. Indeed, without the Imola race victory, it is *extremely* unlikely that either the 750, or for that matter the 900, would ever have been seen in SS form!

The first 750SS was, in fact, simply known as the 'Imola Replica' when it made its public debut in prototype form during March 1973.

Paul Smart's win at Imola had created a state of euphoria at the Bologna plant which resulted in a total revision of priorities. For a short distance of time the factory management, or at least Milvio and Spairani, believed they could continue the conquest of the road racing scene—even at full GP level. When realism returned, it was seen that their best (and more cost effective) way forward was through the 750 V-twin, in desmo form, for both track and road. This entailed the cancellation of not only the 500 V-twin GP bike, but also a fuel-injected 350 three-cylinder engine.

The end of both these racing projects was

Roger Nicholls in action during the 1976 British GP at Silverstone. His machine was a 1974 750SS converted to 900SS engine size

1975 model of the 900SS, at the time intended as a strictly limited production machine. Sales far exceeded the factory's original estimate, thus forcing the machine to become a regular in the factory's range

announced in the winter of 1972—significantly at the same time as general manager Spairani was removed from office.

In the wake of these events Ducati's experimental department (*reparto sperimentale*) was thus left with considerable spare capacity, which they decided to fill by taking advantage of the Imola victory building 25 replicas. It should also be noted that this might also have something to do with the fact that Ducati had assured the Imola organizers that they would be constructing the minimum number of machines to qualify for its racing entries under the FIM's Formula 750 racing regulations. . . .

The 25 machines were to be road legal production versions of the Imola machines. And at the outset, the project was intended as a once-only exercise. However, things didn't go quite the way the factory's management had intended because as soon as the bikes appeared the demand for them far exceeded anything which had been budgeted for, forcing further batches to be produced.

As I have already stated in my earlier book *Ducati Twins* (Osprey), I consider machines from this initial batch of 25 to be the most beautiful of all the Ducati V-twins, differing as they did in several details to the subsequent 750SS models. Unique to them were the front mudguard (retained by hose clips), leading-axle front forks, their total use of Lockheed brake parts (including calipers and master cylinders), the fairing and black engine outer casings.

The engine specification of the 1973 750SS was

identical in bore and stroke and capacity to the unit used in the GT and Sport. But the compression ratio was increased to 9.65:1, and the standard 22 mm gudgeon pins and small-end bushes were replaced by 20 mm components.

In that first batch, the engines were almost exact copies of the actual Imola bikes (but without the works racer straight-cut bevel gears). The specifications included forged slipper pistons and stronger con-rods machined from a solid billet with double webbing at the bottom for extra strength. The offside crankcases even featured a flat to enable the piping for an oil radiator to be mounted.

In SS form, the engine would rev to 8800, and drove through the standard five-speed gear cluster. For owners wanting an even greater level of performance than that offered by the 'standard' SS, there was also a kit to transform the machine into a full Formula 750 racer. This comprised a set of racing camshafts and a special exhaust system with high-level exhaust pipes, a smaller diameter balance pipe than standard, and open megaphones. Also supplied was an oil cooler and attachment kit, as were racing spark plugs, Bosch condensers and a Renolds racing chain. There was a selection of alternative main jets for the Dell'Orto PHM 40 mm carburettors, and eight alternative rear-wheel sprockets, from 34 to 42 teeth. Finally, the purchaser received a full racing fairing, including the screen and fittings.

As related in the previous chapter the 1973 Imola racer differed considerably from the 1972 racers, and therefore the 750SS. The frame was shortened, there were three rear spindle positions, central axle forks, Scarab brakes and a much modified engine with a different bore and stroke—even the valve angle was changed!

Above **The zipped seat on the 900SS—just about enough room for a pack of sandwiches or tool roll, but not both**

Below **Black and gold 900SS with a dualseat, introduced in 1978 (1979 model shown). . .**

When the definitive production version of the 750SS (round-case type) appeared in early 1974 it didn't get either the short-stroke engine or the more compact frame. Instead, the engine and frame were based on the 1972 racer (and for that matter the valve-spring GT and Sport models) with the front forks and brakes from the 1973 machine.

Each 750SS was truly hand built, with the engine assembly receiving special attention from the specially selected mechanics allowed to assemble the batch (totalling some 180 machines). Beside the forks and brakes the other instantly recognizable change between the few 1973 750SSs which had been assembled and the 1974 version, was the former had black engine covers and the latter polished casings.

At 180 kg (398 lb) dry the 750SS was the lightest of all the Desmo Super Sport models and precisely the same as the 500SL Pantah! Compared with a typical modern racer replica from Japan, the 750SS styling is best described as reserved, timeless even, with its lack of gaudy decals or flashy paintwork. The colour scheme was identical to the 1972 works racers with a metallic duck-egg green frame and swinging arm and silver fibreglass ware. In fact, this material was used extensively on the bike—on the fuel tank (which had a clear section like those fitted to the works racers, enabling the fuel level to be determined at a glance), the mudguards, side panels and seat base. A useful, if insecure, feature of the seat design was the provision of

a compartment within the tail section for the tool roll (or maybe a packet of sandwiches!). Access to this was simply by a zip across the back of the seat pad.

Unfortunately, the finish of all the fibreglass components, paintwork and chrome was not in the same league as that of the engine or frame. As *Cycle* commented in their June 1974 road test: 'Bothered by details? You'll be bothered by the Super Sport. Stress cracks spread from every attachment point of the fibreglass to chassis. The bottom of the fuel tank leaks in two places. The front fender cannot be made to fit properly. The seat is tatty. The tachometer, pirated from the Sport, has a red line set at 7800 rpm when it ought to be at 9000. The fairing fits asymmetrically. Rust is intruding through the surface of the frame's rather shoddy paint (that doesn't match the rather shoddy paint on the tank, seat or fender). The fuse box is mounted upside down and is open to the punishment of lousy weather. A hole has been crudely filed in the rear inner-fender to make room for the rear brake line. And there's an honest-to-God Italian fly moulded into the fibreglass fuel tank.'

In stark contrast, the same tester went on to say of the 750SS engine: 'It's absolutely transfixing, from off-idle to mid-range cruising to 9000 rpm (and more) acceleration. Equipped like the rest of the Duck 750 with a 5-pound flywheel bolted to the inside of the primary gear the SS engine is snatch-free, willing, tractable and high-turning. What time the Italians at the Ducati factory haven't spent on the fibreglass they have positively lavished on the engine. It's an ultimate-quality engine in every major respect.'

Like the Mach 1 single of the early 1960s the 750SS was either brilliantly good or downright bad and in the process defined the outer limits for the road rider with sporting instincts. If one could put up with the thin paintwork and the stress-cracked fibreglass, the rest was pure magic.

As *Cycle* said, the time that Ducati didn't spend on the finish was more than repaid by the energy lavished on the engine and chassis. The rockers and con-rods were polished, and the forged slipper pistons carefully balanced. The inlet and exhaust ports were smoothly matched to take advantage of those massive 40 mm Dell'Orto pumper carburettors, breathing directly through large, wire gauze-covered plastic bellmouths.

Such attention to detail added up to an engine which, from idle to maximum revs, produced instant response both in terms of torque and acceleration. This superb power unit was matched to a chassis which held the road arguably better than any other large capacity sportster of its day, creating the legend, which still exists today, that the word Ducati on the tank means a sweet-handling bike with a torquey V-twin motor. Added to

. . . and engine details

Pilot's eye view of the 1979 900SS

the super powerful triple disc brake set-up the 750SS was really, certainly as far as a roadster, 'a bike which stood at the farthest reaches of the sporting world—the definitive factory-built café racer', as *Cycle* put it. Incidentally, the 1974 750SS, with its twin Scarabs at the front and a single Lockheed at the rear, can lay claim to being the first *production* bike in the world to employ triple disc brakes.

A decade after it was launched, Australian *Bike* magazine, in the June 1984 issue, called the 750SS 'probably the greatest sporting motorcycle ever built'. And it was out on the road where the Super Sport Desmo really shone. MRW (Mark Wigan), writing in the May 1976 issue of *Motorcycle Sport*, really hit the button with the following description: 'The entire picture

A combustion chamber of horrors. Even Ducati Desmos can disgrace themselves sometimes

changes within 15 seconds of starting to drive (ride!) the SS. It is simply magical in the manner in which it reaches out for the next piece of road, and then promptly demolishes it.'

Before we leave the 750 to take a look at the larger 900 version which replaced it, I will let Phil Schilling, former executive editor of *Cycle*, have the last word—a quote from his book *Motorcycles*, published in 1975: 'As a well-rounded motorcycle for the everyday enthusiast, the Ducati 750SS is a disaster. As a pure sporting motorcycle, it's a masterpiece.'

The new '900' was once again based on what Ducati,

at least, termed a touring bike, the 860GT. And in 1975 when the 900SS first saw the light of day, this meant it had 'square' engine cases rather than the more pleasing to the eye round cases of the 750s. The factory also offered a new 750SS, again with square cases, mainly for domestic consumption where Formula 750 racing still survived. This square case 750SS should not be confused with the original, being instead a 900SS with smaller bores.

The new bikes were really the result of two earlier developments. In November 1973, the prototype 860, the GTI, had made its debut at the biannual Milan Show. Earlier that year in May, the important Barcelona 24 Hour race had been won by the prototype 860 'production' racer. This machine was actually a round case 750SS bored out to 864 cc and fitted with a dry clutch from the 1973 works Imola racer rather than a completely re-engined bike. Like the smaller Desmo V-twins, the larger capacity model made a historic winning debut by scooping Barcelona, ridden by the Spanish pairing of Benjamin Grau and Salvador Canellas. The machine ran faultlessly from start to finish, finally winning by a massive margin of 16 laps and in the process set new lap and distance records. The pair packed 1,674.58 miles into the 24-hour period. Studying the Barcelona bike leaves the impression that it could almost have been a 1972 Imola race bike, fitted with lights. Nevertheless, the success of the capacity increase and the availability of the new engine inevitably led the factory towards their new SS versions.

The 900 actually had a capacity of 863.9 cc from a bore which had been increased to 86 mm, while the stroke remained at 74.4 mm. The production 900SS which first appeared in mid 1975 was, like the original 750SS, intended as a once-only, small batch, hand-built motorcycle. But things didn't work out like this. Due to the sales flop of the mainstream 860GT (and the new parallel twin 350/500) the factory was forced into making what the bike buying public actually wanted, which meant the 900SS, and so it became 'standard issue'—a model which for 1976 went on general sale as part of the official mass-produced model range. Of course 'mass-produced' is only a relative term, Ducati's annual production would be swallowed up by a single day's figure at Honda!

On the production version the compression ratio was 9.5:1 and the engine would rev to 7900 rpm. Both

Mick Walker's runner Dave Cartwright awaits the off at Silverstone, August 1978

900 (and square-case 750) retained the 40 mm carburettors and the same gearbox and clutch, but the 900 received a new camshaft profile. Electronic ignition replaced the old twin points set-up and, unlike the 860GT, a 200-watt alternator was specified. The space vacated by the distributor on the old 750 was taken up by a definite improvement, a disposable oil filter cartridge which supplemented the primitive nylon gauze filter drain plug used on all previous bevel-driven ohc (valve-spring and desmo) designs from Ducati.

Other engine differences included a complete redesign of the method of bottom bevel gear support. On the round-case 750 series a lot of stress had been placed on the gears themselves, with the consequence that shimming and bearing wear became critical if either was not absolutely perfect, the inevitable result would be the bottom bevels becoming excessively noisy. This was rectified in the larger engine by mounting the bevel gears on a support plate which itself contained three bearings.

The oil pump was updated and although both the 750 and 860 pairs of gears had 11 teeth each, they were *not* interchangeable, and the body and backplate were different. The latter was round on the 750 and elongated on the 860.

The gearbox internals were identical to the 750, including the shafts and selector forks, but were to prove a source of trouble when the larger unit was subjected to high mileages, or racing usage.

The 1975 900SS followed the original 750SS in having polished webbed con-rods, with 20 mm small-end bushes and a straight 36 mm crankpin, with each rod having its own separate cage, with twin side-by-side hardened steel rollers.

Like the early 860GT, these 1975 900SS square-case models suffered a clutch problem and had to be modified under warranty early in their life. The 900SS was also noted for an over-stiff clutch action, and clutch slip.

The changes to the engine were matched by a lesser number to the running gear. Only the first few of the 1975 models featured the large Imola tank, thereafter a smaller capacity steel component was fitted, with the fibreglass item available as an optional extra. In any case, for markets such as Britain the use of fibreglass (or

Cartwright again, this time on the Isle of Man during the Formula 1 TT. He lapped at over 100 mph on what was essentially a standard bike, complete with lights and silencers

Much of the factory's racing effort in the late 1970s was channelled through the NCR concern, whose headquarters were only a stone's throw away. Illustrated is one of NCR's endurance racing bikes

for that matter plastic tanks) was banned for street use. Brembo brakes with drilled discs replaced the original type and the whole machine gained a new colour scheme. Gone was the distinctive duck-egg green and in its place was an overall silver bike with blue decals. The only visual differences between the two square-case SS versions was the colour mix of the fairings, the 750 was silver with a 3 in. thick blue decal in the middle, the 900SS fairing blue with a silver decal.

For those who wanted to take their bikes racing, the Bologna factory still listed the majority of the parts from the original 750SS racing kit, plus new profile Imola type camshafts.

However, the following year, 1976 saw what many enthusiasts consider to be the first in a series of moves which ultimately removed much of the raw sporting stance of the Desmo Super Sport concept. This was the move to a gearchange on the left. Although this may have appeared as simply a cosmetic modification to some people, in practice it meant inferior gear selection. The 860GT had already received this treatment, with a left-hand gearchange from the out-set of its production life and this was recognized to be

poor compared to the 750. To achieve the left-hand change (required for the North American market), a linkage and a long rod had to be fitted destroying in the process the direct link between the gear pedal and the selector box. Quite simply, this detracted from a set-up which had in the past been near perfect.

Not only this but in an attempt to satisfy the various governmental legislation the factory's management saw fit to offer the raw-boned SS in a more civilized form—with restrictive 860GT seamed Lafranconi silencers, large air filters, smaller 32 mm carburettors and direction indicators. However, the outcry from Ducati owners worldwide was so fierce that the factory had to rethink their policy and revert to the 'real' 900SS once more!

There were other changes in 1976, including a stepped 36/38 mm crankpin, substitution of the previous side-by-side big-end rollers with a single straight-across type with a narrow diameter. Other more minor items included relocation of the ignition switch from its former position on the nearside frame at the rear of the fuel tank, to a central console position next to the instruments and a totally new Japanese style Aprilia horn/dipswitch assembly. However, even though it *looked* better than the ancient chrome-tin snuff box affair used previously, it was actually extremely prone to falling apart!

June 1976 was perhaps the 900SS's greatest moment,

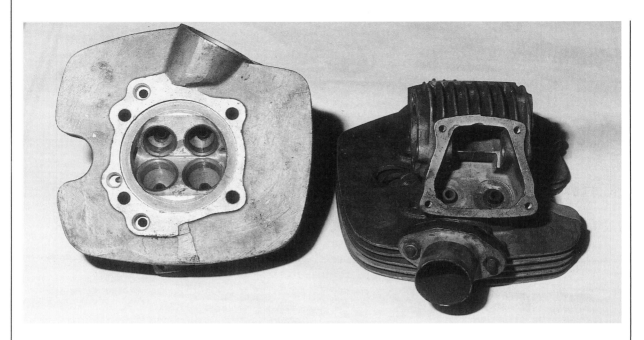

Above **Experiments were carried out in the 1970s with four-valve heads. Here is the proof**

Above right **1977 saw the Darmah SD, a Desmo, but one intended as a sports/tourer, with a higher level of sophistication and finish than any Ducati before it. The screen was an optional extra**

at least in standard trim, on the race circuit when Welshman Roger Nicholls won the Isle of Man Production TT at over 103 mph.

In 1977 the 750/900SS line remained unchanged, but the infamous Aprilia switch was ditched in favour of a more reliable CEV unit.

A black and gold 900SS was introduced in 1978. Besides the colour change, the model introduced cast-alloy wheels which, initially was not a good move. The original wheels were Campagnolo, and both these and their Speedline replacements suffered various problems, notably associated with the cush drive/sprocket carrier mounting. It was not until FPS wheels were fitted that these were finally resolved.

Many other details changes were made at this time. There was a dualseat with fibreglass base and a lockable compartment in the rear. A CEV headlamp replaced the old Aprilia unit but remained at 170 mm diameter and the rearset foot controls were totally redesigned. The biggest change was to the bottom end of the engine and the electrics. This followed the introduction of the Darmah in the previous summer which was an important model for the factory and one which heralded the first touring Desmo V-twin.

With the poor sales of the 860GT/GTS and 900GTS, Ducati realized that their attempt to provide a touring replacement for the popular 750GT had failed. In contrast, the 900SS had proved an instant best-seller and continued to be in strong demand around the world. In addition, the major press criticism had centred around the lack of sophistication and inferior

finish of all Ducati motorcycles, not the basics like handling, performance or braking.

In response to this and in an attempt to improve its less than satisfactory sales record, Ducati senior management came up with the combination of a 900SS Desmo engine (but with 32 mm carbs) in a rehashed 900GTS chassis, but with totally new styling and, it was hoped, a better level of finish.

So the Darmah was born—named after a fabled tiger in Italian children's folklore. Tigerish by name and tigerish by nature, the Darmah was to embody the dual qualities of smooth sophistication and raw power in a single package that had been unashamedly developed to bring the V-twin closer to the Japanese product in all those areas which brought sales, while retaining the essential character that made a Ducati a Ducati. And in this, for once, the hard-pressed Bologna factory's management hit the jackpot.

The Darmah was given its first public showing as early as December 1976 at the local Bologna Show, and it was immediately apparent from the reaction of press and public alike how well the development team had met its brief. By May of the following year the first production machines were on sale in Italy, with export markets getting their first supplies over the next couple of months.

Below right **Darmah SD engine. Note Bosch electrics, comprehensive air filters and hydraulic steering damper**

Above left **Earls Court, August 1977—Darmah SD and (right) 500 Sport parallel twin—both Desmo, but otherwise very different**

The heart of the machine was still the 90-degree V-twin engine, fundamentally as before, with the desmo cylinder heads from the SS, *but* with not only smaller carburettors and inlet tracks, but also a narrower distance between the two inlet stubs (52 mm instead of 58 mm).

Other technical differences included a completely new type of selector mechanism for the left-side change. This was now situated on the nearside within the crankcase, whereas all the earlier V-twins had the selector mechanism in a separate box on the opposite offside location.

Another area which received special attention was the electrics. Except for the old type 200-watt alternator, the 18-watt electronic regulator-rectifier box, the battery, indicators and tail light (all of which had proved generally reliable in service), all the other electrics were new. The policy had been to replace Italian components of dubious quality with components from a truly international array of manufacturers. Bosch from Germany, Nippon-Denso from Japan and Lucas from Britain.

Bosch provided the new electronic ignition pick-ups and lighting, Nippon-Denso the instruments, switchgear and HT coils, and a Lucas starter solenoid superseded the complicated set-up first seen on the

750GT when it had finally been given an electric start option in 1974.

Amongst all these new components, in typical Ducati fashion, was one weak link—this was the sprag clutch, an important item which formed part of the drive from the electric start mechanism—in effect, a one-way bearing that locked in one direction but was free to rotate in the other. This was (and still is) prone to failure, and in extreme conditions has even been known to break up and the resulting mass of particles can wreck an engine if allowed to circulate with the oil for any real period of time—you have been warned!

Complementing the improved electrics was a super powerful 170 mm Bosch headlamp with a 55/60 watt H4 quartz halogen bulb.

Right from the off, unlike the SS models, the Darmah was equipped with cast-alloy wheels, and of course the comments regarding these made earlier still apply.

But however much of an improvement the Darmah was from a technical point of view, it was its style which most observers noticed first. This was the work of Leopoldo Tartarini, who had also been responsible for the Desmo Sport parallel twin. Tartarini, whose Italjet concern was based locally to the Ducati factory, had a special relationship with his much larger neighbours. There were strong links between the two companies, not just because both were based in Bologna but long before Tartarini had played an important part in spreading the Ducati name abroad on his round-the-world trek with fellow traveller Giorgio Monetti, on a pair of 175 Tourist models during 1957–8.

The Darmah Sport made its debut in 1978. This was usually supplied with Contis and 40 mm carbs—in effect, an identical specification to the 900SS. However, someone at Ducati boobed and didn't bore out the

Below left **Sensuous lines of the Darmah SS. Although a great bike it was offered only in 1979 and 1980**

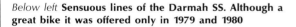

Below **Darmah Sport with black and gold finish and 40 mm carbs. Unfortunately, someone at the factory forgot to open inlet ports to match**

Above left **1981 saw a revised, some say spoilt, 900SS. Alterations included a more restrictive exhaust, air cleaners (although these were usually removed), new seat and different colour scheme**

ports to match the bigger carburettors. The finish was in black and gold.

The spring of 1979 saw the Desmo V-twin range increase yet again with the introduction of the Mike Hailwood Replica (described in Chapter 10) and the Darmah Super Sport. This time the Darmah SS was fully uprated to the same state of tune as the 900SS (and Hailwood Replica) and even shared identical gearing. This meant that to all intents and purposes the performance of the three machines was very similar.

Like the 1979 versions of the Darmah SD and Darmah Sport, the Darmah SS had no kickstarter relying on the electric thumb only (in contrast, the 900SS never received electric start, at the same time the factory also chose to modify the timing cover and oil-pump bush.

Other modifications to convert the Darmah SS for its task were aimed at providing a more sporting riding stance. The top fork yoke was changed for one with no handlebar mountings and the rider was given clip-ons instead, although these were a different pattern from those on the 900SS. Because of the lower bars, the control cables and front hydraulic pipe were adapted to suit the new position. The frame was altered to take rearset footrests and controls, with rear pillion footrests mounted on extensions behind the rider's footrests. Like the standard SS, the Darmah SS featured milled footrests with no rubbers. The rear suspension units were changed over to a type with gas damping.

The bike—one of my personal favourites—looked superb with its SS-type half fairing and slimmer, more rounded, stainless steel mudguards. The seat base, tank, fairing and side panels were all finished in a metallic ice blue, with decals and striping in a contrasting darker shade of blue. Both side panels carried the tiger's head emblem (as did the majority of the standard Darmah models) but with the letters SS, instead of the normal SD.

From April 1979 (with the introduction of the SS version) all Darmahs had the wider carburettor mounting stud spacing, thus rationalizing production. The SD and Sport models also received new seats. These were designed to improve the seat base rather than simply to increase comfort, although in practice it achieved both. The new seat was a more conventional shape, with a plastic rear cover loop, but the Darmah SS continued to use the earlier style throughout its life.

Later in 1979, the factory began to fit Silentium

Below left **1981 900SS engine assembly. This one has had bellmouths fitted**

silencers to the two basic Darmahs, in place of the previous Lafranconis. Few of the red and white versions had these, however, since it was discontinued towards the end of the year, leaving only the black and gold Darmah and the Darmah SS in production.

At the Milan Show in November 1979, Ducati had very little that was new on show except the belt-driven 500SL Pantah. The bevel-driven vees were largely left to stagnate and this was to prove a down point in Ducati's fortunes. In response to falling sales all the factory did was sit on its backside and do nothing except take the best Darmah, the SS, out of production early the following year!

As the 1980s dawned it was the Mike Hailwood Replica, together with the new Pantah series, which largely kept the ailing company afloat.

In Milan two years later, a half-hearted effort was made in offering a full touring version of the Darmah SD. This was finished in a deep, rich ruby red, with colour-matched cockpit fairing, rear carrier and panniers. But although it was an attractive motorcycle it wasn't really in the same league as, for example, the BMW R100RS or Guzzi Spada. None were imported into Britain.

Earlier in 1981, a 'new' 900SS had appeared but this quite frankly had lost much of the style and raw performance of the earlier models. In an attempt to please the bureaucrats, if not their loyal customers, Ducati chose to fit the ultra-restrictive Silentium

The 900S2 superseded the 900SS in 1983. It received a mixed press and public reaction. To many it lacked much of what the original SS concept had been all about. At best it was an attempt to civilize, at worst it illustrated just how far the management could get things wrong

silencers, from the Darmah SD, and air filters. It also received a silver/blue paint job, but with decals more in tune with Harley-Davidson than Ducati!

There were also several smaller changes including a new dualseat, a modified clutch, new front mudguard (based on the MHR) and clutch cover.

In many ways this model acted as an interim machine until a complete revision, called the S2, appeared for the 1983 season. Although the S2 did have the advantage of an improved gearbox, just about everything else was inferior to the original 900SS models. *Motor Cycle News* simply called it: 'The worst Ducati V-twin ever made' and a 'dog'. However, in contrast, rivals *Motor Cycling Weekly* were impressed, although it should be pointed out that their tester admitted to never having ridden a Ducati previously. . . .

The S2 that I tested in August 1983 (the same bike used by *MCN* and *MCW*) had several serious faults. With maximum speed restricted by at least 10 mph— due in no small part to the silencers and air boxes—it still carried the gearing of the *real* 900SS, so that it was quite simply massively overgeared. This also meant less mid-range acceleration! As proof of the restrictive nature of the silencers, both were blued equally, exactly half-way along their length. The combination of handlebars, seat and pegs gave a riding position which had obviously never been tested outside the factory gates—it was the most uncomfortable Duke I have ever ridden and even the fairing-mounted mirrors were in the wrong position. Another fault was the foam seat cushion, not only was this rather uncomfortable, but didn't afford the pillion much grip and was also literally cracking up!

Perhaps, like the *MCW* tester, if you hadn't ridden the real thing you might have thought it good but compared to the earlier SS models the S2 was a mere shadow of what had been a truly impressive sporting motorcycle.

As for performance *MCN* achieved a timed 130 mph, *MCW* almost 124 mph. But they did make the comment: 'The Duke is so long legged it was still accelerating through the timing lights.'

Besides the gearbox, the engine was much the same as before. The majority of the changes were to its running gear. Cycle parts were based on a mix of Darmah and Pantah components with very little true 900SS in the packaging—the swinging arm was one of the few remaining genuine 900SS parts. The fuel tank was similar to the 900SS but with a lockable round black plastic filler cap. The machine's most obviously Pantah-based influence was the fairing (like the late 500SL and 600SL). Also very much Pantah was the excellent folding lifting handle to save the rider getting a hernia when attempting to use the centre-stand.

The S2's colour scheme, of metallic gun metal grey and black was rather spoilt by the garish use of flamboyant multi-coloured red and orange striping. Finally, the S2 was offered with or without electric start.

The Mille S2 appeared in 1985, the year of the factory's takeover by Cagiva. Finally, at the end of its term, the 'old' Ducati team got things right. The engine now had plain bearing big-ends, a much improved lubrication system, gears which did not break, a dry hydraulically-operated clutch and many other worthwhile modifications with a capacity of nearly 1000 cc

Only a few Mille S2s reached Britain. Here is one with Keith Davies, head of Three Cross Motorcycles, who imported it

The final version of the Darmah SD appeared in 1983. This shared the S2's colour scheme, but without the colourful striping. Very few were sold, however, before it was struck off the model list towards the end of the year.

For 1984 the S2 remained mechanically unchanged but gone was the gun-metal grey, to be replaced by a striking combination of red frame and black tank, seat and fairing. But even though the garish red/orange stripes remained the new finish was a distinct improvement.

Then in early 1985, came the final version, the 1000S2. Like the Hailwood Replica Mille, the 1-litre S2 was much more than simply a bigger bore job. For a start, both the bore *and* stroke were changed, 88 × 80 mm, giving a capacity of 973 cc. But Taglioni and his team didn't stop there. They bit the bullet and added Nikasil cylinder bores, a dry (hydraulic) clutch, a revised lubrication system with a full flow, screw type filter, one piece crankshaft with plain bearing big-ends, (with a 45 mm crankpin diameter) and substantially revised engine casings. Perhaps the most significant improve-ment was the oil system—all previous Ducati V-twins had religiously required an oil change every 1000 to 1500 miles. Whereas the 750 and 860 engines had a lowly 22 psi oil flow, the Mille engine was even provided with a healthy 80 psi (18.3 litres/min. at 7000 rpm).

In addition, there were new style cast-alloy wheels, brake discs, electro fuel taps, a totally revised instrument panel, an improved dual saddle, a belly pan and numerous smaller alterations.

The 1-litre job was offered with two levels of performance, 83 and 90 bhp. Essentially, the difference was a two-into-one exhaust system and open bellmouths for the 40 mm pumper carburettors on the more powerful version, in place of Silentium silencers and air boxes. The factory's brochure *claimed* 146 and 137 mph respectively which, if truthful, made the performance variant of the 1000S2, the fastest of the entire SS/S2 family.

Not only this but the larger S2 was a much better bike than the one it replaced. From a reliability viewpoint the Mille engine was perhaps the best of all the bevel-driven V-twins, with the 750 next. The 860 (900), with its list of weaknesses such as big-end and gearbox, can only be rated marginal.

Unfortunately for the S2 and its owners, 1985 was the year of the Cagiva takeover. All the development work which had been put into the 1-litre models was largely wasted as first the S2 Mille was dumped before the end of the year, with the MHR Mille following shortly afterwards in early 1986. No one gained, certainly not the final year of Ducati's corporate balance sheet. Also, for existing owners' spare parts are even now a problem with such a limited production run.

With massive losses being displayed, as a result of the Mille development costs and the company's poor sales record, Ducati as a separate identity had finally reached the end of the road, and a new era—without the bevel-driven twins—was just beginning.

10

Hailwood—return and replica

In Chapter 5 we traced the early career of the man often dubbed the world's finest ever road racer, Mike Hailwood, and his exploits with various Bologna built raceware, which had come to an end in late 1960.

In the following season he won his first world title after riding a privately entered 250 Honda Four to not only scoop the championship series, but also become the first man to win three TTs in the same week. Following this success he was provided with a pair of MV Agustas for the Italian GP at Monza and promptly won the blue ribband 500 cc race, finishing second in the 350.

After a decision to concentrate on the larger capacity classes, in 1962, there came even more glory, which included taking the 500 cc world title aboard the big MV. This was a crown which he was to hold for the next four seasons.

Then, in 1966, he rejoined Honda. With the Japanese team Mike won two 350 cc championships and another on a 250. But his main aim in switching from MV to Honda had been the chance to ride their new 500. But after finishing second to Agostini's MV even Hailwood was unable to master the super powerful, but ill-handling, machine. Mike finally quit at the end of the 1967 season saying, 'The 250 and 350 were fine, but the 500 was a real pig. If it had gone on much longer, I'd have probably killed myself.'

Quitting Honda and the GP scene, effectively brought his full-time motorcycle racing career to an end. By then he had won 76 grands prix and had ridden Ducati, Honda, Mondial, AJS, Norton, NSU, MZ, EMC and MV Agusta, amongst others. He then turned his full attention to cars. Although Mike had flirted with four wheels in the early 1960s, it was not until 1967 that he began to take them seriously.

It is a little known fact that Mike Hailwood tested a Ducati V-twin at Silverstone as far back as August 1971. He's the one hiding behind that dark visor

Also in 1971, Phil Read tested the 500 GP V-twin at Brands Hatch in June. Both Phil and Bruno Spaggiari rode 500s at Silverstone the following August. The bikes displayed a fair turn of speed before retiring

His greatest achievement on four wheels was victory in the 1972 European Formula 2 championship (beating amongst others, Nikki Lauda, and Carlos Reutemann) before he crashed during the 1974 German Grand Prix at the Nürburgring sustaining severe leg injuries which prevented him from racing cars again.

It was on four wheels that he came into contact again with former two-wheel champion John Surtees, when Mike drove for John from 1971 to 1973 inclusive in the Surtees team. It was also as a Surtees team driver that he finished second (his best ever grand prix result) in the 1972 Italian GP at Monza.

Following his 1974 Nürburgring accident he had a series of operations on his badly damaged right foot, but eventually gave up all hope of making a comeback when none of these proved successful, leaving him with little movement in that foot.

But all through his four-wheel racing career Mike hadn't lost his love of motorcycles—even though his time with Honda had often made him less than keen to compete. Even though he had officially 'retired' from two-wheels at the end of the 1967 season, Mike

continued to receive a whole host of offers to race various bikes. Perhaps the most lucrative was one from Benelli. This was not only the possibility of racing *new* 350 and 500 machines against his old foe Agostini, but a fat signing-on fee which Benelli boss Nardi Dei offered to tempt him. This offer, made in the early 1970s, ultimately came to nothing.

More positive, although far less lucrative, were overtones from the British BSA concern for Mike to ride one of their three-cylinder 750s at Daytona in 1970. After qualifying at 152.90 mph, behind Gene Romero's Triumph at 157.34 mph, Mike proceeded to astound everyone by leading the race for the first ten laps until problems with the ignition system forced him to retire.

Twelve months later he was back again. This time Paul Smart and Gary Fisher battled with Mike for the lead until the BSA's engine cried enough with pushrod failure. Undaunted by these events Mike requested that BSA provide him with a bike for the Formula 750 race at the ACU's international meeting at Silverstone on Sunday 22 August (the forerunner of today's British GP).

However, this time BSA didn't want to play ball. The problem was purely monetary. Because of their serious financial problems the company had been made to cut back drastically on their racing programme just five short months after winning Daytona (Dick Mann).

Although Hailwood would not get a BSA for

Silverstone, BSA's engineering director Mike Nedham didn't rule out the possibility of Mike being provided with a works Rocket 3 for the 'Race of the Year' at Mallory Park in September. But *Motor Cycle* reported in their 4 August 1971 issue: 'Without a BSA for Silverstone, Hailwood may ride a 350 TR2 Yamaha in the Formula 750 race as well as in the 350 class. Or he may race a works Ducati that is now on its way to England.' But all Mike would say the weekend before the *Motor Cycle* news story was: 'I haven't got a Yamaha yet and I don't know anything about the Ducati.'

However, under the surface things were really bubbling. For a start Mike had already entered for the Silverstone meeting. And once this became known manufacturers and race organizers were soon beating a path to Hailwood's door. Ducati telephoned their British agent Vic Camp asking him to offer 'bikes' to Hailwood *and* to arrange a meeting with managing director Fredmano Spairani. But when questioned at the time Camp wasn't sure 'whether the factory wanted Hailwood to ride their Grand Prix 500 V-twin or a new Formula 750 machine derived from their recently released 750 GT touring bike.'

The Silverstone outing was to be Mike's first British appearance since switching to cars. And he had made up his mind after riding John Cooper's 250 and 350 Yamsels at Silverstone. On the smaller bike he clipped two seconds off the official class lap record set by Jim Redman on a works Honda. On the 350 he was just outside the record. This was the first time he had raced a two-stroke since he rode a works 250 MZ in the East German Grand Prix in 1964, when he crashed.

Five days before the Silverstone meeting he practised on a Ducati and it turned out to be the new 500 GP bike. But in the event Mike opted to ride a 350 Yamaha borrowed from Paul Smart—a works bike provided by the Japanese company's European base in Holland.

As *Motor Cycle* reported: 'Silverstone had seen nothing like it since the great days of the early 1950s, when Geoff Duke reigned supreme on works Nortons. Every road to the 2.9-mile Northamptonshire circuit was jammed two hours before the meeting was due to start and programmes were sold out before the racing got under way.' There were two main reasons—it was the first major motorcycle promotion at Silverstone for six years and Mike Hailwood was back in action on two wheels in Britain.

Without a Yamaha until the last minute, Mike borrowed Paul Smart's factory TR3 model for the 350 event. But he missed Saturday's official training because of a car-race engagement, and his only pre-race laps on the Yamaha were done during a 10-minute practice on race day morning, when the track was still slightly damp.

And then he fluffed the start. 'I'd practised starting, but out there in the middle of the grid I couldn't hear if

the engine was running or not', he said later. And while Cooper (Yamsel), Jarno Saarinen (Yamaha) and Giacomo Agostini (MV) shot ahead, Hailwood was left struggling way down the field.

After 2 laps he was in 18th place, and at the end of the 20-lap, 58.54-mile race he finished fourth behind winner Agostini, Saarinen and Cooper.

Mike had his second outing in the Formula 750 race but because the new Ducati he had tested earlier in the week was not handling to his satisfaction, he rode the works Yamaha. The race was dominated by the Triumph-BSA winner Paul Smart, setting a new motorcycle record for Silverstone at 104.95 mph. Mike took third, the first rider of a non Triumph-BSA triple.

Above right **Mike on the square-case 750SS he shared with Australian Jim Scaysbrook in the Castrol Six Hour race at Amaroo Park, Sydney on 23 October 1977. The pair finished sixth**

Below **Hailwood inspecting the bike, with Scaysbrook seated. Refuelling is in progress**

Below right **Mike cranks the 750SS over near the limit at Amaroo Park**

Above **Roger Nicholls on the Sports Motor Cycles Desmo V-twin. it was this combination of rider and machine which tempted Mike Hailwood back to the big time**

Below **Nicholls' and Hailwood's bikes prior to Mike's amazing return to the Isle of Man in June 1978**

Interestingly, the 125 race was won by a youngster called Barry Sheene on an ex-works Suzuki twin, who broke the lap record for the class at 93.75 mph, the former holder being none other than S. M. B. Hailwood with his Desmo single at 87.22 mph, set way back in 1960!

Although Hailwood didn't race a Ducati at Silverstone on that August day in 1971, other riders certainly did—none other than Phil Read and Bruno Spaggiari were in the 500 race on the new GP V-twin. Both made poor starts then came tearing up through the field, Read had just snatched third place when big-end failure put him out. Spaggiari took over third spot, then joined Read in the pits when one cylinder cut out completely. (For more details on the 500 GP V-twin see Chapter 6).

Meanwhile, in the week following Silverstone, it was revealed that Mike Hailwood would not, after all, take part in the Race of the Year at Mallory Park the following month. 'I think BSA would have lent me a 750 racer for the meeting. But MCD (Motor Circuit Developments) have said they don't want me. It seems they dropped the idea after I agreed to race at Silverstone', said Mike.

However, there were plenty of others who *did* want him. Benelli, who had offered the nine times world champion complete control of their race department if

he joined them earlier that year, were strongly rumoured to be renewing interest. And, at Silverstone, Hailwood had been offered the new 750 four-cylinder German Münch. In addition, Mike had been reportedly promised 'an enormous sum of money' to race at Pesaro, Italy, the following Sunday.

Even though Mike summed up his Silverstone experience as 'great, I really enjoyed it', in practice none of the other offers came to anything. And except for a none too serious ride on a private Yamaha 250 at Silverstone in 1972 he seemed to have lost interest in racing motorcycles. Then came the accident in his GP racing car at Nürburgring in 1974 and everyone thought his racing days on both two and four wheels were finally over.

In January 1977, Mike accepted an offer to take part in an historic race meeting at Amaroo Park, Sydney, Australia, where he rode a 500 Manx Norton, finishing second in one race to Aussie Jim Scaysbrook. Three months later, he was back in Australia for another historic machine race at Bathhurst. There he finished third on the same Norton he rode at Amaroo—and the man who won again was Scaysbrook. Following this, he competed a couple more times on the machine once owned by former 250 World Champion Kel Carruthers.

But the big news was the announcement in June of that year that together with Jim Scaysbrook Mike had agreed to partner a Ducati 750SS in the Castrol Six Hours production race on Sunday 23 October. This event was acknowledged as one of the world's toughest marathon races because of the strict regulations which prohibited riders from modifying their machines beyond showroom condition.

The man behind the move to get Mike to Amaroo Park on 23 October was Sydney radio announcer Owen Delaney. Delaney and Hailwood struck up friendship following a radio interview the previous January, and it had been Delaney who was instrumental in bringing the multi-world champion to Bathhurst in April.

It was at Bathhurst that first mention of the Six Hours had occurred when Mike was asked if he would like to compete in the marathon and he had replied: 'It sounds like a lot of fun—as long as people don't expect me to win.'

The pairing of Scaysbrook and Hailwood, even with the handicap of running a smaller machine than the majority of the other 40 teams, didn't prove too much of a problem at Amaroo Park. On the 750SS they completed 350 laps of the 1.21-mile circuit to finish sixth overall and at the end Mike said he had 'enjoyed' his ride very much.

It was, in retrospect, the 1977 Castrol Six Hours at Amaroo Park, which set the wheels in motion on a truly remarkable set of events unparalleled in racing history. . . . The significance of this was revealed the following January, when Mike made a surprise appearance in front of 1600 estatic fans at the annual

'Night of the Stars', organized by *Motor Cycle News*, where he revealed the exciting news that he would be riding works Yamahas as well as an 860 Ducati Desmo V-twin in the IoM TT races that June.

A couple of weeks afterwards, in their 25 January 1978 issue, *MCN* were able to bring further details from the official launch of Team Martini Yamaha. This took place on the 16th-floor Martini Terrace of New Zealand House in London's Haymarket where Mike was quoted as saying: 'Nobody must expect miracles. But we're not going to the Island to swan about.'

How did all this come about? Well, whilst visiting Britain during the previous summer, Hailwood had visited the ACU to discuss the possibility of making a return to serious two-wheel racing—notably the Isle of Man TT. He had also visited the British GP at Silverstone, where purely by chance, or so the story goes, he came across the Sports Motorcycles racing team of owner Steve Wynne and rider Roger Nicholls with their 860 Ducati V-twin. Mike remarked that it 'looked like his kind of bike', to which Wynne replied that if he fancied a ride he only had to ask. . . .

Some weeks later (and after his Australian 750SS

Mike chats to a couple of admirers. He might have lost some hair and put on a bit of weight but he was about to prove that he had lost none of his former skill on the track

debut with Jim Scaysbrook) Steve Wynne received a call from Mike's close friend journalist Ted Macauley, asking if a Ducati could be made available for the 1978 TT. To prove that Hailwood genuinely wanted to ride the Italian four-stroke is the fact that his fee was purely a nominal one of £500. So it was most definitely a case of love rather than money, but why?

It was hardly likely to have been for any really nostalgic reason, even though Mike must have had some happy memories of his earlier days on the Bologna bikes. Much more likely is a combination of two reasons. The first one his satisfaction with his ride in the Castrol Six Hours and the performance of his mount *and* the realization that Steve Wynne's rider Roger Nicholls had only just failed by a few seconds to beat the might of the Honda works team with riders of the calibre of Phil Read and Stan Woods with a Ducati V-twin in the 1977 IoM Formula 1 TT race.

Following Macauley's request Steve Wynne, through the British Ducati importers, Coburn & Hughes, had got the factory involved. This amounted to the building of two machines. The cost of these was £10,000, which involved a three-way split between the factory, Coburn & Hughes and Sports Motorcycles. Wynne maintains to this day that the other two parties didn't cough up and he had to foot the total bill.

These two machines, were decidedly 'works specials', with *everything* lightened inside the engines, dry clutches, Verlicchi frames and a special wide swinging arm—so modern, slick tyres could be fitted. Power output was a claimed 87 bhp at 9000 rpm.

Obviously looking forward to the prospects of racing again on two wheels at the highest level, 1978 was none the less a bitter-sweet year for Mike. The biggest disappointment was the death of his father Stan, aged 75, in Barbados on 4 March that year. For tax reasons Hailwood Senior had left Britain a few years earlier and set up two homes, one in Barbados and the other in Cannes in the South of France. He spent a lot of time on cruises and had just completed a round-the-world trip when he collapsed in Miami during December 1977. Stan was flown to his Barbados home where Mike had visited him en route to New Zealand in January, a few weeks before he passed away.

Whatever anyone's opinion of Stan, it has to be said that he supported his son's racing effort 100 per cent but at the same time didn't spoil him. A little known fact is that Mike actually paid Stan back large amounts of money once he had made his way in racing during the early 1960s which was proof of the respect and appreciation he had for his father, who had often bulldozed him during his early racing days.

The race which will live in the memories of all those lucky enough to see it, the 1978 Formula 1 event. Here Mike is seen at Quarter Bridge on his way to creating one of the biggest upsets in motorcycle racing history

The catalyst that made it all happen—at least from a technical viewpoint—the Hailwood engine components displayed for all the world to see!

As a final thought, I would sum up Hailwood Senior in the following way—that for all his ruthlessness he was truly Mike's staunchest supporter and biggest fan.

Without doubt Stan would have been proud and excited at what was shortly to follow, even though the first signs were not too good. 'Hailwood humbled' said the *MCN* headline in their 5 April 1978 issue. This was in response to Mike-the-Bike getting lapped *three* times in his world debut on a 750 Yamaha in the Australian GP at Bathhurst during the 30-lap race over the Mount Panorama Circuit.

There had been two unlimited races at the meeting. The first was held in pouring rain and Mike finished outside the top 12. The following day only 11 riders finished and he was ninth—a far from impressive performance—or so the cold hard results said. Truth revealed a somewhat different story.

With his bike being well below par on speed and state of tune. But in his usual way Mike hadn't wished to play up anything more than 'a get-to-know-you ride'.

In an interview prior to the meeting he said, 'I just hope no one expects me to do anything marvellous. The Yamaha has the gearshift on the other side from what I am used to, so I will have to get used to that.'

Two weeks after Bathhurst, Mike once again

partnered his friend Jim Scaysbrook on the same 750SS they had ridden the previous year. The venue was Adelaide and the event was the annual Three Hour production race. The pair finished seventh, the first 750 home. In the race there was the unforgettable sight of Mike, high up on the banked speed bowl section of the circuit, passing Australia's top riders with effortless ease. Even though he hadn't achieved anything similar with the Yamaha, his Ducati performance was a taste of what was to come.

Then it was back to England, arriving at Heathrow airport on Tuesday 25 April 1978 where he had flown from New Zealand in preparation for his big time comeback during the TT races.

He was scheduled to go to the island at the end of the month to begin refreshing his memory of the fearsome 37¾-mile Mountain Circuit, the toughest in the world.

Although barred by his Isle of Man contract from racing in any pre-TT meetings in Britain, Mike hinted that if he was satisfied with his TT performances, he would also ride in the Mallory Park Post-TT international on 11 June.

But before visiting the Island, Mike had his first ride on 2 May at Oulton Park with the Sports Motorcycles factory-built Ducati F1 machine and adjudged his Oulton laps as, 'very satisfactory'. And it was after this test session at the Cheshire circuit that he finally agreed a deal to race in the Mallory Park Post-TT International on Sunday 11 June.

There he would match himself in a nostalgic duel with Phil Read in the TT Formula 1 race—and the event might even get television coverage so great was the interest.

A good indication of why Mike agreed to race at Mallory, before he had raced the F1 Ducati in anger, is given in a track test the same month (again at Oulton Park) and was by Barry Ditchburn for *Motor Cycle News*.

Ditchburn started by saying, 'The Hailwood Ducati is the first bike I've ever ridden hard against the stop coming out of Esso. (A super-elevated, super-tight right-hander, now no longer used—like a wall-of-death almost.) And as I came out of Knicker Brook I thought how good it will be down the Cronk-y-Voddy straight'.

He went on to recall: 'The last time I raced a four-stroke twin was back in 1969–70 when I rode a Weslake-Triumph. And the fantastic engine braking of the big Duke brought memories flooding back.'

The special dry clutch

Ditchburn found: 'Handling was taut but good enough to make me feel at home on the bike immediately', but the bike's great attribute, 'is the flexibility of the engine'. He noted that, 'it seemed the sort of engine which never needs maximum revs. I took it to 8500 rpm in top. And although it never dropped below 4000, the engine was at its best at around 6000 rpm.'

This meant that it was virtually impossible to arrive in a corner in the wrong gear. Ditchburn put it this way: 'The power of the Ducati is beautifully progressive. You don't get the kick of the Yamaha—just real gutsy strength.'

There are obviously some things which don't go down too well with testers. In this instance there were two. For a start, 'Suspension was a bit stiff for me but the special Girling shockers are claimed to be 100 per cent better than the original Marzocchis' and 'I would not have the bars as steeply raked as Hailwood, but the bike was not tailored for me.'

Overall Hailwood's Ducati came through the test with flying colours. Barry concluded as follows: 'The Ducati is deceptively fast. There was no fuss or vibration and it never felt it was really moving. It may not be the quickest in the world but the big Duke is sheer pleasure to ride. I think it has ideal power characteristics for the Isle of Man. I don't know about Hailwood but, on last year's performance alone, the bike is a potential winner.'

The bike itself was clearly based around the standard production 900SS of the period but with a lot of special work and new parts and/or modification. The engine retained the original's 864 cc (86 × 74.4 mm) capacity, and was *claimed* to produce some 88 bhp at the rear wheel—this was around 5 bhp more than Nicholls' 1977 TT bike. Good for 9000 rpm, the engine also retained the original 900SS 40 mm pumper Dell'Ortos, but had been gas-flowed and fitted with larger valves, the inlet going up 43 mm (39 mm) and exhaust 39 mm (36 mm). The compression ratio of the three-ring forged slipper pistons was 11:1, compared with 9.5:1 on the Nicholls' 1977 TT mount.

Combined with a vast amount of lightening of the engine's internals these changes gave more usable power at lower engine revolutions. The standard ignition system was discarded in favour of a Lucas Rita transistorized system. An air-cooled clutch was the most obvious difference in the transmission but the gearbox had also been modified, with dogs removed from fourth gear to give a slicker shift.

Much care had been taken with the left-side mounted gearchange operation on Hailwood's bike—this may seem strange but there were two *almost* identical 1978 works prepared TT F1 bikes, one for Mike and the other for Roger Nicholls. Unlike the production 900SS of the period both these machines used bottom ends based on the earlier 750, rather than later 900 type engines. This not only meant that the air-cooled clutch and straight-cut primary gears from the 1973–4 Imola racers could be used but also that as standard the gearchange was on the offside (right), rather than the nearside (left). This meant that because Mike's right foot had been badly damaged in his 1974 Nürburgring car crash, the gearchange had to be transferred to the left. This was achieved with a crossover shaft inside the swinging-arm pivot and not the totally different method on the production machines.

Like the Imola racers, the TT F1 bikes used fibreglass petrol tanks with a transluscent strip which gave an instant reading of the fuel level and an oil cooler.

For several weeks prior to his comeback ride in the TT, the world's motorcycle press had devoted more column inches to Hailwood than anyone else. This prompted the following comment from the man himself in *Motor Cycle* dated 29 May 1978: 'Trouble with my comeback is that it's all got a bit too serious. This was not my original intention. I just wanted to race in the TT again. Maybe I should have done it incognito.'

And the following week on the eve of the races, again in *Motor Cycle*, Mike commented: 'And I must admit that to bring the whole thing down to earth I played a nasty little joke on my old friend Ted Macauley who has put in such a lot of work behind the scenes to organize the whole effort. I rang him up and told him I'd fallen off and broken my leg! Of course I couldn't keep it up. I just burst into laughter after a few seconds of awful

silence. He told me he had gone all the colours of the rainbow and broken into a cold sweat as he'd seen the whole carefully built plan, which now involves so many people, crumble. Makes you think, doesn't it?'

The above comments reveal one of Mike's traits, the practical joker, the live-wire prankster.

But even with the huge publicity the racing experts still thought success highly unlikely—well, it had been 11 years since the name S. M. B. Hailwood had graced a TT programme. And racing over the demanding 37¾-mile Mountain Circuit was different to anything else. So these cynics had time on their side, but to be fair several were to be the most lavish in their praise afterwards. In any case, it was expected that if the 'old man' (he was then 38) was going to do anything it would be aboard one of the three Yamahas, rather than the Ducati.

But how wrong those so-called experts were. Throughout his practice sessions for the 1978 TT, Mike and Ducati continued to amaze, ending up with a fastest lap of 111.04 mph—unbelievable but true. How could a man, the world asked, who had last raced on the circuit more than a decade ago, put up such a mind-bending performance?

In retrospect it was probably a combination of things—the will to win, course knowledge, determination, fitness, and with the F1 event the most suitable bike for the task in hand.

Bearing in mind the fact that the Yamaha Mike used in the 500 (Senior) TT, with a best practice lap of 107.57 mph, against a speed of almost 4 mph faster with the Ducati says a lot, especially considering the fact that the Yamaha was a full works GP bike built for Agostini! Even on the 750 Yamaha his best practice lap was only just faster at 112.36 mph.

Record crowds had jammed the Isle of Man for Hailwood's return and before the F1 TT, held on Saturday 3 June, sunkissed fans were claiming the best vantage points *seven* hours before the race began. But their efforts were to be rewarded with a history making race. As the *Motor Cycle News* headline said simply: 'MIKE! Hailwood lands a fairy-tale comeback victory.' Going on to say, 'With tears of emotion streaming down his cheeks Mike Hailwood climbed the winner's rostrum for the 13th time in his legendary TT career after six record smashing laps with a 900 Ducati in Saturday's Formula 1 World Championship race.'

It was unreal . . . fantastic . . . but he had done it. He had won the greatest gamble of his life with a devastating victory that captured the imagination of the thousands of fans who waved him to his tenth world title. And in the process he stunned his rivals with a race record of 108.51 mph and a lap record of 110.62 mph. He had set a scorching pace during which he forced favourite Phil Read to push his works Honda to

Mike (right) with second placeman John Williams after his Formula 1 TT victory

Right **Mike at Silverstone in 1978. Years of racing both two and four wheels at the highest level are etched into his features**

destruction. Not only this but Mike's race average was only fractionally slower than his old record lap of 108.77 mph on the Honda 500 Four with which he won the Senior TT back in 1967.

Except for an instant on lap 1, Mike led the race throughout. But it was the way Hailwood caught and passed Phil Read and the Honda that sent the crowds delirious. He had started 50 seconds after Read and pursued him so relentlessly that before the half-way mark Hailwood was leading on the road! On lap 3 at Ramsey the pair were neck and neck but by the Bungalow Hailwood was 100 yards ahead of the Honda team leader. It was as *MCN* put it, 'the most exciting comeback the TT has ever seen'.

And with the battle at full pitch the pit crews prepared to refuel their riders. Hailwood took on three gallons in 41.2 seconds but Read was quicker. The Honda fired instantly but the Ducati needed an extra push to help the limping Hailwood. The situation on the road was reversed but the Honda was on the blink.

Puffs of tell-tale smoke told their own story as Hailwood hounded his rival throughout the fourth lap. As they began their fifth lap, Read was still a few yards ahead on the road—but not for long!

His engine smoking badly, Read was behind through Union Mills, his leathers smothered in oil, he gave up at the 11th Milestone after a couple of hectic slides—it was all over.

Below **As great as his triumph had been the previous year, the 1979 TT, at least the Ducati part, was a great disappointment to Mike and his myriad fans. Quite simply the bike wasn't fast enough, or good enough, to win again**

With some 60 miles left, Mike couldn't afford to slacken the pace until well into his last lap which was still completed at a speed of 105.84 mph. On that last lap Mike cut the revs right down and said he 'cruised'.

How fast could he have lapped on the Ducati? His reply was, 'Certainly over 112 mph, maybe more'. Of all the other Ducatis in the race only one other finished. This was my own rider Dave Cartwright on the Mick Walker Motorcycles 900SS production bike, who came home in 16th spot averaging 94.94 mph. Roger Nicholls, on the sister bike to Hailwood's, retired after the sight glass of his oil sump shattered and the hot lubricant soaked his legs.

George Fogarty and Eddie Roberts, also entered by Sports, both retired and Jim Scaysbrook, Hailwood's Aussie racing partner, laid his bike down at Governor's Bridge after a full throttle fright caused by a broken coil bracket. The coil shorted the throttle cable!

A sea of fans and photographers greeted the winner at the finish, then followed the ceremonies on the rostrum and the pictures to record the event. Afterwards, Mike made his way back to his hotel and the first man to knock on the door was none other than Phil Read. He still had his leathers on and had come to congratulate Mike. It was a very sporting gesture and afterwards both riders went down to the bar for a well-earned drink. Mike to celebrate, Phil to wash away his disappointment.

Next on the TT list was Monday's Senior but Mike's hopes were dashed with a broken steering damper after the first lap. He'd opened the race with a burst of 108.54 mph and was riding well enough to have climbed the winner's rostrum again. In the 250 race he finished a subdued 12th and maybe his biggest disappointment, but he looked set to do well in the Classic (not what it might appear—but an open unlimited megabike race!) until he holed a piston on his big Yamaha when 10 seconds behind race leader Mick Grant. It is true that Mike was none too pleased with the machines the Japanese company provided for him, and said, 'Yamaha were a disgrace compared to the Sports Motor Cycles effort'.

Following this amazing performance came another a week later at Mallory Park, Leicestershire, at the Post-TT meeting. Following a poor start, Mike and the Ducati V-twin overcame not only both the works Hondas (Read's engine problem had now been rectified), but the additional challenge of British TT F1 champion elect John Cowie, to prove that it wasn't just in the Isle of Man that he was still a force to be reckoned with. He was also able to take on and beat the current crop of British short-circuit stars.

Even an accident at Donington Park a few days later couldn't dim the superb performances achieved both on the Isle of Man and at Mallory Park.

Mike's final British meeting in 1978 was the international at Silverstone, where the speed advan-

tage enjoyed by the Japanese megabikes really showed itself. Even so, Mike brought the Ducati Desmo V-twin home in third spot.

The year 1978 was supposed to have been a 'one-off' return and as things were to turn out it would have been best left that way. But Mike's will to go racing again was too strong. And armed with promises of factory bikes from Ducati and Suzuki the temptation was too great.

A pair of Ducatis, for the F1 TT and the open class Classic TT, were *supposed* to be delivered for final preparation and testing in January 1979. But by the beginning of April they had still not arrived. Finally, they were ready and Mike was called to Italy for testing. This took place at Misano. Almost at the end of this—after reporting that he was satisfied with the bikes—an accident occurred which caused all sorts of problems. The machine being tested had had its gearchange reversed from one up four down (opposite to normal Ducati practice, which by then had adopted the Japanese inspired left foot, one down, four up approach). Mike's mistake was to go *down* rather than

Hailwood near the spot at Hilberry where the bike stopped on the last lap, only a couple of miles from the finish, with a broken battery connection. He was able to repair this and ride on to the finish

The original roadgoing Mike Hailwood Replica (MHR), introduced in 1979, featured plastic tank, one-piece fairing and no side panels

up, with the result that he came off breaking three ribs. Worse was the reaction by the Italian press, with banner headlines of the accident. This meant that the government-appointed financial controllers, who were effectively running Ducati at that time, saw these stories and instructed the factory personnel not to continue with their racing programme, due to potential claims for possible injury which might be sustained by someone riding a machine which the company had built!

With less than a month to go before the TT practice commenced, this was the last thing anyone connected with the racing effort wanted to hear. Although the issue was finally resolved allowing Mike to race (who had recovered sufficiently), the stop-go racing policy had meant that the development of the machines was not of the standard it should have been. This was to prove disastrous. . . . Not only had the factory's effort been blunted but Misano was a smooth circuit quite unlike the Isle of Man, and the special frame constructed for the open Classic TT didn't handle (shades of earlier days!).

The F1 bike (like that of previous years) retained the production model's 864 cc capacity, but the special bike not only had the new frame but a larger 949 cc (90 × 74.4 mm) engine.

All this was to no avail and after clocking less than 90 mph in practice on the Classic TT bike, Mike was so annoyed with its poor performance, 'It was all over the road', he said later, that he flatly refused to ride it opting instead for his Senior Suzuki.

In the F1 TT on the 864 cc Ducati, his best practice time was 105.88 mph, well down on the 1978 figure. And in the race this showed, for he was definitely slower, before he lost top gear at the start of the last lap. The extra engine revolutions caused severe vibration—although the engine didn't explode as it might have done without its desmo valve operation—instead, the battery leads fractured under the extra stress, causing

1984 version of the 900 Mike Hailwood Replica

Ducati's 1980 brochure featured the MHR and 900SS together—but with the emphasis firmly on the fully faired bike

the machine to stop. Thinking it was the engine which had cried enough, Mike got ready to push home (he was some 2 miles out at Hillberry). It was then that he spotted the loose connections. Luckily, he reconnected the wiring and it worked—well enough to limp home taking fifth place. Even with these problems his average speed for the race was still 106.06 mph, with a fastest lap of 109.45 mph. But Mike was far from happy with what had happened behind the scenes and although he had entered for some British short-circuit meetings after the TT on the pair of Ducatis, he refused point blank to ride the Bologna machines—as he felt the factory had caused many of their problems.

Having won the 1979 Senior TT on an RG500 Suzuki Mike rode this in England. But a practice crash at Donington on the Japanese machine brought the curtain finally down on the career of the rider who is held by many to be the greatest road racer of all time. And Desmo Ducatis played an important part in this story—both at the beginning and end of the long, distinguished career.

As his wife Pauline later revealed in the foreword she wrote for the commemorative booklet, *Tribute to Mike Hailwood*, for the Mike Hailwood Day at Donington Park on 11 July 1982, that triumphant comeback at the 1978 TT was a very special moment in what was by any standards a fantastic roll of honour of over more than 20 years' racing on both two and four wheels.

Pauline Hailwood wrote: 'We mourned the fact that Stanley (Mike's father who died of cancer earlier in 1978)

had not been there to see him win, but we both felt that he had been there in spirit. Mike told me that as he stood on the winner's rostrum, with tears in his eyes, filled with unbelievable emotions, he had dedicated the race to Stanley.'

The Mike Hailwood Day had taken place as a mark of respect for Mike himself, who had tragically lost his life, together with his daughter Michelle's, in a horrific accident whilst driving the family's Rover SDI car home after a humble fish and chip supper on Saturday, 21 March 1981. The Rover was badly damaged in a collision with a heavy lorry. It was particularly ironic that a man who had ridden and driven some of the most potent racing machinery in the world for over 20 years should meet his end in a road accident near his home.

Perhaps the biggest tribute to his name was the Ducati model which the Bologna company put into production a few months after that historic 1978 TT victory.

From a commercial point of view, Hailwood's win was a huge stroke of luck. As the company had been going through one of its financial problem periods, the Isle of Man victory generated a fantastic amount of publicity at just the right time to lift its flagging sales. For once the Ducati management made the right move and capitalized on it with a machine named after this great racer and his magnificent feat, and so the Mike Hailwood Replica was born.

Even though in reality it bore little resemblance to the TT winner this didn't matter, it had the magical name and shared the same colours so who cares . . . buyers certainly didn't. In fact the demand was so great that the initial production batch was an instant sellout.

These first models of the MHR, some 500, of which

The 1000 Mille Hailwood Replica on the company's stand at the 1985 Milan Show

200 were exported to Britain, all came with a certificate. But it soon became evident that the model was just what the public wanted so it was made a standard production model for 1980. For several years thereafter it was to be Ducati's best-seller not just in Britain but notably in Japan, and West Germany too.

Motor Cycle, testing one of the original batch shortly after it was released, called it, 'The cat that's got the cream'. Tester Graham Sanderson was obviously impressed saying, 'When riding the muscley 864 cc V-twin one can't help getting the impression that for all their industrial might and expertise in motorcycle design the Japanese have gradually wandered off course. They can, and do, build bigger, faster, harder accelerating rocket-ships than the Ducati. Some are cheaper and a few can be ridden around the turns at speeds which only a few years ago would have been unthinkable to the road rider. But none can compete with a Hailwood Replica when it comes down to doing things in style.'

Meanwhile *Bike*, who tested the Replica (they referred to it as the *Duplicati*), said shortly afterwards: 'It is one of those rare bikes which successfully achieve the two highs of owning a big bike—it poses well and goes well.' Editor Dave Calderwood was so impressed that he actually went out and bought one himself—what higher recommendation could you have?

Motorcycle Sport was equally enthusiastic: 'The Hailwood Replica must be regarded as a classic performance bike, a pure thoroughbred for the money, even at £2,900. Purchased primarily as a Sunday flier, it is difficult to imagine a better buy.'

But as already mentioned, the Hailwood Replica was in fact different from the standard 900SS only in a very few details apart from the obvious cosmetic changes. It had brake calipers which were anodized, a nice trick looking gold. Instrumentation was from the Darmah SS, with Japanese Nippon-Denso clocks and switches and warning lights, instead of the all-Italian bits of the 900SS. The original batch came with different cast-alloy wheels with thinner spokes and less webbing,

compared to either the standard Campagnolo, Speedline or FPS assemblies.

As soon as you sit astride a Replica, it's easy to imagine the racer since it has that same cobbled together feel—even though it's a factory-built machine. The fuel tank was also different on the first batch which featured a massive 24-litre fibreglass affair or, as in Britain, a smaller 18-litre metal inner tank, with a fibreglass cover. Either way it looked massive.

One of the cleverest ideas on the MHR was the seat which could be converted from a single large-humped racer to a dual bum-pad. A foot-long portion of the rear hump had three screws holding it (and the seat) in place. Remove these and the rest of the seat was revealed. Replace the three screws and you're away.

But at the other side of the spectrum the box spanner supplied in the tool kit, which was supposed to reach the crankcase oil-level dipstick, couldn't. Unfortunately, the one-piece (later modified to three) fairing wrapped right underneath the bike and didn't have quick release fasteners such as Dzus catches. It also suffered from water collecting in the 'chin' at the base of the fairing, but this was something which could easily be cured with ten seconds and a small drill bit, but why didn't Ducati resolve these minor irritations before marketing the bike?

Obviously, being enclosed by a full fairing, engine noise tended to be reflected back at the rider. Even so that fairing was still good news, it allowed the rider to make full use of the performance at higher speeds and offered protection far in excess of that to be found on almost any other motorcycle of its era. Even a decade later the Japanese are only just starting to make use of proper fairings to beat the old bogey of wind buffeting and drastically decreased fuel consumption at higher speeds. And on standard 15/36 gearing (which it shared with the 900SS) the full fairing showed its worth in the aerodynamics stakes, by allowing the Replica to run up to the red line in top gear easily during any speed tests. There is, however, a higher 16-tooth gearbox sprocket available and a range of rear-wheel ones, from 32 to 40 teeth inclusive, so no owner should be stuck for selecting the best ratios to suit his particular needs.

The 12-volt Yuasa battery visible beneath the seat moulding on the offside was a blemish on the machine's otherwise relatively smooth lines.

As for performance, *Bike* got 132.1 mph, *Motor Cycle* 133.49 mph which rather went to prove that the Replica, offered for an extra £400, gave poseurs' rather than performance advantages over the 900SS. In fact there are many, like myself, who actually prefer the looks of the cheaper machine.

The MHR remained much as before in 1980 but for the substitution of a three-piece fairing—which made life easier for owners with a mechanical nature.

There were more changes in 1981. Quieter Silentium silencers were introduced, side panels, a larger 24-litre

Early 1986 and the last of the bevel-driven vees rolled off the Bologna production lines. These were Mille MHRs, a fitting tribute to both man and machine

metal tank for all markets and a few other minor differences. By now all Ducati V-twins were leaving Bologna with FPS cast-alloy wheels after a spate of problems with the Speedline variety. Ducati claimed that performance remained unchanged, but I would question this.

Then in 1983 came a major revamp—at least cosmetically. For a start there were redesigned side panels, fairing, front mudguard (now black to match the rear mudguard which had been a black one from the previous year), a larger rear light and yet again a different design and make of cast-alloy wheels, oblong direction indicators both front and rear (which were no longer mounted integrally at the front in the fairing), a new instrument console and a black chainguard (formally in polished stainless steel). And the engine now sported revised outer casings.

A hydraulic clutch appeared in 1984. Then the following year, in line with changes made to the S2, the engine capacity was enlarged to 973 cc (88 × 80 mm) and the machine renamed the Mille Replica Desmo (although it still retained the colourful Mike Hailwood decals used since the original 1979 version). Cosmetically, however, the 1985 model was the same as the previous year's bike.

Unlike the S2 Mille, the Mille Replica continued after the Cagiva takeover in May 1985. And it was still

available and on show, at the company's stand at the Milan Show that November.

The end came early in 1986, when the new owners abandoned an idea to once again relaunch the bevel-driven V-twin engine and the last Mille Replica rolled off the Bologna production line that spring, bringing to a close a famous era both on road and track.

It is in many ways fitting that this model should have been the last of the line, if for no other reason than the man whose name signified the bike, the late, great Mike Hailwood, who had done more than his share to create the Desmo legend at Ducati Meccanica.

Italian Ducati enthusiast Gerolamo Bettoni's Mille Replica. The youngster is Paul Grillmayer, son of Ducati Club Austria President, Ewald Grillmayer

11

Belt-driven vees

When Ing. Taglioni and his development team first conceived the 750 V-twin back in 1970, they had largely remained loyal to engineering practices evolved with the single-cylinder models—this meant that drive to the overhead-cams was by tower shafts and bevel gears, and the crankshaft was a two-piece affair with caged roller big-end bearings. Whilst both these might have been state-of-the-art in the 1950s, by the Superbike age of the 1970s they had become obsolete to say the least.

For a start, the shaft and bevel gears were much more expensive than the much cheaper to produce cam chain, so beloved of the Japanese. Whilst with a modern high-pressure lubrication system, a one-piece crankshaft with plain white metal bearings could do everything the more expensive multi-piece roller bearing crankshaft could, even at racing level.

By 1973, Taglioni had proved with his 500 Grand Prix racing V-twin that a system developed in the car world, the toothed rubber belt, could be just as effectively used for two wheels. It had three important advantages—cost, reliability and noise. Indeed, local rivals Morini had just put their 350 twin into production, using this very principle.

In the middle of the decade, under yet another management team, authorization was given for the production of a totally new breed of Ducati—the 350/500 parallel twins. Strangely, although Taglioni was only responsible for the valve gear of the desmo version of this design the parallel twin engines were to play a vital role in the birth of another new engine design, the Pantah series.

For one thing it was the dismal failure of the parallel twins to attract a viable level of sales which led to Taglioni being asked to come up with an alternative *and*, ironically, it was the parallel twins which finally

Part of the original modular belt-driven plan called for both V-twins and singles. Pictured here at the 1977 Milan Show is the 350 Rollah roadster. . .

introduced Ducatis to a one-piece, plain bearing big-end crankshaft.

Before studying the Pantah in detail we should also mention the positive-valve operation versions of the parallel twin roadsters—the Desmo Sport. This was produced in two forms, the 350 and the 500. The smaller bike had a capacity of 349.82 cc (71.8 × 43.2 mm) and the larger machine 496.95 cc (78 × 52 mm), so both were very much short-stroke units.

Their valve-spring brothers, the GTLs, had first seen the light of day in 1975 but their reception was anything other than enthusiastic, with their square lines which closely followed the 860GT—both styled by car stylist Giorgetto Giugiaro of the Italdesign Studio in Milan. In an effort to rescue something, Ducati management called in Taglioni to design a desmo top end and Leopoldo Tartarini to wave his artistic magic on the appearance of the machine.

The result went on sale in 1976. Tartarini's re-styling had been successful in completely changing the look of the machines, producing something almost like a miniature Darmah, with its integrated flowline of tank and seat—not surprising as the same man was responsible for both. The prototype of the Sport (a 500) had appeared for the first time the previous November at the Milan Show and even though it had a *white* exhaust system, it looked 100 per cent better than the valve-spring GTLs.

٠. .and the futuristically styled Utah trail bike

However, despite these changes and the Desmo tag, Ducati's new parallel twins were no more of a sales success than the original had been. Although they were basically a sound design, the Sport Desmo parallel twins just didn't attract enough of Ducati's traditional customers. Even though the design was largely abandoned in 1978, limited production continued until as late as 1982 when the last batch of some 50 500 Sport Desmos were constructed showing, if proof were needed, the less-than-positive management approach to production during that period at the Bologna plant.

An even more amazing version, using the Italian designed 496 cc engine, was not only produced under licence at the Mototrans factory in Barcelona but after Mototrans went under in the early 1980s, a Spanish dealer was still offering new examples in 1988 but that's another story!

With the failure of the middleweight parallel twin 350 and 500s the Ducati management, not for the first time, had to eat humble pie and request Ing. Taglioni to save them by producing something once again from his designer's hat—and so the Pantah was born.

Although many observers believe the Pantah to have originally been conceived as simply a 500 V-twin, in reality the new design had a much broader design brief—or at least that was the way Taglioni saw things (and in a way he was ultimately to be proved correct). The great designer's reason for using the belt drive in the Ducati range was based very much on a modular concept, in which a whole group of machines would be

Right **Rollah's crankcases; note belt, oil filter cartridge (as on Pantah V-twins), and recess at the front of the crankcase for an electric start motor**

able to share common aspects of design and have the maximum number of interchangeable parts.

This was evident in 1977, when at the Milan Show prototypes of the new Ducati were unveiled. Besides the precursor of what would become the 500 Pantah SL, there were also prototypes of a 350 single in two guises. These were based on the rear cylinder and numerous other parts of the V-twin. One, known as the Rollah, was a conventional roadster and the other, the Utah, a futuristically-styled trail bike. The models were intended to spearhead a comprehensive range of modular engined Ducatis with toothed-belt desmo valve gear, which would complement the existing bevel-driven 860 series.

It was planned that the 350 single would later be joined by a 250, while the 500 could also be produced in 350, 600 or 750 sizes.

Below **Earlier in 1977 the prototype belt-driven V-twin engine was mounted in a Sport Desmo parallel twin chassis. Also in the picture is Ing.Taglioni (in dark glasses) talking to American journalist, long resident in Spain, Dennis Noyes (with helmet)**

Pre-production 500SL Pantah on display at the Cologne Show, September 1978. Note fairing which has a shape not dissimilar to the 900SS

But more mismanagement was to see the singles aborted and consigned to the scrap bin. Instead, only the 500 V-twin was authorized for production—with the pre-production model being first shown to the public at the West German Cologne Show in September 1978.

However, as the 1977 prototypes played such a vital role in the future development of the company's motorcycles it is worth looking at them in some detail. All three machines had finned cast-alloy cam-belt covers which gave the engines a far more pleasing appearance then the smooth type fitted on the production versions of the Pantah. The Pantah's twin cylinders displaced 498.9 cc, while the Rollah and Utah were 346 cc. All the engines had Gilnisil (the Italian equivalent of Nikasil)-coated cylinder barrels and forged semi-slipper three-ring pistons. The 350 barrel was virtually the rear pot from the V-twin, bored and stroked to 84 × 64 mm (the 250 would have shared the 500's dimensions of 74 × 58 mm).

As the original concept demanded, many of the components were identical, including much of the transmission. Prominent amongst shared parts though were, of course, the toothed-belt mechanism itself, and the cylinder-head valve gear. A worthwhile feature of the new design was the use of a 60-degree valve angle providing more scope for tuning, although conversely the valves themselves were smaller than the old bevel-driven singles which had a 36 mm exhaust and 40 mm inlet, while the new engines had 33.5 mm and 37.5 mm respectively.

The crankshaft was one-piece, with the traditional Ducati caged roller big-end bearing (used on both the singles and V-twins) being replaced by split con-rod caps and British Vandervell white metal shell bearings. Not only was this much cheaper to produce but also, with a new lubrication set-up, it offered a cure to the spate of big-end troubles experienced by the bevel-driven V-twins—notably in the more highly-tuned 860 engine.

At the same time, a new oil pump was introduced, because of the plain bearings' need for a constant high-pressure supply of lubricant, at 70 psi almost *four* times that of the 860. Although the 860s and parallel twins used a disposable cartridge oil filter for the first time in Ducati's history, the modular design concept incorporated a full-pass, car-type, screw-in oil filter.

But nobody was actually able to buy a belt-driven Ducati until the first production 500SL Pantahs went on sale in 1979. Much of the bike was identical to the original prototype, which had appeared back in Milan almost two years previously. The engine had the same capacity and bore and stroke measurements. The 68-tooth belts were made for Ducati by Uniroyal and each had its own tensioner. Although the engine was virtually all new, surprisingly, the rocker covers were

Production 500SL from the first batch—finished in red, rather than ice blue—at Earls Court, August 1979

exactly the same components as used on the larger, bevel-driven V-twins.

With a compression ratio of 9.5:1, it produced its peak power of 52 bhp (at the crankshaft) at 9050 rpm. Its effective power at the rear wheel peaked rather lower, 48.87 bhp being developed at 9000 rpm. The transmission featured a five-speed gearbox, operated by a rearset lever to make the most of this potent middleweight unit.

The general tightening up of noise-level restrictions meant that the Pantah was fitted with very much quieter Silentium silencers than those seen on previous Ducatis. These, together with a greatly reduced engine noise, at first astounded existing Ducati owners, whose own models seemed (and were) so much noisier. One of the contributing factors which gave the Pantah its civilized note was the adoption of rubber silencing plugs for the cylinder and head finning. These, more usually found on modern two-strokes, reduced resonance or fin ring. Induction silencing was taken care of by a large, single paper element air filter. This was mounted in its own moulded plastic container with a pair of rubber hoses feeding the twin Dell'Orto 36 mm PHF carbs.

This oh-so-civilized package was still capable of turning in a class leading performance, hustling the SL up to a maximum speed of 122 mph. To enable the rider to take full advantage of this potential, its chassis offered unsurpassed handling from an unconventional new design.

500SL Pantah engine. Note how the engine hangs in a trellis type chassis. . .

The frame was little in evidence to the casual onlooker, much of it being hidden from view behind the tank and enveloping side panels. In fact, the Verlicchi built device was a beautifully triangulated trellis consisting almost entirely of straight tubes. The engine unit was suspended beneath the frame, hanging from only three bolts, but held extremely rigidly. The suspension was as steady and efficient as the frame. At the front, 26 × 52 × 15 mm ball race steering-head bearings (the same size as the larger V-twins) supported the 35 mm Marzocchi fork legs. The design of the rear swinging arm was a combination of old and new practice. At the front was a completely new method of mounting the pivot bushes (still in phosphor-bronze) in the engine crankcases, both these and the pin were lubricated by the engine oil and a seal at each end prevented the oil from leaking out around the pin. In service this has proved a much more efficient system than the previous method used on the Bologna machines. As the pivot point was not concentric with the gearbox sprocket, a chain protector pad was fitted to the top of the swinging arm at the front to avoid

. . .and here with cam covers removed to expose toothed belts

otherwise harmful contact with the chain during suspension movement. The rear of the swinging arm was suspended by Marzocchi AG Strada five-position shock absorbers, with separate reservoir. The chain adjusters were the 'Seeley' type, as used on the 750, 900SS and the MHR.

Front and rear 18-in. wheels were by FPS in cast alloy with seven pairs of spokes and were finished in gold paint. Both carried 260 mm Brembo discs, made in cast iron and drilled with a pair at the front and a single disc at the rear opposite the 38-tooth sprocket. The brake caliper and master cylinders were smaller than those which the larger V-twins carried, and the square Brembo pads were the same size as those used on the parallel twins.

The electrics were as refined as those on the larger V-twins had become by this stage. The alternator was a 12-volt, 200-watt unit, which charged a 14-amp hour Yuasa battery. Ignition was by a Bosch BTZ system which sparked at extended-nose plugs. However, the bike had no kickstarter and therefore relied solely on the efficiency of its electric starter. This was unfortunate, for although the motor itself was reliable the Achilles heel of the Pantah, like the Darmah, was the sprag clutch which is described in Chapter 9.

Not so the other electrical components and controls. Lighting, instrumentation and switchgear were in keeping with the standards set by the Darmah and were seldom unreliable. As the bike came complete with a fitted half fairing, the 150 mm Bosch headlamp and oblong front indicators were fitted directly into the moulding, while the rear lights were standard CEV offerings, individually mounted.

For the first time on any Ducati the fuel tank employed a locking cap, although the lockable compartment within the rear seat hump was a familiar feature. The SL also shared the clever one/two seat with the Mike Hailwood Replica, where by simply removing a plastic wrapover cover the rider could opt for a dual configuration in place of the single racing style.

The first models came in red, soon followed by the definitive colour of the 500SL, ice-blue metallic.

The styling of the razor sharp fairing and square edge tank, seat and panels was very much a matter of taste—some loved it, others (like me) were less keen.

Also, the early versions of the Pantah (up to the middle of 1981) were not entirely without mechanical problems. Besides the troublesome sprag clutch on the electric start mechanism, other faults came to light, notably the gearbox (which used several components from the parallel twins) and premature main bearing wear. Notably, even in high mileage models, the crankshaft was extremely sound.

When the '600' version of the SL was introduced midway through 1981, its styling had been revised to give the machine more market appeal. The fairing lines had been relieved giving a less angular appearance and not only this but the ugly crude black plastic front

Pantah SL seat with detachable plastic section to convert to dual when needed

mudguard had been replaced, and an attractive silver finish had replaced the ice blue. Detailing was now in red only, in place of the red and blue striping that had distinguished the previous 500.

The machine's 600 status had been achieved by boring out the 500 cylinders to 80 mm, giving a capacity of 583 cc. Power was now up by 6 bhp at the crank to 58 bhp, good for 52 bhp at the rear wheel. With dry weight up by 5 kg to 188 kg (413.6 lb), the maximum speed was also up to 126 mph.

But there was more to the 600 than just a capacity increase and a new look, for it also improved on some of the mechanical shortcomings of its predecessor. The biggest advantage of the larger engine was its superior torque—now 5.17 kg m at 7500 rpm—against 4.07 kg m at 8000 rpm on the 500. Not only did this provide much better mid-range power and acceleration, but it also meant that the 600 needed a new, stronger gearbox—which it got, together with the adoption of a hydraulic clutch. These components were thereafter standardized on the 500 and 600SL models.

It was also around this time that the new Pantahs were beginning to make their impact in competition. Following Hailwood's final retirement in 1979, many pundits believed that the day of the race-winning Ducati was over, for on the face of it how could a V-twin, however good, expect to compete against the rising tide from the land of Nippon? How wrong these observers were to be proved with the debut that same year of a new type of Ducati V-twin—the racing Pantah.

At first, it must be admitted, the new 500 looked anything but a world beater in serious competition, however well it might perform out on the street. Although it quickly established itself as a popular machine for someone wanting a middleweight sporting roadster, the bike in its original form did not seem to have much hope of being campaigned in anything other than Italian Junior racing or similar European events, such as the Coupé Pantah in France.

As had happened so often in the past it was left to a privateer in the shape of a German engineer, Alfred Baujohr, to show the way things could shape in the future. Baujohr had already produced a big-bore version of the 900SS engine, and this had found a ready market amongst a number of wealthy Ducati enthusiasts in Germany. Now, he decided it should be possible to do the same thing with the Pantah and constructed a 600 version for the recently announced Formula 2 racing class. In Baujohr's hands, the basic engine's 74 mm bore was taken out to 81 mm and to prove its capability he arranged to race it in the 1980 Isle of Man TT. Sadly, the machine failed to show well in its race, which consisted mainly of Yamaha two-strokes but the basic soundness of the idea was more than indicated by its practice performance, where it was sixth fastest and set a maximum lap speed of 94.19 mph.

Above **The 600SL introduced in 1981. Not only did the engine design give greater strength and more torque but its styling with the help of new fairing and front guard was greatly improved**

The 350XL, first of the 'small' Pantahs intended mainly for domestic consumption, made its debut in 1982

Baujohr was not the only one to realize the potential of the Pantah with a larger capacity engine, for Ducati themselves had always intended it to be manufactured in a larger size. But strangely, when they did get round to it they did not opt to use the engine dimensions used by Baujohr, but went instead for 80 mm pistons which meant that the new engine's actual capacity was only 583 cc.

There things might have stayed, for as a Formula 2 racer, the Pantah was still in a class dominated by two-strokes and four-cylinder four-strokes. And then fate stepped in to lend a hand when the sports governing body, the FIM, changed their rules for the 1981 racing season, effectively barring the pukka racing Yamaha TZ 350s, which had previously dominated the class, almost killing it in the process.

But the real key which unlocked the door to an era of Formula 2 World Championship success was a meeting in September 1980 at the Cologne Show between two of Ducati's senior management team and a director of British dealers' Sports Motorcycles (the company which had played such an important role in the return of Mike Hailwood in 1978).

The Ducati personnel were export sales director Franco Valentini and commercial director Dott. Cosimo Calcagnile. Sports Motorcycles' negotiator was Pat Slinn who was able, after a lengthy meeting, to return to Britain with news that Dott. Calcagnile had agreed that Ducati would provide limited assistance if Sports Motorcycles could find a rider capable of winning the 1981 Formula 2 TT.

Initially, the only commitment made between the two parties was for a Pantah-based machine to be built, entered and raced in the Isle of Man. Ducati had other racing obligations—especially the Italian Formula 2 Championship—and could only provide a complete engine assembly. However, this was to be free of charge and supplied with a pair of special pistons, camshafts and racing exhaust system.

As a rider for the project, Sports chose the Midlands veteran Tony Rutter. Rutter's vast experience, on a wide range of machinery, from four-stroke single-cylinder Manx Nortons to water-cooled Yamaha TZ/TR two-stroke twins and an equally large number of circuits, including the Isle of Man's $37\frac{3}{4}$-mile Mountain Circuit, made him a particularly wise choice as subsequent events were to prove. Maybe Rutter couldn't be labelled a 'superstar', but at least he had more than ample ability and unparallelled experience.

The next stage in our story came in February 1981 when Pat Slinn travelled to Italy and spent a couple of days at the Bologna works learning all he could about the factory's racing Pantah engines. Back in England once more, work began in earnest on the engine the factory had shipped over. This turned out to be a well-used, test-bed engine that had completed some 22 hours running on the testing house 'brake' and had a

small crack in the crankcase around the front right-hand engine mounting boss. However, it was otherwise complete and Sports had about 12 weeks in which to transform it into a racing Pantah, capable of winning the Isle of Man Formula 2 Trophy.

Work on the engine itself absorbed nearly 90 hours in the ensuing weeks. During this time, a standard roadgoing Pantah frame and swinging arm had been given to frame specialist Ron Williams, of Maxton, with a simple brief—to adapt the parts as he saw fit and to supply racing forks, rear suspension and wheels. After a lot of midnight oil had been spent, it was finally ready for testing at the nearby Aintree and Oulton Park circuits before being shipped over to the Isle of Man.

Its race debut couldn't have been better and except for suffering a minor gearbox problem during practice week, it was still possible for Rutter to lap the mountain course at over the ton—101.26 mph. With final tuning, all was now ready for the race proper.

As soon as the race got under way it was evident that the combination of Rutter's experience and the belt-driven Desmo V-twins' speed and reliability were in a class of their own. With a superb display of controlled riding, Tony Rutter took the chequered flag at the end of the 4-lap race with over $1\frac{1}{2}$ minutes' time advantage over second place man Paul Odlin's overbored 550 Honda four-cylinder, setting new race and lap records of 101.91 and 103.51 mph!

The Ducati factory, to quote Pat Slinn, were 'over the moon' promising that Tony would be provided with a full works 600 TT F2 racer in time for the Ulster Grand Prix (the next round in the Championship). In fact, when Rutter and the Sports team arrived in Northern Ireland, there was not one but *two* factory bikes, together with top race mechanic Franco Farnè and Franco Valentini, sent out from Italy to look after the machinery.

Such support ought to have perhaps guaranteed a win but as if to prove the fickleness of racing a quirk of ill luck cost the team victory. Because of the very bad conditions with mist and rain reducing visibility, Tony thought that the pit board flashed to him as he sped past 'plus 14 seconds'. Unfortunately, it read '*minus* 14 seconds' so when he decreased speed slightly, instead of upping the tempo, it ultimately cost him the race. However, the second place which he secured was enough to give him his first world championship—and Ducati their second.

The red and yellow masterpiece which Tony Rutter rode to second spot at Dundrod was one of five almost identical works, so-called TTF2, racers which Ing. Taglioni and his team had originally conceived for the 1981 Italian Formula 2 class championships. Although

The red and yellow beauty that Tony Rutter rode at the 1981 Ulster Grand Prix. His second placing in the Formula 2 event clinched his first world title, and Ducati's second

drawing heavily on the roadster's design these were purpose-built racing motorcyles, built with all the skill that the factory could muster, and not converted production machines.

These TTF2 bikes were works of art in their own right. For example, the special Verlicchi-constructed frame weighed a mere 7 kg. It featured, unlike the production roadster, a monoshock rear end with a special Marzocchi shock, while up front were Marzocchi adjustable racing forks with magnesium sliders. Completing this superb chassis were Campagnolo magnesium wheels, fully floating discs and Brembo gold line brake equipment.

The engines were equally special. Unlike the roadgoing Pantah 600, these pukka racing versions used Baujohr's engine dimensions of 81 × 58 mm, giving 587 cc rather than 583. The forged semi-slipper pistons used gave a higher (10.5:1) compression ratio, and high-lift camshafts, together with larger diameter valves. Carburation was by 36 mm Dell'Ortos on

The first ever Battle of the Twins race in Britain, at Donington Park, August 1982. Nearest to the camera on the front row of the grid is multi-Formula 2 World Champion Tony Rutter and his 600 Pantah

Right **Tony Rutter, then aged 41, on his way to his third successive Formula 2 TT—and ultimately his third world title, in June 1983**

Rutter's Ulster GP bike, although 40 mm units were used in Italian events. There were many other differences, both for weight-saving and extra power. Among these was a specially cast magnesium outer cover for the hydraulically operated dry-clutch assembly. The ignition system used was a Bosch electronic set-up. With these, and other detail modifications, maximum power was up to a very healthy 78 bhp at 10,500 rpm—a true rear-wheel figure.

Besides the works 600 machines, Taglioni also produced a 500 version. This made its debut at Mugello in October 1981, when factory rider Massimo Broccoli finished a superb seventh against the cream of the domestic two-stroke brigade, headed by Marco Lucchinelli and Franco Uncini.

The bike was identical to the world championship-winning 600, except for converting the engine capacity to that of the roadster 500SL, giving dimensions of 74 × 58 mm.

The following year, 1982, the factory pledged its support to both Italian and world series right from the

Above **Rutter in action during the 1983 Formula 2 TT**

Below **Two years on and Tony downs a can in one after gaining his fourth Formula 2 TT victory**

Rutter in action at Brands Hatch. A few weeks later he was to suffer severe injuries in an accident at Montjuich Park, Barcelona, on his bigger F1 Ducati racer

start. In Italy, this was rewarded by Walter Cussigh again carrying off the title which was first won by Broccoli in 1981.

For world championship duties, Tony Rutter was signed again, but this time the factory was to provide him with works bikes for all three rounds of the series, as the Portuguese Grand Prix joined the Isle of Man and Ulster events.

This new venue was at Vila Real in the north of the country, where although the level of organization left something to be desired, it none the less became a popular date in the F2 calendar.

Ducati's decision to mount a works supported effort was to pay off handsomely, for in taking his second World Formula 2 title, Rutter succeeded in winning all three rounds. The first victory came in early June in the Isle of Man, where he easily exceeded his own lap record with a speed of 109.27 mph—a remarkable achievement for a 600 twin! This was followed by similar performances in Portugal in July and the Ulster in August, proving that the Desmo vee was unbeatable in its class.

This fact was to be underlined the following year when Tony took the 1983 title as resoundingly as he had in 1982. And 1984 was to be yet another Ducati/Rutter benefit, although by now the competition was mounting something of a challenge. The 1984 series was staged over four events—the Northwest 200 in Northern Ireland, Vila Real, the Isle of Man and Brno in Czechoslovakia. Rutter campaigned and finished in all four and although he retained his title it was a close run thing, with a pack of 350 Yamaha-engined machines in hot pursuit.

Meanwhile, Taglioni, Farnè and the engineers back in Bologna had not been idle for they were only too aware,

Above right **Final SL variant, the 650, it was only manufactured in 1983**

as is always the case in racing, that the 600 Pantah could not remain unbeatable forever. . . and in any case the Formula 2 class seemed likely to lose its world status before long.

This led to the development of a Formula 1 (750) version. A bigger bore Pantah with the larger capacity had already appeared in the hands of American rider Jimmy Adamo who had ridden it into 13th place in the 1982 Imola 200. The larger machine's 748 cc displacement had been gained by increasing both the bore *and* the stroke, to provide an oversquare 88 × 61.5 mm. This took the rear wheel bhp figure up to 94.8 at 10,500 rpm, increasing the 145 mph top speed of the 600 to almost 155 mph.

During the winter of 1983–4, this bigger bore belt-driven Desmo V-twin was produced in a strictly limited number intended for pure racing use and besides being used in Italy the following season, they also found their way abroad, including one to Tony Rutter—who had by this time ended his association with Sports Motor-cycles, although not with Pat Slinn who was now his race mechanic.

Although the 750 did not achieve the level of success enjoyed by the 600 in the world F1 series, it none the less made a significant impact in both endurance events and the newly instigated Battle of the Twins series on both sides of the Atlantic.

Sadly, whilst taking part on his F1 machine at Montjuich Park, Barcelona, in August 1985, Tony Rutter crashed heavily suffering multiple injuries including severe ones to his head. At the time the worst was feared, many publications reporting him to be near death. But they hadn't made allowances for the man's fighting qualities because not only did he eventually recover but he recovered sufficiently to even race again.

On the production front, several new additions to the Pantah family were introduced in 1982.

The first of these, the 350XL, made its debut at the Milan Show in November of the previous year. This was largely intended for domestic consumption as the 350 class was favoured with a much lower tax bracket than larger bikes in Italy.

Production versions of the 350XL began reaching dealers' showrooms in the spring of 1982. It retained the basic specification of the 500/600SL series, including the belt-driven desmo heads. The 66 × 51 mm bore and stroke gave a capacity of 349 cc. At 10.3:1, the

Below right **The 600TL. Poor sales forced Ducati to sell off its remaining stock at knockdown prices. None the less under the 'banana' styling there lurked an excellent middleweight machine. The 600 shown here was tested by the author for** *Motorcycle Enthusiast* **in early 1985**

compression ratio was well up on the larger models at 10.3:1, although it had much smaller 30 mm Dell'Orto PHF carbs. Peak power was 38.53 bhp at 9000 rpm, giving a maximum speed just short of 100 mph. The XL retained the larger machine's triple Brembo discs and cast-alloy FPS wheels. Distinguishing features were a small 'bikini' fairing, different silencers without a kink, and a red/black paint job.

The front forks were by Paiolo (still 35 mm), although Marzocchi units were retained at the rear. Handlebars were a flat, touring bend, and the seat was dual with no single option. The bike was fitted with an oblong headlamp and new, square flexibly-mounted black indicators.

Later in 1982, an SL version of the 350 was offered. In appearance it was simply a smaller engined 500SL 'Mark 2', but with an attractive red/green finish. Although power output was identical to the XL, the full, more comprehensive streamlining increased maximum speed by 2 mph, to 101 mph.

At around the same time, a touring version of the 600 was launched. This was the TL and it shared much of its specification with the 350XL. Mechanically, the newcomer was similar to the 600SL but without the hydraulic clutch. A range of matching accessories, including German Krauser panniers and crashbars were also offered as optional extras.

But unfortunately for Ducati, lacking the charisma of its SL brother, the TL proved a poor seller. As proof of this, several months *after* the machine was taken out of production in 1983, British dealers Moto Vecchia offered the TL at a knockdown price of £1999 in 1984 (almost half what the *real* price should have been). Totalling some 100 examples, the final TLs were sold in Britain during 1985 for £2199.

At these prices the TL represented excellent value and with the exception of some relatively minor faults (such as an overhard seat), proved popular with their British owners. Even against such class-leading bikes as the Kawasaki GT550 and BMW R65 the TL stood up well, with its excellent handling, torquey engine and superb brakes. What let the TL down most was its somewhat weird 'banana' styling, even though underneath there lurked a basically excellent motorcycle—once again Ducati got it wrong.

In 1983 came the 650SL—the last of the original Pantahs, before a major update in engineering and capacity. Very few of these were produced, these were the uncertain days following the Cagiva/Ducati press conference in early June of that year. The 650SL had even more torque than the 600 version. And although its lines were unchanged it had an attractive red/yellow finish—the same colours used by Ducati on their works TTF2 racers. Bore and stroke were both revised, 82 × 61.5 mm, to give 649 cc and 66 bhp.

The real question being asked, demanded even, by Ducati's countless enthusiasts around the world was:

You've got the colour right, why not the looks and specification? This was in reference to those who wondered why the factory hadn't got around to producing a street legal version of its world championship-winning TTF2 bike!

Those long-suffering individuals were catered for by certain dealers, notably in Britain, who produced a number of replicas but if you wanted a factory produced bike it was not until another couple of years later (1985) that Ducati finally came up with what everyone wanted, the F1.

To the true believers the F1 represents the last of the real Ducatis, in other words the traditionally raw-boned sporting motorcycle, without an ounce of fat to be seen anywhere. With its razor-sharp styling, the F1 evoked a passion with Ducati lovers whether they resided in Milan, London, Cologne, New York, Tokyo or Sydney— or anywhere else for that matter!

In the very year which saw Cagiva become the factory's new owners, as the American magazine *Cycle*

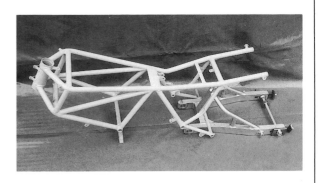

Above **Verlicchi monoshock frame kit used by several enthusiasts to convert their roadgoing Pantahs into a racer or super sportster**

Below **Also available was a range of tuning parts such as these straight-cut primary gears**

This 750 TT1 Replica was constructed (and available) before the factory got round to offering a complete machine themselves. It used the Verlicchi frame kit as a base. Several companies, notably in Britain, offered similar machines

World put it: 'Ducati must have known a line was about to be drawn in the history books and the people there must have wanted to leave a last entry. Because the F1 is everything an Italian sports bike is expected to be and so seldom is.'

Fraser Stronach, testing one of the very first F1s to reach Australia, headed his write-up for *Motorcycle International*: 'Extinction with Distinction', going on to say, 'If the Formula 1 Replica is the last Ducati it's a hell of a way for the name to go out.'

The first batch of some 300 machines, destined for Japan (by now Ducati's top market), began to roll off the Bologna factory's production lines in April 1985 and more deliveries to Japan and a few to Australia left Italy shortly afterwards. Less than a month later the Cagiva takeover became a reality. But this didn't stop the F1 production, if anything it actually *increased* it with not only Italy, but other markets getting the new machine before the end of the year.

In any case, 1985 had got off to an excellent start on the racetrack, with Marco Lucchinelli gaining a magnificent second in Daytona's Battle of the Twins race in March, just losing out to the sheer horsepower of Gene Church's works Harley, the legendary *Lucifer's Hammer*. As Fraser Stronach recalled in his test, 'the first impression you got of the F1 in the flesh, was of a short, small motorcycle with a solid compact feel'.

The F1 shared the longer 61.5 mm stroke with the 650SL Pantah and employed 88 mm pistons to get the capacity up to 748 cc. These vastly oversquare dimensions allowing the larger engine to rev higher than might have been expected. A pair of open mouth Dell'Orto 36 mm pumper carburettors supplied the gas. A well silenced and certainly street legal 2-into-1 Conti exhaust system had the single silencer existing on the left (nearside). Like the 600/650SL, the F1 featured a hydraulically operated clutch. There were other differences too and these all added up to a delightfully smooth and punchy motor.

But in many ways, as with the racers, it was the chassis rather than the engine which created the real interest. Like the works bikes, this followed the basic principles of using the engine as a stress member thanks to its very strong gravity diecast crankcases. The

Above **The factory's Formula 1 and endurance racers predated the ultimate F1 sports roadster. This is the full racing version, used in the period 1983-5**

Above right **1985 version of the F1 sportster, being ridden in Australia**

round section swinging arm pivoted in the rear of the crankcases (as on the earlier Pantahs), before coming up to meet the cantilever rear suspension. Even in appearance, the frame dominated the bike rather than the engine.

Perhaps this was to be expected when one realizes that with 57 bhp (or up to 63 bhp depending on which dyno you believe) the F1's straight-line performance was significantly down compared with the Oriental opposition. But a low frontal area, narrow width and effective streamlining made the very best use of what power there was, with a timed maximum of 127 mph (*Performance Bike*) the F1 was identical to BMW's K75S—which needed 75 bhp to achieve the same result.

At this point, combined with effective penetration, the chassis takes on more importance. It steered and handled like a thoroughbred racer and this enabled it to score heavily over the more sedate three-cylinder BMW. So, between points A and B the Ducati was considerably quicker, even though it had less power and an identical maximum speed! This ability brought

the F1 back into the region of performance occupied by the latest generation of Japanese sportsters.

Fashion dictated a 16-inch front wheel. But Ducati were loath to forsake their traditional stability, so kicked out the steering angle (rake) to 28 degrees with a long 155 mm of trail. Consequently, the steering was a touch on the heavy side, not helped by a hydraulic steering damper. Hidden amongst the fairing brackets and frame tubes this was, however, needed as really heavy bumps could set the front tyre kicking.

Another slight disappointment was how easily the centre-stand would ground when the bike was being ridden in the manner for which it was intended—at least with a heavy rider aboard.

These were the only two faults though, otherwise the handling and roadholding were beyond reproach performing in the same impeccable fashion, whether threading its way through a city street, or negotiating high-speed swerving at over 120 mph.

Below right **The hand-built 750 F1 Montjuich, at 136 mph almost 10 mph faster than the standard bike, on display at the 1985 Milan Show**

The Marzocchi PVSI rear shock was used in a rear suspension system which closely followed the early Yamaha single shock pattern. This might not have been of the modern rising rate type but was none the less extremely compliant, once the unit had bedded in, and matched any of the more sophisticated Japanese types. Compared to their earlier bevel-driven V-twins, such as the 900SS or Hailwood Replica, the F1 could be ridden anywhere, anytime, and not have to unduly avoid pot-holes or similar road irregularities. This fine combination of increased travel and softer spring rates was one of the biggest bonuses on the whole bike—the old bogey of overhard Italian suspension deleted at a single stroke.

The 38 mm Marzocchi forks were not dissimilar to those on the final bevel twins, the Mille Replica and S2. Likewise, the Brembo discs and calipers—this meant that the latter were only the standard (cheaper black) rather than the more exotic gold line type.

Open road riding was made more pleasant by the comprehensive endurance-replica fairing. As the *Motorcycle International* test said: 'It offers good wind and weather protection, even to the hands, but you have to lie on the tank to get out of the breeze completely. Only the cramp induced by leg positioning limits the bike's long-distance comfort.'

The quality of finish, especially paintwork, fibreglass and alloy work of the tank were streets ahead of any previous production Ducati offering. Only the poor quality finish of the black exhaust system marred an otherwise superbly finished product. Many preferred the F1 to Bimota's similarly engined DB1 of the same era.

The final comment on the F1 must go to Fraser Stronach, with the words he used to conclude his July 1985 test: 'The F1 looks and is the part. It's not just a concept copy of a race bike as is the RD500 (Yamaha), but a machine that's very close to the real thing. For me it confirms Ducati's status as the world's finest sports motorcycles. You can keep your GSX-Rs and FZs, I'll take the Ducati F1 every time.'

For anyone wanting more performance than the F1 offered there was, depending upon the dates they were offered, the Montjuich, Laguna Seca and Santamonica. These were truly *hand*-built super sportsters, for either racing or fast road work. And because of their strictly limited production, they were at least 25 per cent more expensive than the standard F1 and can be viewed as the modern successor to the original Imola Replica 750SS of the early 1970s.

These were clearly based on the works Formula 1 and endurance machines, with 40 mm (some Montjuichs retained 36 mm instruments) Dell'Ortos, 10:1 compression pistons, larger valves, fiercer cam profile and less restrictive exhaust. They produced power from 7500

Ducati team with F1 racer at Misano, 19 April 1987

Final F1 variant, the Santamonica, axed in early 1988 to make way for the new 851 Superbike

through to over 10,000 rpm, which was transmitted via the stock gearbox, with straight-cut primary gears instead of the helical type used on the other production Pantahs.

The gearbox was fully capable of withstanding the need to keep the engine on the boil between 7500 and 10,000—which itself was quite an achievement considering the gearbox problems on the tuned larger bevel-driven vees. And complementing this was the chassis which also proved itself capable of coping with the extra punch.

More often than not, these special F1s came shod with pukka slick racing covers indicating, at least as far as the factory was concerned, that they had been built for the racetrack, rather than the road.

For North American roads the specials, or for that matter the standard F1, were effectively outlawed as there was no place in the mid 1980s Stateside for a bike with such a raucous exhaust note and a complete lack of air filtration, let alone emissions controls. So to get around the legislation, all the F1s imported into the States came shorn of their lights and turn signals and marketed 'for racing use only'.

Even so, demand exceeded supply and they were quickly snapped up. After all, as *Cycle World* said: 'They

may be bargains. This last Ducati (not strictly true!) is a throwback in spirit to the 750SS of 1973, the F1's most famous predecessor. Like the 750SS, the F1 is the Italian sportsbike of its era.'

When *Cycle World* tested a Montjuich in their August 1986 issue they got a timed maximum speed of 136 mph and the headline read: 'Who says twins are not fast?' But although the tester loved it he made the following statement: 'Perhaps like the Rolling Stones, the Montjuich's true home is in the past, in a 1960s setting where it could run with side-piped Corvettes and open exhaust GTOs. Certainly, the safe and sane and noise-controlled 1980s will restrict it to closed-circuit use.'

Cycle World also concluded that the Montjuich none the less pointed to the future and to Cagiva honouring Ducati's commitment to the Ducati V-twin engine concept. They saw that the next motorcycle in the belt-driven Desmo V-twin story, the Paso, as a machine that 'promises to have some of the Montjuich's out-of-the-past character without offending present-day sensibilities'. And so the era of the fully civilized Ducati had finally arrived. Under the old management the factory had tried and failed several times over the previous decade. But now, under Cagiva, could they at last get it right?

A pair of these futuristically styled machines in 350 and 750 capacities, together with the semi-chopper styled Indiana custom bike, made their public debut at the Milan Show in November 1985. With an all-enveloping plastic bodywork, which you either loved or detested, the curvaceous Paso was named after the late, great Italian roadracing star, Renzo Pasolini, who although he may never have ridden a Ducati, was very much a folk hero at Cagiva's Varese headquarters.

In many ways the Paso was a tribute, by the new owners of the Ducati factory, to a man who had lost his life on that fateful day at Monza, in May 1973, in the horrific accident which also claimed the life of the Flying Finn, Jarno Saarinen.

Although the basic engine was very much the work of Taglioni and updated by his heir, Massimo Bordi, the frame and cosmetics were down to Massimo Tamburini—one of the originators of the famous Rimini superbike concern, Bimota. Not only had Tamburini co-founded Bimota but in the all-important first decade of its life it had been he, above all others, who had been responsible for its rise from a small unknown specialist frame builder, housing engines such as the 750 Honda Four, to a marque of worldwide acclaim that it enjoys today.

Close friend Graeme Simpson summed the Paso's

appearance up by saying, 'When it first came out I didn't like it, but the more I see of it, the more it grows on me'. Graeme rides a Kawasaki GT750 . . . which rather goes to prove that Tamburini succeeded in his task of giving Ducati a machine with an appeal much wider than the company's traditional buyer.

After Tamburini had left (fallen out with) his Bimota workmates, he joined the Roberto Gallina grand prix

The 750 (foreground) and 350 Paso prototypes displayed at Milan in November 1985

Below **The 350 Paso prototype, late 1985**

racing team in 1983 before eventually opting to join the Castiglioni brothers' Cagiva empire as a designer two years later. However, Tamburini carried on his activities well away from the Varese and Bologna factories.

Just as significantly for the future of Ducati, Taglioni's protégé, Bordi, used the Paso to officially launch his own career and come out into the open from under the wings of the master.

A production 750 Paso heads a line of Ducati models at the BMF Rally, Peterborough, May 1988

Bordi chose to incorporate several important changes to the short-stroke 88 × 61.5 mm engine (the 350 was only for Italy), most notable were the inclusion of a stronger 14-plate dry clutch and Japanese Kokusan electronic ignition. The latter was clearly at the behest of Ducati's new masters who had always pursued a policy of superior quality, not national pride, when it came to choosing component suppliers. Even so, the triple Brembo discs and Oscam cast-alloy wheels were Italian—as quite simply they were of the best quality.

But it was the bike's styling which really set it apart, along with Honda's CBR600 and 1000, the first of a new breed of modern, fully enclosed two-wheelers.

Strangely, it had been Bimota and Tamburini's successor, Frederico Martini, who had originally been commissioned by Cagiva to build a prototype of a machine very similar to the eventual production Paso back in early 1985.

When Tamburini himself joined the Cagiva-Ducati setup he took the design a step further with a new set of clothes and many modifications—almost a totally new motorcycle, in fact.

Below **Underneath its plastic bodywork the Paso sported a rather crudely finished square tube frame with single shock and rising rate suspension**

Ing. Bordi's modified engine sat in an ugly Japanese-style full loop rising rate square-tubed steel frame, equipped with the latest rising rate monoshock rear suspension offering variable adjustment through reverse Honda Pro-Link type lower linkage and a Swedish Ohlins gas-filled unit. At the front a pair of Marzocchi MIR 41.7 mm forks employing a 25-degree steering head angle, coupled with a 105 mm trail offered taut and flex-free handling. The forks had anti-dive in one leg only with adjustable air assistance. And as with other Pantah-engined models, the alloy swinging arm (something with which Cagiva had wide experience from their succession of motocrossers) pivoted through the rear of the crankcases.

Steering, thanks to the twin 16-in. wheels, was quick and totally different to previous Dukes. The ride was much smoother than any Ducati before, making nonsense of the Italian-means-hard brigade (wheels were later enlarged to 17 in.).

Unlike the F1 and its variants, the Paso was intended from the outset as a mass-market bike. Hence, to meet the strict emission and noise-level controls in markets such as the USA, the rear cylinder head was reversed through 180 degrees and a single Weber 44 DCNF 107 carburettor fitted. This also had the advantage of endowing the Paso with a much lighter throttle action thanks to a butterfly, rather than round or square conventional slides of the types previously used on the Bologna vees—and of course a single cable.

Likewise, the single Weber allowed a much more efficient air box and filter element which, combined with the super quiet Silentium silencers and comprehensive bodywork, enabled the design team to easily meet the various governmental regulations around the

Above right **Introduced in 1988, the 'new' 750 Sport became an instant sales success**

Below right **Given a restyle and capacity increase, the 906 Paso was new for the 1989 season**

world. On the standard 15/38 gearing, maximum speed was just over 130 mph.

Generally, even if the Ducati traditionalists were not keen, the press lavished its praise on the Paso. Summed up by the following comment in *Motorcycle International*'s *New Bike Buyers' Guide*: 'Quite unlike any other Ducati so far, the Paso manages to combine Japanese civilization with Italian style and emerge unscathed at the other end as the best Duke ever.'

By comparison, the Indiana custom bike made much smaller headlines. In any case there was much less technical change under its mass of shining paintwork, polished alloy and sparkling chrome plate. Initially shown in 350 and 650 engine sizes, the larger capacity was soon superseded by a 750. However, none of the Indianas used the Paso's reversed rear head and single Weber, relying instead on twin Dell'Orto PHF 30s (350) or German Bing 64/32/379s on the larger two models. Neither did the Indiana use the Paso square tube chassis.

Somehow, even with their desmo heads and Ducati badges the Indianas are poles apart from the sporting heart of the marque, intended instead to appeal to a breed of rider not normally associated with the Bologna factory's line-up.

At the beginning of 1988 the F1, in all its forms, was finally discontinued. Quite simply it was no longer able to meet the ever more stringent approval laws in the majority of Ducati's export markets. Many were sorry to see its demise. Simon Fenning of the then British importers, Moto Vecchia, commented, 'This model has been our top selling Ducati'. The final F1 offered in Britain was the limited edition Santamonica which sold for £8295, against the £5995 for the Paso.

But a new range leader was just around the corner, waiting to make its entry on to the world stage in a blaze of glory at the bi-annual Milan Show later that year. . . .

The Indiana custom bike. Like the Paso this made its debut, in 350 and 650 sizes, at Milan in 1985. In 1987 it gained a capacity increase to 750. It was intended to cater for a totally new breed of Ducati customer

12

The brothers

Most enthusiasts know at least something of the various old and well-established Italian marques—names such as Benelli, Gilera, Morini and Moto Guzzi, not to mention Ducati. But how many can really relate much about the modern day powerhouse of the Italian motorcycle industry, Cagiva?

Born as recently as September 1978, Cagiva had by 1982 risen to the very top of the Italian domestic motorcycle sales table, even though the mighty Piaggio still made more two-wheelers than anyone outside Japan, but the vast majority of these were mopeds and scooters.

By 1985 Cagiva had started to buy up rival manufacturers, first came Ducati, followed by the Swedish Husqvarna concern in 1986 and Moto Morini in 1987. On the sporting scene the name Cagiva has reached the forefront in the majority of off-road activities, whilst on the road the company has spent a massive fortune over the last decade in providing the only alternative to the massed ranks of the Japanese giants on the starting grids of the blue ribband 500 cc World Road Racing Championship arena.

So who are Cagiva and how have they managed to

The brothers Castiglioni, Claudio (left) and Gianfranco (right), head a vast motorcycle empire which includes not only Ducati but Cagiva, Morini and Husqvarna

achieve such an amazing array of success in the production and sporting fields in a mere decade? Read on and all will be revealed.

The Cagiva story is a fascinating one, not only because it is one of the very, very few success stories in the modern motorcycle industry but also because it is an extremely complicated one, in reality a 'phoenix which has risen from many fires' as the American journal *Cycle World* described it.

To fully understand just what lies behind their success it is necessary to go back as far as 1912. It was in this year that a company called Aeronautica Macchi was formed to specialize in the manufacture of seaplanes.

These early flying machines were built on the very site which years later was to become the headquarters for Cagiva's original motorcycle operation. Located on the outskirts of Varese at Schiranna, the factory, some 30 miles north of Milan, with its slipways into the lake and its massive hangar still exist. The location is idyllic—more imaginable as the perfect setting for a luxury holiday hotel than a manufacturing plant, with the tranquil waters of Lake Varese lapping on the shore and the breathtakingly beautiful Swiss Alps in the background.

At the outbreak of World War 1, Macchi found themselves building French Nieuport fighters under

Aermacchi were for many years one of Italy's leading aircraft manufacturers. Pictured is a Macchi C200 Saetta fighter over North Africa in 1940

licence for the Italian army, in addition to the flying boats of original design.

After the end of the hostilities, the Varese concern successfully continued in the aviation sector specializing not only in flying boats but seaplanes including successful participation in the famous Schneider Trophy races culminating with a new World Aircraft Speed Record at the then amazing speed of 440 mph in 1934. This feat was achieved over Lake Garda by one of the Macchi MC72 seaplanes, powered by a specially built supercharged dual Fiat piston engine.

In the dark days preceding World War 2, Mussolini's Italy embarked on a massive armament building spree and Macchi found themselves once more constructing military fighter planes. Starting with the MC200 Freccia (Arrow), the Varese Company produced a succession of important and competent designs, including the MC202 Folgore (Lightning) and MC205 Veltro (Greyhound). Used by the *Regia Aeronautica*, these were widely accepted as the finest fighters produced by Italians during the period.

Following the end of the conflict, however, there was a total ban on aviation products and so Macchi had to diversify, like several other similar companies, or go under. Macchi, together with Agusta and Piaggio, chose two wheels but this was not before the famous old Varese organization had designed and begun to

market a three-wheel truck—which incidentally became a best-seller in its own right and is still currently manufactured, albeit by a totally separate company.

But more importantly to our story, Aermacchi's management, anticipating the motorcycle boom which was to come in the late 1940s and early 1950s, and intending to have a stake in it, began the task of procuring the services of a leading designer. Their ultimate choice was Lino Tonti (now chief designer at Moto Guzi), who had worked at Benelli and had spent the war years employed on aircraft engine design.

Tonti's initial design for Aermacchi, first offered for the 1950 season, was distinctly unorthodox. It was an open-frame lightweight with a 124 cc two-stroke engine pivoting in unit with the rear suspension. The luggage or tool container, shaped like a conventional fuel tank, featured a hinged mounting at the steering column so that it could be fixed near the saddle to give motorcycle minded owners something to grip with their knees. This machine enjoyed some considerable success and later a sports version appeared which had the frame encased by a real tank. This was also used in trials, including the ISDT (International Six Day Trial) of 1951. This event, the 26th in the series, had its headquarters in Varese and was also the local marque's international sporting debut.

Rather unsuccessful, on the contrary, was a 250 twin (two 125s coupled together) which was offered during 1953–4.

In 1955, Tonti designed a record-breaker, making full use of the wind-tunnel and other resources of the

Long-stroke, wet-clutch Aermacchi Ala d'Oro 250 over-the-counter racer of the early 1960s. Machines like this were largely responsible for building the factory's two-wheel reputation

factory's aviation department (the company had by then re-established aircraft production). Powered by dohc engines of 48 and 75 cc capacity, this was one of the first examples of a 'flying cigar', being very low and almost 10 ft long. Placed behind the driver, the engine had the peculiarity of having its cylinder inclined *rearwards* at an angle of 20 degrees. The overhead-camshafts were chain driven, with 9 bhp for the 73 cc and 7 bhp for 49 cc—good figures, considering the period and the low octane petrol which had to be used. The engines, which had wet sump lubrication, were in unit with a four-speed gearbox and final drive was by chain. Weight (wet) was around 210 lb with 18-in. tyres and a frame which used space frame construction and a fully sprung body.

The record attempts were made in the spring of 1956 along the Milan–Varese *autostrada*. Staged under far from ideal weather conditions on 4 April, rider Massimo Pasolini (father of racing star Renzo) broke the world's 50 cc standing start mile record with a speed of 51.5 mph. Using the larger engined model on the same day, he captured the flying start kilometre and flying start mile records in the 75 cc class with speeds of 104 mph and 100.5 mph respectively, breaking, by a considerable margin, the records set up only a few months previously by Germany's Adolf Baumm with his NSU feet forward streamliner.

Soon after the successful record bid Tonti left to join rivals FB Mondial. The man chosen to replace him as technical director was one of Italy's leading designers of the day, Ing. Alfredo Bianchi, previously with Alfa Romeo and Parilla and a very keen motorcyclist himself before the war. He had designed the ohc 250 Parilla sports and racing models, which were so successful in Italian events just after the war, and also manufactured his own Astoria engines and complete machines, the single ohc and two-stroke units, 125 and 175 cc, enjoying quite a lot of popularity as proprietary components by some of the country's smaller manufacturers.

Bianchi's first task after joining Aermacchi was to evolve a production machine from a sketch of an 'ideal' motorcycle which had been executed by Count Revelli, a well-known car stylist who had himself been a racing motorcyclist and had actually won the 1925 Italian GP at Monza on a GR machine of his own design and manufacture.

The new model, the all-enclosed 175 Chimera (Dream) was publicly launched at the 1956 Milan Show.

But although it aroused a vast amount of media attention the Chimera never sold particularly well, either on the domestic market or outside Italy. So it was decided to undress it to produce a more orthodox machine. Ing. Bianchi went back to his drawing-board, expressly charged to make as few changes as possible in order to avoid further heavy manufacturing costs. This explains the single-tube backbone and the horizontal disposition of the engine, both obligatory features of the original design. What differed though was the rear sub-frame. On the Chimera there was a single rear shock à la Vincent style, whereas the undressed model featured conventional period twin suspension units.

When first introduced the Chimera was a 175 cc machine, but before long a 250 version had appeared. And it was not long before their sporting potential was being explored.

In 1957, a tuned 175 model, giving 15.5 bhp instead of the standard model's 13 bhp (at the same 8000 rpm), was being made available for use in Italian sports machine races. Thereafter the performance of the 175 cc production racer was increased to 20 bhp, even though it was largely shelved in favour of the more popular 250. The latter appeared later than the 175, the prototype being given its debut in the 1960 German GP by Alberto Pagani (son of 1949 125 cc World Champion Nello). It made such a good showing up against the cream of grand prix racers that Aermacchi decided to go ahead with a small batch of similar machines for sale to private owners. The first of these 250s, the *Ala d'Oro* (Golden Wing) as it was called, still had the long-stroke 66 × 72 mm bore and stroke dimensions of the Chimera, a four-speed gearbox and it churned out 22 bhp at 8000 rpm. One of the few obvious external changes to the roadgoing sports version, the *Ala Verde* (Green Wing) was an increase in wheel size from 17 to 18 in.

The low initial cost of the Ala d'Oro, together with its ease of maintenance (needed rather often as the original models were none too reliable), and the ready availability of spares, made it immediately popular as a private owner racer, not just in Italy but in export markets around the world too. And it soon proved itself to be no mean performer, particularly on short, twisting circuits, where its lightweight and rapid acceleration paid handsome dividends.

No doubt it was the international success of this model, coupled with the achievements of the motocross version (Lanfranco Angelini was five times Italian champion on an Aermacchi) that led to a crucial development in our story. This was a joint 50/50 commercial shareholding with the American Harley-Davidson company in 1960.

With a lightweight boom developing in North America, Harley badly needed a good 250 that could be sold in touring, sports, racing and also motocross versions. This coincided with the Italian company being

more heavily involved in their aviation sector than at any time since World War 2, so it suited both companies for the commercial union to go ahead. Certainly, during the early years of the agreement it proved a highly satisfactory *and* profitable venture for both parties, with more and more of the products being shipped across the Atlantic. By 1964 75 per cent of the factory's production was going to Harley-Davidson for distribution in America and the following year saw the launch of a 50 cc moped also largely intended for Stateside consumption. The European market was therefore becoming less important. Aermacchi not only offered the various ohv flat single models throughout continental Europe in the early 1960s but also the strange *Zeffiros* (Zephyr). These were a combination of motorcycle and scooter with a choice of 125 or 150 cc engines and even a full blown scooter. Only the latter and the four-strokes appeared in Britain, imported via Bill Webster's Italian Imports company, based in Nantwich, Cheshire.

Shortly after the merger, the increased production which had resulted made it necessary to separate the motorcycle and aircraft companies in Italy. The aeroplane plant being in Varese itself, whilst the old lakeside location was modernized and enlarged to handle the growing output of two-wheelers.

By the end of 1962 Bianchi realized that no more power could be squeezed from the long-stroke 250, so he changed the bore and stroke to over-square dimensions of 72 × 61 mm. Up went the power to 28 bhp at 9500 rpm (more than the world championship

Aermacchi–Harley-Davidson folk hero, the late Renzo Pasolini, killed in the horrific accident which also claimed the life of Jarno Saarinen, in the Italian GP at Monza, 20 May 1973

winning double-knocker Guzzis of a decade previously) and the adoption of a five-speed gearbox allowed full use to be made of this boost in performance. By 1965 the power was up to 30 bhp at 10,000 rpm—not bad for a quarter-litre push-rod over-the-counter single!

Bianchi was also coming to realize that it would be increasingly difficult to make much of an improvement on this and therefore came up with a double-knocker version of the flat single. But, even though a prototype was built, Harley-Davidson were utterly opposed to having a racer which differed fundamentally from the roadster machines—they even used one of the ohv Ala d'Oro engines in the Aermacchi powered Harley-Davidson 'flying cigar' on which Stormy Mangham broke the American 250 cc mile record with a speed of over 156 mph in the summer of 1964. So the dohc project had to be shelved and the prototype sold off.

Changes thereafter to the Ala d'Oro mainly centred around larger capacity versions—first 293 cc then 344, right up to over 400. But these were mainly because the competition in both the 350 and 500 cc classes at the time was largely restricted to ageing British singles, such as the AJS 7R, Matchless G50 and Manx Nortons.

Strangely, the larger capacity hadn't been intended for road racing at all. It was first prepared for competition in 500 cc motocross and devised at the end of 1962, by coupling a short-stroke piston and cylinder to a long-stroke bottom end. The resulting

square 72 × 72 mm bore and stroke measurements gave a displacement of 293 cc and this machine, by virtue of its light weight and easy handling, was reasonably successful in Italian dirtbike racing, in much the same way as the BSA Victor was in British scrambles.

As history records, competing in the larger road racing classes, notably the 350 category, the Aermacchi flat singles were effective even at grand prix level piloted by the leading privateers until the advent of the Japanese two-strokes, notably the Yamaha TD/TR twins. They were also campaigned with reasonable success by factory development riders including Pagani, Gilberto Milani and Renzo Pasolini.

The parent Harley-Davidson company in America was taken over by the giant AMF (American Machine and Foundry) Corporation in 1968, and although nobody realized this at the time it was to signal the end of the harmonious Italo–American co-operation which had existed between the Milwaulkee and Varese factories.

Even so, development of new models proceeded apace, 1967 had seen an all new eight-valve street motorcycle which was marketed in America as the ML

The Varese factory directly following its liquidation and closure by AMF in August 1978. No one could have guessed what was to follow

and MLS. This was also known as the Rapido. The engine capacity was 123.5 cc (56 × 50 mm) and it was this powerplant which was to prove a vital link in not only the evolution of the Aermacchi/HD story, but of the early days of Cagiva.

Originally, the Rapido had a four-speed box and single backbone frame with no front downtube. In July 1967 a racing version made an impressive appearance in the hands of Alberto Pagani who gained a third place against top opposition at Zingonia. One year later the racer went on sale to the public. By then it was producing 20 bhp at 9200 rpm and had a five-speed gearbox, 27 mm Dell'Orto carburettor and a full cradle duplex frame, Ceriani forks and Oldani brakes.

The following year Kel Carruthers came home second in the IoM TT and in 1970 fellow Aussie Johnny Dodds gave the Varese marque its first ever world championship grand prix victory in West Germany.

Meanwhile, a 100 cc street bike based on the larger 'stroker' had made its debut. There was even a tuned version, called the Baja, which was intended for desert racing (hence the name)—a popular sport in the southern states of America and Mexico.

As the new decade dawned a whole string of variations of the 100 and 125 two-strokes appeared. By 1973 the most popular were the X90/Z90 and TX125. That year had seen the introduction of oil-pump lubrication via the Japanese Mikuni pump, and an alloy cylinder on the larger engine. Both these features were to be found on subsequent roadster models.

The racing department had also been busy. By 1970 the ageing flat single four-stroke was becoming obsolete even in the larger classes. So the factory engineers, now headed by engine specialist Ezio Mascheroni, had come up with a new twin-cylinder 250 two-stroke, using a pair of the early 125 racing strokers' cylinders. This had its first outing in February 1971 at the Modena Autodrome, and Renzo Pasolini was the first man to race one. The model got water-cooling in 1972 and was soon followed by a 350. It was not long before both bikes began to display real potential, even at GP level. But the race effort received a major blow when Pasolini was killed in the 1973 Italian GP, in the same accident which claimed the life of Jarno Saarinen.

But the following year the newcomer to the team, Walter Villa, scored the first of three consecutive 250 world titles and in 1976 he added the 350 title.

Harley also offered a limited amount of replicas known as the RR250 and RR350, however, these never lived up to the expectations of Villa's world championship mounts.

With racing becoming ever more specialized all this track success had very little relationship to the standard production roadsters. It was in this latter area that the factory's problems really centred. In 1972, AMF had purchased Aermacchi's remaining 50 per cent share in the Italian plant. Quite simply Aermacchi had by then

Cagiva's first brochure, September 1978—simply overprinted Harley material

lost interest in two wheels and just wanted out, to enable its efforts to be concentrated on its main business—selling aircraft.

Even though a record 45,000 motorcycles left the Varese factory in 1974 (largely for the North American market) the writing was clearly on the wall. A combination of AMF's 'maximum dollar profit, minimum quality' production tactics and Japanese competition, saw sales of lightweight Harleys slump dramatically in the USA market almost overnight. This was even though brand new 175 and 250 trail bikes had made their debut in 1974 followed by street versions the following year.

Things were little better elsewhere. Outside the States, AMF had set up HD International, with its headquarters in Geneva, Switzerland. This was simply a set of offices for the sales operation—the motorcycles themselves were still built in Varese, with excess stock stored at the warehousing facility in Holland.

Like the parent management, AMF International viewed motorcycles in the same way as any of their other leisure products, which ranged from tennis rackets to ten pin bowling alleys.

Another problem was that to cope with the record production figures in 1974 extra labour was brought in,

much of it unskilled, the result was inevitable—the machine quality was often less than perfect. The most serious defects centred around unreliable electrical components, poor plating and painting and scant attention to build quality.

Throughout the period 1974–7 the poor quality led to dissatisfied buyers, excessive warranty claims and ultimately less customers. AMF even ran a rather stupid advertising campaign in Europe illustrating the latest version of the 250 two-stroke single, the SST250, comparing it directly with Villa's world championship winning twins—of course any reasonably knowledgeable enthusiast realized the difference straightaway. . . .

By mid autumn in 1977 the production quality and durability had begun to improve with not only superior chrome and paintwork, but superior components and quality control. AMF had been forced into realizing that warranty claims didn't do anyone any good and ultimately affected that magic word *profit*.

A whole host of improvements came in 1978 with a new 125 road model, the SST125. This came with a disc front brake, electronic tacho, all new instrument console and improved electrics. The list continued with new Ceriani forks, new headlamp, flatter handlebars, more comprehensive air filter and improved kickstarter. The other models in the range were also updated in a similar manner.

Above **One of the first bikes built after Cagiva gained control was this prototype 294 cc ohv flat single based on the old Aermacchi design, together with a sporting version it never entered production**

The previous year had seen the debut of a production motocrosser, the MX250, but for the States only. For 1978 it was planned to market this worldwide, plus an enduro version, the RX250, also new 350s in street and trail form. But only a few of these had actually been built before the shattering news in May 1978 that AMF were pulling the plug on the Varese operation and in future would be limiting its two-wheel activities solely to North America—which meant no more lightweights, only the large capacity V-twins.

At the time it seemed to observers close to the scene, that just when they had finally sorted out the problems of the previous few years and with some exciting new models in the wings, the Italian arm of the company was to be cut off. However, as events were to dramatically prove, even though AMF carried out their threat of closure this was to ultimately benefit the motorcycling world and lead to a brand new marque, which amazingly would in a short time challenge the world not only on the sporting front, but also in production figures too.

As the British Harley-Davidson lightweight importer I

am perhaps in a unique position to relate the chain of events which were to follow the AMF closure bombshell. In fact, Mick Walker (Holdings) Ltd was among the interested parties who carried out talks with AMF about purchasing the Italian setup but eventually the lakeside factory went back to Italian hands under the control of President Battista Lozio and brothers Claudio and Gianfranco Castiglioni.

The Cagiva name was an amalgam of CA for Castiglioni, GI for Giovanni (the father of the two brothers) and VA for Varese. Giovanni Castiglioni had created a vast industrial empire based in Varese specializing in small metal pressings, and his organization was one of the region's largest employers. The family had made their fortune making items such as locks, belt buckles, clasps and all those dinky pieces of metalwork to be found on luggage and handbags. The Castiglioni metal-pressing operation was so efficient that it could actually beat the foreign competition on both price *and* quality!

The sons of the founder had helped build this organization and with their entrepreneurial ability were ideally suited to turning around what had been a financial disaster for AMF. Not only this but as the elder son, Gianfranco revealed shortly after the takeover in the autumn of 1978, in answer to just why they had purchased the factory, his reply was direct and simple: 'Because we love motorcycles of course'!

Above **Early British Cagiva publicity material stressed backup, rather than sales**

Below **The author at his Wisbech headquarters during his 3½-year reign as Britain's first Cagiva importer**

Indeed the Cagiva name had already been seen, even at grand prix level, when Marco Lucchinelli had taken his Cagiva-Suzuki to a series of excellent results in the 1978 500 cc World Championships, including a fourth at the Austrian GP, third in the Italian, seventh in Belgium and finally a fourth at Silverstone, the home of the British round. All these results came in *before* the takeover of the former HD-Aermacchi factory.

Incidentally, Lucchinelli's machine, which was basically a Suzuki RG500 with a heavily modified engine, was sold to another top rider Scot Alex George, who although retired in the Senior TT went on to win the prestigious post TT meeting at Mallory Park in 1979.

This enthusiasm for the sport has remained a constant feature of Cagiva policy ever since, including a mega budget which had been thrown at the largely unsuccessful attempts at taking on the might of Japan in the 500 cc road racing world championships, with superstar Randy Mamola being signed for the 1988 season.

By contrast, their less publicized but far more rewarding ventures into off-road sport have paid massive dividends, with trials, enduro and motocross. It is in this latter field that the real sporting successes have been accomplished with Cagiva becoming World Moto Cross Champions in both the 125 and 250 categories.

In fact, one of the very first projects undertaken by Cagiva's development team following the takeover was the development of a water-cooled 125 cc motocrosser. The prototype made its bow in 1979, with production versions going on sale the following spring—the Japanese didn't have their water-cooled dirt racers ready for the market until 1981. . . .

An enduro version, albeit air-cooled, was the next 'new' Cagiva off the stocks, making its debut in early 1981. Although they had no real experience of modern two-stroke dirtbikes, the Cagiva 125s were a match for anything in the world, being both fast *and* reliable—no mean feat for a company which had been founded only a few short months before.

But besides these two machines, the balance during those early months were motorcycles constructed from designs and parts already existing in the Varese factory before AMF's closure. These included revised versions of the Harley MX and RX250 comp bikes and updated versions of the various two-stroke street and trail machines.

Displaying their links with the past the Cagiva emblem for the motorcycle division was an Italianized version of Harley-Davidson's Number 1 logo, but with

The world's first water-cooled production motocrosser, the 1980 Cagiva WMX 125. Don't be fooled by the fins on the barrel—it was air-*and* liquid-cooled

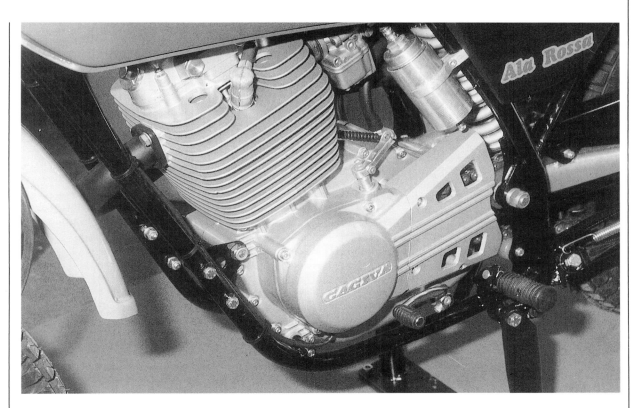

November 1981, and Cagiva showed their first autonomous four-stroke—the 350 Ala Rossa

the Cagiva corporate logo—an elephant. Originally this was *white*, until I explained the significance this would have in English-speaking countries and from that day on it became a grey elephant!

In addition, for an interim period of one year following the takeover in September 1978, the petrol tanks of all the machines produced carried the name 'HD Cagiva'. Thereafter the Harley name disappeared entirely. However, this didn't stop the Cagiva management from taking full advantage of their purchase—for example, instruments carrying the logo 'AMF Harley-Davidson' adorned the machines until all the stocks were fully exhausted on the SST/SXT models into the early 1980s. In fact, for the low outlay—put in some quarters at £2 million, the vast amount of buildings, plant machinery, bikes and spares which came with the deal was without doubt the main source of profit in those early years and the fuel which stoked the fires of expansion in the years which followed.

So, for the first three years of its life, except for the limited production motocross and enduro machines, the new company lived off what it had inherited from Harley. Then at the Milan Show in November 1981 a whole series of new models appeared including a completely new 125 trail machine with up-to-the-minute styling and a six-speed reed valve engine, clearly

based on the successful dirtbikes, several off-roaders including a water-cooled 125 enduro and an enlarged version of the motocrosser for use in the quarter-litre class. There was also a 500 cc motocrosser and perhaps most exciting of all, the company's first four-stroke design, the 350 *Ala Rossa* (Red Wing), a single-cylinder trail bike. The concept of this latter machine, with its chain-driven ohc engine, clearly showed that Cagiva were not worried about borrowing ideas from the Japanese.

Meanwhile, a brand new 500 two-stroke four-cylinder grand prix road racer had made its debut at the West German GP in May ridden by Virginio Ferrari.

In August 1981, Cagiva smashed the 125 cc world speed records in the flying kilometre and mile. Piloted by a 24-year-old Dutchman, Bart Smith, the cigar-shaped projectile named *Ala d'Oro* (after the Aermacchi flat single road racer of the same name), set the record for the flying kilometre on 1 August and for the mile three days later on 4 August. The speeds achieved were 159.74 mph and 154.54 mph respectively and subsequently ratified as world records by the FIM.

The machine used by Smith had been developed at Amsterdam University and built by two Dutchmen, Pet Blumper and Jan Nyheues, with full co-operation from the Varese factory.

The engine was essentially a largely *unmodified* production WMX water-cooled motocross unit, although the gearbox was fitted with electromagnetic control. In 1981, the factory also won not only several important motocross championships around the world, including the Italian title and top British schoolboys event, but also took several gold medals in the ISDE staged on the island of Elba.

You may ask, how did Cagiva get under way so quickly with the development of new machinery for both production and sport? Besides many less significant reasons the main answer was commitment *and* money—lots of it. Another was people. When Cagiva commenced production back in the autumn of 1978 a mere 130 workers remained from the original 500 HD staff (which had already been drastically slimmed down from the boom years of 1973–4). Of those over a quarter were employed in the R & D department. Not only this, but the Castiglionis spared no effort in recruiting the right personnel. Included were several technicians who had formally been employed by the MV Agusta race team, West German engine designer Peter Durr, top Dutch two-stroke tuners Jan Thiel and Jan Witteveen and of course the former HD staff who had built and tuned the machines which had brought Walter Villa his four world titles in the mid 1970s—men like Mascheroni and Milani.

To fully appreciate the real achievement, one must realize that when Cagiva entered the two-wheel world as a manufacturer, it had no new designs, no image and

outsiders gave it no chance of success (as I know from personal experience) in a highly competitive market.

Another reason was that although the Castiglioni's loved motorcycles, they still thought like successful businessmen. By emphasizing the fundamentals—efficient manufacturing, high quality, competitive pricing (by Italian standards), and authorizing the development of new models, the fledgling company was able to achieve the seemingly impossible task of growing from nothing to be a world power within a decade—something no one except the Japanese have managed in recent times.

But all this would have been an impossibility without the buoyant home market. Here Cagiva was fortunate, at the time of their launch there was no competition from the Japanese as they were barred from the Italian market in the classes Cagiva were concentrating upon—up to 350.

And as already mentioned there was a considerable amount of profit generated by selling the old designs and stockholding of bikes and spares which existed when AMF shut the doors. But perhaps most fortunate of all, it was a revised Harley, the SST125, which became

First fruits of the Cagiva–Ducati agreement signed in June 1983 were the 350 and 650 Alazzurras which employed Pantah V-twin engines

a best-seller on the domestic market during the period 1979–82. And most surprising of all the SST used a development of the 1967 ML/MLS engine!

Another reason for the marque's early success was its willingness to examine, and copy where necessary, the latest Japanese advances in motorcycle engineering. During my visits to the Varese factory over the first three years of the new management it was a frequent sight to see several brand new Japanese motorcycles in the R & D shop, brought in so that the Cagiva technicians could see exactly what the opposition amounted to. . . .

In their first full year Cagiva built 9000 bikes, the following year this was up to 13,000 and by 1982 it had increased to 40,000. There were now 300 workers, of which 50 were R & D staff.

There was another development in 1981, again copying the Japanese, the opening of the first foreign factory—situated in Venezuela. This was responsible for producing Cagivas for the South American market, initially solely from parts made in Italy.

This was subsequently followed by several other overseas projects and as early as 1981 the first talks had taken place with the Soviet government into the

A section of the Ducati factory in Bologna shortly before Cagiva gained total control in May 1985

possibility of supplying Cagiva expertise to the USSR in the same way as Fiat had done earlier in the four-wheel market.

However, to date, although further meetings have taken place, the only concrete results of this Italian–Russian co-operation came in 1982 when Russian riders campaigned the new 500 cc motocross bike in the world championship series. But the possibility of a tie-up in the future shouldn't be dismissed. It could well be that the go-ahead Italian company will benefit from the commerical and industrial changes which are currently taking place in the Soviet bloc.

Cagiva have also set up a number of associated companies to distribute their motorcycles in foreign markets, including North America. However, one notable failure has been Britain, where the subsidiary they established in Birmingham in 1982 lasted only just over a year.

But ever since they took over the old Aermacchi/Harley-Davidson facilities in September 1978, the Castiglioni brothers have dreamed even grander dreams.

They envisage Cagiva as the European choice, the company whose dealers would be able to present a viable alternative to the Japanese. But in this they needed larger capacity machines—which effectively

meant *four-strokes* and these would have proved not only exceptionally expensive—even for Cagiva to develop, but would have taken years to conceive. But the Castiglionis realized there was a way round this problem—why not go out and find another company and form a partnership in much the same way as Harley-Davidson had done with Aermacchi?

Throughout 1982 the Italian company scoured Europe and beyond in their search. This even led them to take a detailed look at the British Hesketh operation which had gone into liquidation that summer. Hesketh proved a non-starter when Cagiva sales director, Luigi Giacometti, discovered during a visit to Hesketh's Daventry factory that outside suppliers provided most of the components used in the V1000 V-twins' construction. Giacometti commented: 'They (Hesketh) had nothing to offer us. The receiver wanted £150,000 for a pile of drawings and papers.'

Amazingly, Cagiva were to find the answer to their quest in their own backyard with Ducati the legendary state-owned marque whose reputation had consistently exceeded its ability to generate any profit.

On 2 June 1983 the two companies jointly called a press conference in Milan. The outcome of discussions between the two parties, or so the gathered press were told at the time, centred around Ducati supplying Cagiva with engines of 350 to 1000 cc in contracted quantities for an initial period of seven years—starting with 6000 in 1984, 10,000 in 1985 and 14,000 in 1986.

The leading Italian magazine *Motociclismo* headlined the meeting '*Il Matrimonio Cagiva-Ducati*'. Others were less sure, notably foreign journalists, and ran headlines like: 'Ducati in the balance', 'Ducati merges' and 'End of the line'. Most predicted the end of Ducati motorcycles but not for the first time the pundits were to be proved wrong.

The June 1983 Cagiva–Ducati agreement centred around the supply of engine units, but there were other issues, some of which the two parties subsequently appeared to have differing views on. The most important of these was that Cagiva took it that *any* motorcycles produced either by themselves or Ducati would in future be marketed by the Cagiva sales organization. In contrast, Ducati officials and the majority of their importers took the agreement to mean that the Bologna company were only supplying Cagiva with engines and could therefore still produce and sell *complete* Ducati motorcycles through their existing channels at home and abroad. For several months thereafter confusion reigned. This uneasy peace lasted for almost two years (23 months to be exact) before on 1 May 1985 the control of Ducati Meccanica S.p.A. passed from the VM Group—in other words, the Italian government—to the private hands of the Castiglioni family, and a new era was born.

Funnily enough, before the June 1983 press conference it had been Ducati, through its state-controlled management in Rome, which had made the first moves *not* Cagiva. For several years the Italian government had been trying to rid itself of Ducati, but had largely been frustrated by the combination of strong unions and the close liaison they enjoyed with local government officials. The central government would probably have closed Ducati or at least stopped motorcycle production years before but for the fear of what industrial anarchy might ensue in the Bologna area which had for a long time been a political hotbed controlled by the Communists.

Ducati's production figures had been dropping to new lows during the early 1980s as they found themselves less and less able to mount a challenge on the world's markets. This was not helped by the failure of their two most important export outlets—North America and Britain, where both importers had seen sales crash overnight. So it was Cagiva who held the strongest cards when it came to the hard bargaining.

Quite simply, the VM negotiating team eventually just threw up their hands and surrendered—the Castiglioni brothers Gianfranco and Claudio had won and in the process finally solved the problem which had got them interested in Ducati in the first place, at a lower price than they had had to pay AMF for the Varese factory—a reported 3 million US dollars.

Initially, the brothers planned to retain the Ducati name for a short period only, as they had done with HD Cagiva, but soon realized the good commercial sense which meant that riders around the world already knew and respected the Ducati name, whereas Cagiva was still largely unknown outside the Italian borders. Therefore, except for a small grey elephant the Ducati name lives on and appears set for many years to come.

The Castiglionis now had the ability to market a comprehensive range of motorcycles, from 125 through to 1000 cc, but felt they still lacked one vital ingredient, style. Another bold decision was taken, to find a top man. That man turned out to be Massimo Tamburini, co-founder of Bimota and its chief designer for over a decade. Tamburini came to Cagiva via race specialist Roberto Gallina who was a close friend of the Castiglioni brothers. His brief was to conceive the most exciting roadster around and his early results were the futuristic Ducati 350 and 750 Paso and the Cagiva 125 Freccia.

The next target was the giant North American market but here Cagiva, and even Ducati, had a problem. Cagiva itself was little known across the Atlantic and Ducati's long time importer, the Berliner Motor Corporation, had quit prior to Cagiva gaining control. In short, both marques had virtually no established distribution and dealer network. In typically

Cagiva were able to celebrate in style, winning the 1985 125 cc World Motocross Championship, its first ever world title

Campionato Mondiale Motocross cl. 125 cc. 1985
CAGIVA Campione del Mondo

effective and simple style the Castiglionis solved the problem by purchasing the Swedish Husqvarna company in 1986. Actually, not only did Husky have a loyal network of dealers throughout the States but it was also highly respected. It also solved another problem, prior to the Husqvarna takeover, Cagiva were having to build their off-road bikes at the former TGM motocross factory in Parma, due to lack of space in Varese.

Then in 1987, yet another famous and long-established motorcycle marque came under Castiglioni control, Ducati's near neighbours in Bologna, Moto Morini. Again there was logic, if one looked behind the new move. Not only were Ducati and Morini in the same city but the Ducati facilities at Borgo Panigale had excess space, whereas the Morini plant in Via Bergami was in need of modernization. Morini also had a new middleweight V-twin engine with belt drive to single overhead-cams and four valve heads at an advanced stage of development. Ducati's own latest development, also with four valves, was the 851 Superbike. This was intended as a 750 or larger, whereas the new Morini was envisaged as a modular design from 250 to 500.

Another development which took place during 1987 was the opening of Cagiva Commerciale, which was intended to house the entire spare parts stockholding under one roof for the four motorcycle marques now under Castiglioni control. (This was based within the Ducati factory's Bologna complex.) It would also appear that the brothers had been able to wave their wand

Cagiva has always placed great importance on its research and development facilities

over both the local government and trade unions to ensure a peaceful co-existence—otherwise it is unlikely that Bologna would have been chosen as the new centre for Cagiva's motorcycle activities.

The bi-annual Milan Show is always not only a centre-piece in any Italian manufacturer's approach to publicity, but also a show-case in which to display his very latest wares. And so the fiftieth such event, staged at the end of November 1987, witnessed the combined might of the four marques with not only the largest stand, but also some of the most impressive hardware in the exhibition.

Amongst a myriad of Cagiva, Ducati, Husqvarna and Moto Morinis, was a motorcycle hailed by the world's press as the most sensational exhibit of all—the brand new Ducati 851 Superbike.

As the next chapter reveals this machine is truly a very special motorcycle which signals a new dawn for not just Ducati but the whole Castiglioni motorcycle empire.

And so Cagiva marches on. The day to day running of the motorcycle side is now under the control of Claudio Castiglioni, with his brother Gianfranco overseeing the whole group of companies. These include not only the four motorcycle marques but Cagiva's other industrial interests in Italy and around the world.

Currently, the Cagiva group in all its forms employs some 3000 workers and is still growing. As fellow journalist and Ducati enthusiast Alan Cathcart so correctly stated in the August 1985 issue of *Motor Cycle International*: 'Cagiva's purchase of Ducati gave rise to fear and anguish in some Italophile quarters, but for my money the only ones who should worry are the Japanese factories. The brothers mean business and they're succeeding in their aim to provide a creditable alternative to oriental hardware: Cagiva—the European motorcycle.' The same year the American journal *Cycle World* said, 'Cagiva: Today Italy, tomorrow the world'.

All this sums up in a few short words the tremendous progress made by the Castiglioni brothers who in a decade have achieved what a vast majority of observers would have thought impossible. The future looks interesting to say the least.

Aerial view of the commercial headquarters of the Cagiva motorcycle empire now situated in the Ducati plant in Borgo Panigale, Bologna

13

New dawn—Bordi and the 851 Superbike

Without any doubt whatsoever the 851 Superbike, the latest in a long line of Desmos in the Ducati family, is the most significant motorcycle in the Bologna company's recent history. Why? For a start it was the first *production* Ducati to feature four-valve heads, it was also their first *production* model to use water-cooling, fuel injection and an engine management system. But perhaps most important, it was the first all new design for the company by the man selected to replace the legendary Ing. Taglioni, Ing. Massimo Bordi.

Following the takeover by Cagiva in 1985, there has been a new vitality about Ducati's Borgo Panigale plant. Not only have machines, such as the F1 and Paso, rolled off the Bologna production lines but the racing department has been given a new importance. This is in stark contrast to the early 1980s, when despite winning a record four world F2 titles, the race shop had been starved of cash and race shop chief Franco Farnè and his loyal team had worked miracles on a spartan budget.

But after the Castiglioni brothers gained control one of their first deeds was to authorize the *reparto sperimentale* (experimental department) to proceed at full speed with a totally new concept V-twin, which was to later emerge as the 851 Superbike, intended for both road *and* racing use.

The Bologna factory was still using the venerable air-cooled, two-valve head belt-driven V-twin in early 1986, but bored out to 850. With this Marco Lucchinelli not only won the prestigious Battle of the Twins race at Daytona, but proved this was no fluke by promptly winning the first round of the World Formula 1 championship (but on a 750) back home in Italy. He then went on to score more success Stateside by taking the flag at the Laguna Seca Battle of the Twins event on the larger engined bike.

Later in the year a trio of Spaniards—Juan Garriga, Carlos Cardus and multiple winner Benjamin Grau won the Barcelona 24 Hour race on 26 October, around the twists and turns of the ultra-demanding Montjuich Park circuit, again with the big bore job.

The significance of the larger capacity was not recognized by the media at the time, but its main purpose (as with most of the factory's racing in the past) was to prove a new development on the track before offering it for public consumption.

The larger capacity V-twin was also used that year in the Cagiva works enduro bikes, which not only included the Paris–Dakar Rally in January but the Pharoah Rally in October. In the latter event the Italian Ciro de Petri *averaged* an amazing 105 mph over some sections of this largely off-road dirt bash.

But an even more significant sporting occasion was the 1986 Bol d'Or 24 Hour race, staged over the weekend of 12/13 September. It was at this event that the world at large first saw the prototype of what was to later emerge as the 851 Superbike.

After proving that the larger capacity worked at Daytona in March, Ing. Bordi and his development team, led by Franco Farnè, had got down to work. The following month (April) the first detailed drawings were being issued to foundries and machine shops around Bologna. And by early September, after some 150 hours running on the factory's dynamometer, the prototype engine was ready for its first serious track test. And what a test!

Installed in a modified F1 chassis, the prototype engine (which produced in excess of 100 bhp at 9500 rpm) stayed together for 15 hours, which was longer than most could have reasonably expected of an engine only completed a few days previously! It should be noted that this first prototype was a 750 and not a larger capacity unit.

At the time of its retirement the new water-cooled eight-valve V-twin was in seventh place, when a gearbox bearing disintegrated and the bike was sidelined. Even so, the whole effort was a tremendous achievement—from drawing-board to track in just over five months—fantastic!

Strangely enough, it was the success enjoyed by the new futuristically styled 750 Paso which had played a major part in the Castiglioni brothers authorizing the new project. The Paso had been given wide critical acclaim by the world's press the previous November when displayed at the Milan Show. This proved that a high-tech V-twin in a stylish overcoat still had plenty of appeal.

Contact with the British Cosworth company in Northampton also played an important role. Massimo Bordi realized that four-valve heads were the best way to achieve more power *and* double overhead-camshafts, but building both with desmodromic valve operation posed massive problems. He attempted a co-operation scheme with the Northampton concern who were acknowledged as world leaders in four-valve dohc engine designs. But after three meetings Bordi realized that 'I would have to go it alone—they (Cosworth) know four-valves with springs, not with Desmo. We (Ducati) found a good solution without them'.

And that solution turned out to be a real accomplishment representing a combination of the state-of-the-art dohc four-valve cylinder heads with desmodromic operation and a new computer controlled electronic fuel injection and ignition system.

Bordi freely admits that a number of possible alternatives were investigated, including conventional 'spring' four-valve, 'spring' four plus one (like the FZ750 Yamaha) heads and various other methods. And during his meetings with Cosworth (which included design chief Keith Duckworth), what he had seen and heard (even though the British engineers had never acted as full consultants to Ducati) was enough, when combined with his own engineering skills, to enable him to combine the very latest in four-valve technology with the intricacies of the desmo valve operating system.

Ing. Taglioni, although by this time officially retired (at the end of 1982), was still around to offer advice and guidance on the latter. In many ways this was a suitable

Sensation of the 1987 Milan Show, the eight-valve 851 Superbike. Shown here is the Strada form

final tribute to the man who had made the word Desmo his very own over the previous 30 years.

Of all the men who might have succeeded Ing. T, Massimo Bordi is perhaps the most fitting as he earned his degree in mechanical engineering with a thesis outlining the advantages of the desmodromic valve system in four-stroke engines. Bordi was born in Bevagna, Perugia on 9 May 1948. After gaining his university degree in 1974, he joined Ducati in January 1978—following previous employment as a teacher and later as a quality controller at Terni S.p.A.

Like an artist, Ing. Bordi plotted all the suitable configurations in single sketch drawings, over several weeks, of the various designs before choosing the one which he thought best, prior to actually committing his final choice on to canvas (read drawing-board). He then completed his work at fever pitch in a mere seven days or so, with help from his understudy, Luigi Mengoli.

Credit should also be given to chief development engineer, Franco Farnè. A native of Bologna, where he was born on 15 October 1934, Farnè had been a loyal servant to the Ducati marque, whom he joined way back in 1950 straight from school. He also proved himself a rider of world class before a serious accident brought his racing career to a premature end in 1963.

The result was a truly superbly crafted and cleverly designed water-cooled top end which on the prototype, sat atop a pair of modified Pantah crankcases.

Eight-valve, fuel injected, water-cooled, six-speed V-twin powerplant at the 1987 Milan Show

Above right **Rider's eye view of 851 Superbike kit controls**

Bordi considered water-cooling absolutely necessary to provide relatively constant thermal conditions that would not have been possible with the production sohc air cooled power unit. The modification of the prototype's crankcases consisted of a revision to the location of the cylinder throughstuds, which had been relocated outwards to allow for the larger bore sizes, which were to follow, and the water-cooling.

In that first engine, the standard 750 Pantah bore and stroke of 88 × 61.5 mm had been retained but it was always intended to increase the capacity upwards to near 900 cc.

Special effort had been lavished on combustion chamber shape in the new engine, with the very latest 'clean' appearance and valves set at an inclined angle of 40 degrees. Bordi admits that he would have preferred to use a narrower angle so an even flatter combustion chamber shape would have resulted in a flatter, possibly concave, piston crown.

This would have allowed a very high level of thermal efficiency *but* would have also congested the mechanical layout in the head to an unacceptable

Below right **Superbike kit. More go, more money**

degree, upsetting the ideal operating angle of the rockers on the valve stems, thus compromising camshaft profiles and lift. And therefore had he followed this route, the bonus of the Desmo system would have all but been lost.

In addition, if the valves had been set at a steeper angle the inlet ports would lose their ideal straight configuration and protrude from the heads at such an acute angle that the inlet for the front (horizontal) cylinder would have interfered with the steering head location and that of the rear (vertical) cylinder with the fuel tank.

A compression ratio of 11:1 was used during early testing (and at the Bol d'Or) with flat top pistons which had only minor valve relief pockets in them. Valve sizes were 34 mm for the inlet and 30 mm for the exhaust but these, like all the other specifications, were the subject of an updating process prior to the definitive production version.

The engine, which gained a completely new set of purpose-built crankcases in early 1987, also saw its capacity change several times until finally settling for 92 × 64 mm bore and stroke, which computed out to 851 cc. But one detail which was largely unchanged right from the off, was the Weber-Marelli integrated electronic fuel injection and ignition system.

Ducati chose this system in preference to others for a number of reasons. In the first place, the choice was expedient: Weber were based on Ducati's doorstep in Bologna and could therefore be expected to not only provide the very best level of service to their neighbours, but perhaps even more importantly could be reached quickly as and when any problems showed up during the machine's development phase.

Not only this but practically all the component's required by Ducati were available 'off-the-shelf' from existing fuel-injected car setups, so they were comparatively cheap and readily available. (The injectors, for instance, were the same as on several Fiats and Lancias, which was one of the reasons why it had been possible to develop the original racing prototype so quickly).

But perhaps most important of all, the Weber system was known for its reliability *and* the great advantage of being not only able to meet the various emissions and fuel economy regulations that Ducati might have to face, but also to deliver the maximum power required.

The Weber-Marelli system Ducati chose was of the 'open loop' type and was derived directly from the type first used in Ferrari Formula 1 racing cars. This injection system features a limited number of sensors and in some ways resembled the type used on Kawasaki's GPZ1100 B2. The sensors monitored air temperature and density, coolant temperature, engine revolutions, throttle position and ignition combustion (or detonation).

There was no box-like flow meter as used in the Bosch F1 system to BMW's K series bikes, nor a lambda probe, commonly used in sophisticated (and ultra-expensive) car injection systems.

In the Weber-Marelli computer memory, a number of 'maps' have been encoded and on the basis of the engine's running conditions, combine with information coming from the sensors, the computer plotting the optional ignition advance curve as well as the timing of the injectors. Fuel is supplied at a pressure of 43.5 psi (3 bar) by an electric pump and is thence squirted directly into the inlet tracks by a pair of injectors for each cylinder, in a phased mode.

In comparison, the Bosch F1 system employs a 'gate' to measure the weight and flow of air entering the engine unit. Put in layman's terms, the system's 'brain' then decides, subject to load, engine speed and other factors, just how much fuel the injectors should throw into this measured mass of air for optimum combustion. Although the Bosch system is highly accurate its gate none the less restricts air flow into the engine, and outright performance therefore suffers.

BMW might not be too concerned with every last ounce of performance but Ducati certainly were. Bordi therefore appreciated that the Weber-Marelli system with its 'mapped' system didn't rely on measuring the air flow directly, but reacted to feedback from the powerplant.

The basis of the system is what is known as the Alpha angle—the degree of opening of the throttle butterfly varying from 90 degrees, with the throttle closed, to 0 degrees flat out.

Using a dynamometer, Weber's designer, Aureliano Lionello, connected the dohc four-valve water-cooled engine to a flowmeter and exhaust gas analyser, then tuned the injector system and ignition advance to deliver optimum performance at 16 different angles and 16 different rev bands. The resulting mass of data was then plotted into graphs referring to possible operating conditions, using a special computer. Aureliano then mapped the Weber system's microchip to conform to the lessons learnt from this data during actual operation.

The system's microprocessor (brain) also corrects for water (or oil) and air temperatures, atmospheric pressure, fuel pressure and changes in battery voltage, choke function and injection timing and duration are also varied subject to the microchip's map. The programming can be varied to improve engine braking, fuel consumption and exhaust emissions.

Any changes to an engine's specifications—different camshaft, for instance—will usually require a reprogrammed chip, so a works racer is harder than a standard production unit to reproduce.

One of the most visually obvious signs of the system

Ducati 851 brochure, with Lucchinelli modelling the Strada

Weber injector assembly

on the 851 Superbike are those massive 50 mm inlet tracks which feed dead straight to the paired inlet valves. Previously, the largest choke size Ducati could get away with, even on their factory racers, was around 42 mm—any bigger and at low rpm air speed through the carburettor just wasn't sufficient to pull the fuel up from the float bowl quickly and accurately enough. In contrast, fuel injection, because it uses external pressure to push the petrol into the engine, suffers no such drawbacks.

Without doubt, it was the machine's computerized fuel injection and ignition systems which was to play a vital role in its successful combination of old world virtues of the 90-degree V-twin layout and the leading technical innovations of the late 1980s. As already mentioned, the prototype of what was ultimately to emerge as the 851, first saw the public light of day at the 1986 Bol d'Or. Water-cooling, two sets of double overhead-cams and four valves per cylinder made it unlike any previous Ducati.

Bike described the Bol d'Or prototype thus: 'In fact its rat's nest of hoses resemble nothing so much as the back of a plumber's van. Now that, from a firm as idiosyncratically traditional as Ducati, was hard enough to swallow. But there was more—this Duke dispensed with great, gulping Dell'Orto carbs in favour of yet another rat's nest of hoses, wiring and injectors—the veins and tendons of an electronic fuel injection system. Boy, did we laugh at the thought of all that spaghetti wiring.' *Bike* then went on to say: 'rash optimism, it seemed, would always find a home in Bologna. Much to everyone's surprise the bike survived most of the Bol's 24 hours.'

Yet it did surprise, and in big doses. The Bol d'Or had proved that here was something special. And even though a series of production delays meant that serious production didn't start until the spring of 1988, when it did the press went wild. With headlines such as 'Ducati

fantastica' (*Superbike*), 'One over the VIII' (*Bike*) and 'Granducati' (*La Mota*).

Prior to this, two other important developments had taken place in the story of the 851 Superbike; its launch at the Milan Show in November 1987—both versions, Strada and kit (the latter was the track version) being displayed, together with an engine unit; then in early April 1988 former Italian 500 cc world champion Marco Lucchinelli scored a sensational victory on a works racing version of the 851 at the first ever round of the new Superbike World Championships, staged at Donington Park.

The 851 was developed as an exclusive sportster (well, with a 1988 British price of £10,995 for the Strada and £12,500 for the kit version it is obviously going to remain that way). It was also meant to provide the well-heeled Ducati enthusiast with a machine with which he could compete at any level, from club to international, on the world's race circuits.

In addition, Bordi and his team now had a machine with which the factory could compete and win races to show that the V-twin concept was still viable up against multi-cylinder engines. The World Superbike Championship is a series of great importance to all factories,

Co-designer of 851, Franco Farnè—a Ducati employee since 1950

Ducati in particular. Its significance in the future is likely to approach that of grand prix status. Realizing this, Ducati were reported as providing Lucchinelli with a total of *ten* bikes for the 1988 season and the racing budget for the 851 was around £250,000.

Additionally, Ducati planned to construct 500 *production* 851 Superbikes (in 1988), the first 200 were the race-kitted version. It was these bikes which the factory hoped would re-create the aura which surrounded the 200 or so Imola Replica 750SS models which were sold during 1973 and 1974.

Lucchinelli's bikes were one-offs, weighing some 30 kg lighter at only 145 kg—the World Superbike minimum. Ducati offered some of the special parts as an additional racer kit—thinner bodywork, lighter front and rear subframes, flywheel and generator and provision to ditch the electric start. The chassis was also slightly different, with taller ride heights at each end and front disc sizes up 40 mm to 320 mm. There were obviously a few *special* engine bits . . . my guess is the works bikes produce 130–135 bhp. Then there were the production 851s which Joe Public could buy.

As *Bike* so rightly put it: 'The first thing to strike you

Marco Lucchinelli—851 World Superbike Series contender and now race team manager

about this ultimate Duke is just how well made and intelligently detailed it is. Ducatiphiles raised on Artex paint, hairy fibreglass and legoland components should look elsewhere. The 851 shrieks of high quality which, if it ain't quite up to Bimota standards, at least deserves space in the same room.'

And *Bike* had this to say about the chassis design: 'In an age of high profile, foot thick aluminium beams, this Duke scarcely appears to have a frame at all—just a few abbreviated but fully triangulated thin-wall chrome-moly steel tubes forging a more-or-less direct path from headstock to swing arm.'

Tying this lightweight structure together was the V-twin engine acting as a stress member itself—a policy used by successive Ducatis down through the years. The frame had a steering angle of 26 degrees, caster off set of 105 mm and a steering column angle of 27 degrees 30 minutes.

Sitting astride the engine was an airbox, complete with a pair of the largest bellmouths probably ever to grace a production two-wheeler. Almost as striking was a veritable maze of wiring and plumbing—thankfully much, much neater than that of the original Bol d'Or prototype. Yes, this could certainly not be labelled as just another Ducati.

Mechanically, the kit and street versions of the production 851 Superbike were surprisingly similar—at least in appearance! The cooking version churned out 100.5 bhp at 9250 rpm, whereas the kit bike pumped out 119 bhp at 10,500 rpm, but as *Bike* discovered, 'Run back-to-back, however, both bikes make similar power until around 9000 rpm when the Strada runs out of puff and the racer clears off.'

The differences responsible for this are a fifth of a ratio more compression, no air filter element (although the air box is retained), less restrictive exhaust system and hotter cams (133 degrees of overlap rather than 74!). Valve sizes at 32 mm inlet and 28 mm exhaust are the same, but Ducati claim that the kit bike has harder-wearing nimonic valves. The kit version also sports closer ratio gears from third to top inclusive in its six-speed gearbox.

But the most impressive thing about both versions is how they produce their power. Ducati V-twins have always been renowned for the high level of brute torque produced, but with the 851 this is replaced by a sweet and tractable personality.

Bike again: 'Dial in any amount of revs and any degree of throttle, however unlikely, and the fuel injection's microprocessor steps in to give smooth, glitch-free power. No spitting back all over your right trouser leg, no sulking on part throttle, no transmission snatch—perfect.'

Superbike tester Grant Leonard put it this way: 'The power came on and on, progressively, no lunge or flat spot, the tacho needle arcing around the clock so quickly I still couldn't believe that it was a twin I was

Lucchinelli's 851 racer, Milan 1987

riding. It revved cleanly straight up to the 10,500 (he was riding the kit version) redline where the rev limiter—an automatic fuel cut-off—smacked my wrists.'

Both production versions of the 851 shared the same basic engine with its four-valve, desmo heads with belt drive, aluminium alloy cylinder barrels with silicon carbide inner coating, forged slipper pistons, one-piece crankshaft, double-webbed 'H' section con-rods machined from solid and with split plain bearing big-ends. The crankcases themselves, although clearly based on the Pantah, were none the less suitably different but still retained the external cartridge oil filter element (with a sump capacity of 4 litres) and front mounted electric start motor.

The dry multiplate clutch was again hydraulically operated but featured straight-cut gears with 62 × 31 teeth. The six-speed gearbox had the following ratios: (Strada) 1st 37/15, 2nd 30/17, 3rd 27/20, 4th 24/22, 5th 23/24 and 6th 24/28. The kit bike had the following changes: 3rd 28/20, 4th 26/22, 5th 24/23 and top 23/24. Final transmission was via Regina ($\frac{5}{8} \times \frac{1}{4}$ in.) chain.

The suspension on both versions was identical. The front end was taken care of by a set of robust 41.7 mm

diameter Marzocchi MIR 100 mm stroke forks, while at the rear there was a full rising rate (unlike the F1 and Paso) Marzocchi Supermono single shock with 50 mm of travel. And apart from preload and rebound adjustment, there was an ingenious snail-cam for varying the monoshock linkage ratios. This all added up to a previously unheard-of level of suppleness for any roadgoing Ducati.

Chassis-wise the Strada and kit 851s were almost identical apart from the latters' 17-in. wheels where the Strada had 16-in. This is strange because although Ducati claimed it was because of tyre consideration it would have been best to opt for 17-in. on both bikes, because the kit bike definitely seems to have an advantage in the handling stakes. Both used Marvic wheels, although the street bike had Marvic spokes bolted to 16-in. Akront rims which was strange. Incidentally, the kit machine came with Michelin tubeless slicks—12/60 17 front and 18/67 rear, whereas the Strada had tube radial from the same source—130/60 VR16 front and 160/60 VR16 rear.

Stopping was taken care of by a pair of floating bi-

Works 851 engine of type used by Lucchinelli, 1988

metal 280 mm diameter discs at the front featuring four-pot P4.32B calipers—with a single 260 mm disc at the rear with a double piston P2.T08N caliper. However, fuel capacity was different although both tanks were in aluminium—the Strada's tank held 22 litres (4.9 gallons), the kit's 20 litres (4.4 gallons). The majority of electrics, including the 12-volt 16-amp/hour battery were crammed into the space beneath the seat hump. In fact, there was so much that *Bike* commented: 'Enough electrics for a dozen Mk 3s.' Both versions had, like a few of the Japanese race replica megabikes, a roll-on paddock stand and no conventional centre or side affairs.

The difference in price between the kit and Strada can also be explained, not just by the level of performance but by the former's comprehensive 'kit' of goodies which came with the machine. As delivered, the hot version of the 851 was complete with an extremely comprehensive spares kit including pistons, valves, electronic box, injectors, sender units, shims, sprockets, special tools and a workshop manual. In addition, it retained the electric start, lights (which

remain on all the time), no speedo (only a tacho) and a temperature gauge.

Both versions came with a very comprehensive workshop manual, but no rider handbook.

An instant give-away between the Strada and kit models' external appearance (besides the wheel size) is the former's direction indicators and built-in mirrors and of course its Paso type silencers, whereas the kit version has no indicators or mirrors, and straight-through track pipes.

As for performance, the Strada is good for over 140 mph, the kit a genuine 160 mph—well, *Performance Bike* got an electronically timed, 159.7 mph (on highest option gearing: 36 × 15), with Lucchinelli's works specials approaching 170 mph on optimum gearing.

Dry weights of the production bikes: Strada 178 kg (81 lb); kit 165 kg (75 lb). The engine unit alone tipped the scales at 65 kg (30 lb).

So why did Ing. Bordi choose to continue with the V-twin and desmo layout, even though in doing so he has broken so much new ground with water-cooling and four-valve heads? In his own words: 'It is the best engine configuration, a V-twin at 90 degrees. It has reduced dimensions, is balanced so there is no vibration and it is light. I continue with desmodromic valve operation for traditional reasons and for image, yes, but the real reason is performance. Because the valves are closed mechanically rather than by a spring, valve actuation is more precise; the duration of valve opening can be longer so more mixture can be taken in and we can achieve higher rpm.'

David Woolsey (seated) and the author at Snetterton, May 1988, with the first 851 to be campaigned on British circuits

In an interview with *Superbike* magazine Bordi confirmed that Ducati would still go on building two-valve heads, but with a new cooling system, even though the top-of-the-range 851 used four-valve assemblies. In addition, he said that by 1990 many of Ducati's models would be fuel injected, as the factory had to take into consideration emission regulations. However, he was also opting for injection on the grounds of performance, saying: 'It is ideal for a big displacement twin which depends on

New for 1989, the superb Lucchinelli 851 racing replica for wealthy track customers

high torque; it gives a much better power curve than when it is used on a four-cylinder; the engine runs more sweetly. We chose the fuel injection system for the 851 because the Superbike Championship rules only allow the same diameter carburettors as on the homologated road bike. For the big twin, we need very big carbs for racing. The injection system is suitable for road and for racing.'

However, as if to confound the traditional Ducati enthusiasts and to provide a guide to Ducati's long-term plans Bordi also made the following controversial statement: 'For emission laws we must consider a *four-cylinder* engine in the future. But it is a problem to come up with something different. BMW found a good solution. I wouldn't like to do anything which the Japanese have done, although I like the Yamaha FZ engine. It is a better engine than the Honda V4. It is narrow but I don't think the five-valve head is better than the four; the chamber is better with four valves in my opinion. A transverse four is a very good engine configuration, I think this is the only possibility.'

A transverse four-cylinder Ducati for the 1990s—we will have to wait and see. . . .

Appendices

851 Superbike kit
Spare parts with motorcycle

036139666 Brake pads pair   3
037038500 Regulator   1
079950195 Free wheel   1
090549960 Oil cartridge   2
11210011A Half bearing   8
19020011A Clutch disc set   1
21010011A Inlet valve   4
21110011A Exhaust valve   4
28040011A Injector   4
28340011A Regulator   1
28540011A Coil   2
28740011A Marelli Group   1
28740021A Relay   2
38920011A Fuse set   1
42540011A Fuel filter   2
51010111A Wiring harness   1
55240051A Sensor   4
57310011A R. H. Silencer   1
57410011A L. H. Silencer   1
61340021A Brake pads pair   4
67040021A Champion spark plug   10
67110011A Wiring Harness   1

67110021A Wiring harness   1
69810011A Accessories box   1
66910011B Valve half ring   20
700010001 Sensor   1
700010002 Sensor   1
700010003 Sensor   1
770010001 Champion spark plug   10
77910071A Screw   8
79120011A Gasket set   2
82910151A Support   1
84010031A Adjustment 2,10   10
84010091A Adjustment 2,40   10
84010171A Adjustment 2,80   10
84010251A Adjustment 3,20   10
84010291A Adjustment 3,40   10
84010531A Return cap 2,80   10
84010591A Return cap 3,10   10
84010631A Return cap 3,30   10
84010671A Return cap 3,50   10
84010711A Return cap 3,70   10
80020011A Rubber coupling   1

851 Superbike kit
Service tools with motorcycle

067503210 Filter wrench   1
887005644 Wrench   1
887005749 Assembling cap   1
887130123 Advance control tool   1
887130137 Pinion locking wrench   1
887130139 Pulley nut locking wrench   1
887130144 Extractor   1

887130146 Clutch drum locking wrench   1
887130710 Alternator locking wrench   1
887130768 Cylinder-head nut wrench   1
887130833 Tool   1
887130844 Punch   1
887130847 Camshaft timing tool   1
887130862 Rocker pin extractor   1

Owners clubs

Ducati Club Denmark
Norre' Alle' 19D, 4/264
2200—København N.
Denmark

Ducati Club Finland
Petri Makijarvi
Vvorimiehenkatu 14 A 16
0014 Helsinki
Finland

Ducati Club France
Section Nord
Lionel Regnat
2 Allee F-V Raspail
91270 Vigneux S/Seine
France

Ducati Club Sweden
Lars Ekeman
Sandviksvägen 5
16240 Vallingby
Sweden

Ducati Owners Club of Victoria
PO Box 16
Box Hill
Victoria 3128
Australia

Ducati Owners Club Japan
1-4-30-101 Miyawaki-Cho
Takamatsu-Shi
Kawawa-Ken 760
Japan

Ducati Club Schorndorf
Lothar Fredenreich
Mulstr 23
7067 Pluderhausen
West Germany

Ducati Club Hanover
Wolfgang Riess
Weidemannweg 8
D 3000 Hanover 91
West Germany

Motoclub Ducati ADM
Via Bentini
38-40128 Bologna
Italy

Ducati Owners Club Switzerland
Marcel Aebi
Dorfstrasse 141
8424 Embrach 2H
Switzerland

Ducati International Owners Club
PO Box 650857
Miami
Florida 33265-0857
USA

Ducati Owners Club GB
Martin Heather
51 Pochard Drive
Altrincham
Cheshire WA14 5NJ
Great Britain

Cagiva group structure

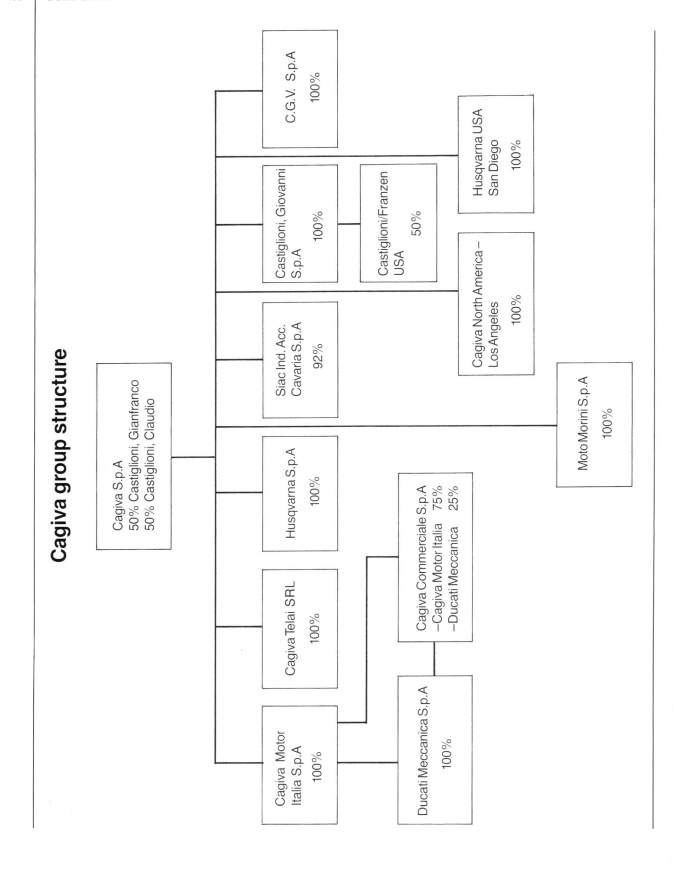

Cagiva S.p.A
50% Castiglioni, Gianfranco
50% Castiglioni, Claudio

Cagiva Telai SRL
100%

Cagiva Motor
Italia S.p.A
100%

Husqvarna S.p.A
100%

Siac Ind. Acc.
Cavaria S.p.A
92%

Castiglioni, Giovanni
S.p.A
100%

C.G.V. S.p.A
100%

Castiglioni/Franzen
USA
50%

Husqvarna USA
San Diego
100%

Cagiva North America –
Los Angeles
100%

Moto Morini S.p.A
100%

Cagiva Commerciale S.p.A
–Cagiva Motor Italia   75%
–Ducati Meccanica   25%

Ducati Meccanica S.p.A
100%

Other motorcycle titles from Osprey

Osprey Collector's Library

AJS and Matchless – The Postwar Models
Roy Bacon   0 85045 536 7

Ariel – The Postwar Models
Roy Bacon   0 85045 537 5

BMW Twins and Singles
Roy Bacon   0 85045 699 1

British Motorcycles of the 1930s
Roy Bacon   0 85045 657 6

British Motorcycles of the 1960s
Roy Bacon   0 85045 785 8

BSA Gold Star and Other Singles
Roy Bacon   0 85045 447 6

BSA Twins & Triples
Roy Bacon   0 85045 368 2

Classic British Scramblers
Don Morley   0 85045 649 5

Classic British Trials Bikes
Don Morley   0 85045 545 6

Classic British Two-Stroke Trials Bikes
Don Morley   0 85045 745 9

Classic Motorcycle Racer Tests
Alan Cathcart   0 85045 589 8

Ducati Singles
Mick Walker   0 85045 605 3

Ducati Twins
Mick Walker   0 85045 634 7

German Motorcycles
Mick Walker   0 85045 759 9

Gilera Road Racers
Raymond Ainscoe   0 85045 675 4

Greeves
Rob Carrick and Mick Walker
0 85045 882 X

Honda The Early Classic Motorcycles
Roy Bacon   0 85045 596 0

Moto Guzzi Singles
Mick Walker   0 85045 712 2

Moto Guzzi Twins
Mick Walker   0 85045 650 9

MV Agusta
Mick Walker   0 85045 711 4

Norton Singles
Roy Bacon   0 85045 485 9

Norton Twins
Roy Bacon   0 85045 423 9

Royal Enfield – The Postwar Models
Roy Bacon   0 85045 459 X

Spanish Post-war Road and Racing Motorcycles
Mick Walker   0 85045 705 X

Spanish Trials Bikes
Don Morley   0 85045 663 0

Triumph Twins & Triples
Roy Bacon   0 85045 700 9

Villiers Singles & Twins
Roy Bacon   0 85045 486 7

Continued on next page

Yamaha Dirtbikes
Colin MacKellar   0 85045 660 6

Yamaha Two-Stroke Twins
Colin MacKellar   0 85045 582 0

Osprey Colour Series

Fast Bikes
Colin Schiller   0 85045 761 0

**Japanese 100hp/11 sec./150 mph
Motorcycles**
Tim Parker   0 85045 647 9

Road Racers Revealed
Alan Cathcart   0 85045 762 9

Restoration Series

BSA Singles Restoration
Roy Bacon   0 85045 709 2

BSA Twin Restoration
Roy Bacon   0 85045 699 X

Matchless & AJS Restoration
Roy Bacon   0 85045 755 6

Norton Twin Restoration
Roy Bacon   0 85045 708 4

Triumph Twin Restoration
Roy Bacon   0 85045 635 5

Restoring Motorcycles

1 Four-Stroke Engines
Roy Bacon   0 85045 787 4

2 Electrics
Roy Bacon   0 85045 788 2

3 Transmission
Roy Bacon   0 85045 859 5

4 Two-Stroke Engines
Roy Bacon   0 85045 860 9

General

Ducati Motorcycles
Alan Cathcart   0 85045 510 3

Ducati – The Untold Story
Alan Cathcart   0 85045 789 0

**Geoff Duke
In Pursuit of Perfection**
Geoff Duke   0 85045 838 2

**Motorcycle Chassis
Design: the theory and practice**
Tony Foale and Vic Willoughby
0 85045 560 X

Road Bike Racing & Preparation
Ray Knight   0 85045 807 2

**Track Secrets of Champion Road
Racers**
Alan Cathcart   0 85045 774 2

Winning Motorcycle Engines
Vic Willoughby   0 85045 926 5

*Write for a free catalogue of
motorcycle books to:*
The Sales Manager,
Osprey Publishing Limited.
59 Grosvenor Street,
London W1X 9DA